Philosophic Grammar of the English Language

Without pretension to high attainments, it has been the author's fortune to become slightly acquainted with some branches of knowledge, the principles of which, he considered valuable, in their application to the structure of speech. The reasons which led him to change his opinions, and yield the prejudices of instruction and habit, may possibly have some effect on the minds of others.

The contradictory, deficient and inapplicable directions, observable in the most popular works on grammar, are different from any thing to which we are accustomed, at the present day, in other scientific pursuits. These were very perplexing, in practice, to the author, as they doubtless are to others who claim the right of thinking for themselves, and of rejecting what they find untrue. The remarkable difference of writers from each other, even in the same language, and still more, the evident variance from philosophic truth, showed that there must be some thing very defective in the manner of conducting the inquiry. Every extension of research to determine where the error lay only accumulated the mass of inconsistency, under the name of learning. Uniform experience proved that what is directly opposed to fact, and good sense, in plain English, can not be made true, by the best quotations from Latin and Greek. Under all these perplexities, it appeared too daring to suppose that the persons to whom the civilized world looked up for instruction in language, while differing from each other in such numerous particulars, were all wrong alike, in the main points; and that the causes of their endless disputes were the improper assumptions on which their whole train of reasoning was founded. The mass of evidence, however, which tended to this belief, was constantly increasing.

After the many years spent by Mr. Locke, in writing his "Essay on the Human Understanding," the limited and mistaken views of that truly great man, respecting the connection of the intellect with language as the instrument it must necessarily employ, could leave no doubt that the exposition, on one side or the other, was wrong. Even J. Horne Tooke, the prodigy of genius and learning, in his favorite "Diversions," so luminous, so interesting, beyong all others, in etymology, as soon as he attempts the philosophic structure of speech, is entangled in the grammatical snare. Those eminent scholars and fine writers, Dugald Stewart and Adam Smith, barely venture to hint at an important work which it would be a vast public benefit to have performed; but they appear to shrink from an undertaking for which it can rarely happen that any other person can be so well qualified as themselves. These facts, and their inferences, which the writer of this performance could not fail to observe, became the subject of deliberate thought. One degree of conviction led to an other, and to the notice of new testimony which was constantly presented. The most important rules laid down as principles of speech, are evidently opposed to the plain understandings of men in their daily practice. In the thousands of verbs represented as expressing "neither action nor passion," even children habitually make the proper application of them in the imperative mood; not only independent of grammar rules, but in direct opposition to their erroneous teaching.

Here a new query arises. How is it possible that so many illustrious scholars, in places of the highest trust, and possessed of ample means, should have been enthralled by mischievous impositions, and the fallacy of such doctrines remain for ages undetected? The humbling fact, implied in the question, has, in the course of human affairs, more parallels, and more answers than one.

The false principles, by which the writers on language have misled the rest of the world, are not dissimilar to those of the Ptolemian astronomy. That system was matured under a succession of kings, most liberal patrons of learning. A confederacy of talent, supported by the royal treasury of Egypt, long employed all the means which science could afford, to ascertain the courses of the spheres. For many centuries, all the prescriptive tribunals of Europe were united, to support this inconsistent theory, and ready to pour down the wrath of their authority, on the unsanctioned heretic who should dare to question its truth.

This delusion has passed away; and the high fed astrology which it nurtured, is reduced to a skeleton, on the leaf of an almanac. Inculcations as delusive and pernicious, in other things, still remain, in full traditional force.

When, at this period, which is sometimes called enlightened, a grammarian lays his penknife on the table, and asks the question, with an air of triumph, " Does that knife *perform* any *action*, in *lying still*," it is the same philosophy which pertinaciously demanded, a few years ago, whether this mighty world could fly a thousand miles in a minute, and no one feel the motion; and if it ever turned upside down, why the water did not spill from the ponds, and the people fall headlong to the bottomless pit? Such querists will find their own answers, in learning the meaning of words, and the laws of nature; and will, more and more, admire that wisdom which gave, every where, the true scientific adaptation to the language of men, notwithstanding their own ignorance and perversity of opinion.

A valuable discovery may occasionally fall to the lot of the humblest votary of science, even where those of prouder name have failed. There is a loftiness in official station, or in long admitted pre-eminence, which sometimes leads men to overlook the simplicity of truth; and the pedestrian, lingering in his twilight course, may stumble on the treasure which the dignitary in his coach rides over without deigning to regard.

The science of speech seems to have been obscured by a system of false reasoning from which most other branches of knowledge have in succession been rescued. The department of instruction, under the abused name of grammar, has become almost peculiar in its degradation at the present day; for in hardly any thing else, could such technical mystery be unblushingly offered for explanation, or contradictory opinions for demonstrative proof. It appears to be time also that, in classic literature, the veneration for antiquity should be limited to its appropriate subjects. The Grecians, whatever might have been their genius in works of taste, made but little progress in researches of exact science. It seems to have been common, in all ages, for linguists to become somewhat familiar with set lessons, before habits of close investigation are acquired. Having, in some degree, learned the forms of words, and grown tired of the task, these persons are afterwards too busy or too indolent to resume the subject, or too limited and prejudiced in their views, to comprehend its bearings and importance.

From causes like these the progress of learning, in this department, perhaps, more than in any other, has been retarded by artificial theories; for it is the misfortune of such theories, that when once adopted, they are very difficult to change ; because they contain within themselves no just principles of investigation. The position being assumed that they must be right, they are received, with trusting submission, as a task for the memory, and imposed on each age in succession, merely because they are not understood.

Gross absurdities are the necessary consequence of attempting to explain either ideas or words, independent of things. To the eye of sound reason, what can appear farther removed from matter of fact, or useful knowledge, than the old college logic which professed to guide the mind, by systematic rules of art, in the way of science and truth?

The neuter verb grammar, with its multiplied and unfitting appendages, as still forced on learners, is made up of the same bewildering technicalities, the unreasoning pedantry of scholastic forms, without meaning or application: for it will be seen by those who may examine the subject, that, with the endless variety in the details of exposition, these sets of arbitrary rules are, in reference to general plan, hardly more than transcripts from each other, through a period of eight hundred years.

It is fortunate for mankind that the proper use of language is substantially preserved, independent of such rules, and in spite of their false teaching.

Human nature derives some credit, also, from the
fact, that, notwithstanding the extent of implicit error
on this subject, many individuals are found, who were
not " *born under the influence of the right planet*," and
who have, not too little, but too much, talent to understand the distinctive character of the *nine parts of
speech*. Such persons will not depend on the " *favor
of their stars*," nor the effect of *unoperative actions*, but
on a more efficient agency, to advance their own knowledge in scientific truth.

As a specimen of the theories which have puzzled
the world to so little purpose, it is common for
European critics to praise the recompilers of grammar,
for " skill in abstract knowledge." This is the most
degrading commendation which a writer on language
could well receive ; but, unfortunately for the cause of
learning, the eulogy, as intended and understood, is
very appropriate.

These compilations of opinions, as now generally
taught under the name of grammar, received their main
cast during the dark ages, when the colleges were
chiefly employed in vague metaphysical disputes ;
when the pretended oracles of science were striving by
whimsical rules of alchemy to transmute baser metals
into gold ; and to produce the medicine by virtue of
which each sage should determine for himself, how
many thousand years he would condescend to remain
on the dirty *platform* called earth.

The fountains of doctrinal authority were running together, in a strong current, before any thing like a rational philosophy could oppose its course. Positions, at first held by assumption, are now defended as time admitted rights ; and so strongly immured is this literary Babylon, that the unscreened assailant, before the frowning towers, can only hope, in imitation of a loftier model, to turn, in part, the stream aside, and march under the walls.

. If the system of teaching in language hitherto pursued is false in its essential principles, it is of great importance, in a national point of view, that it should be set aside. In such an attempt, many opposers must, of course, be expected, both from the prejudice of inculcation, and from the still stronger motive of direct self-interest, as among the devotees and shrine makers, at the Ephesian temple, those who might have relinquished the worship of the goddess, rose to secure their "craft" from the danger they feared. On the other hand, a portion will certainly be found, who are disposed to act in the spirit of free investigation ; and who will consider it a more important question whether proffered opinions are true or false, than whether they are new or old.

Limited, therefore, as the circulation of this volume may be, it will doubtless meet with two sorts of readers. Some will examine for themselves, whether its state-

ments and deductions are just. They will either detect
their fallacy, or will candidly adopt them, if they find
them correct. Others will only inquire whether the
ideas advanced agree with what they have been
told before, or have read in supposed orthodox books.
These persons are not expected to reason; but to
denounce the work, as a matter of course, when they
suspect it to vary from the dogmas of those by whom
they are led.

If the principles here faintly sketched should be
found incontrovertible, the last resort of opposition
will be, to say that they are unimportant; and that the
former manner of teaching will answer as well, or even
be more easy for learners to comprehend. Why, in
language more than in any thing else, should error be
plainer than truth? or how, on any subject, can a
volume of nonentities and perversions form a body of
useful instruction? Such inconsistencies as would, at
once, be rejected in every other department of tuition,
it is hoped will not be retained in language, which is the
instrument of all.

Whatever is opposed to philosophic correctness, will
prove as mischievous and inapplicable in practice, as it
is incongruous in theory. Who, in teaching arithmetic,
would say " nine times nine make a hundred ;" and
then offer, as a reason for this mis-statement, that a
hundred is a round number, and easier to remember

than the real product? It is still worse to tell the scholar that, whenever the "*neuter auxiliary to be*" stands in any way connected with a past participle, the two words together are to be called one "*passive verb;*" as, "The Almighty *is clothed* or *girded* with majesty," and "*is exalted*" above the influence, or adequate conception of all created beings. This remark will equally apply to the chief part of what is given for explanation, on "*Articles, Pronouns, Adjectives,* the *different sorts of Verbs, Moods, Tenses, Participles, Adverbs, Conjunctions, and Syntax.*".

In an epitome for learners, extensive proofs and illustrations are not to be expected. To those who wish for something farther respecting the philosophy on which this system depends, with corroborating authorities from foreign tongues, the writer takes the liberty of mentioning his "*Essay on Language, as connected with the Faculties of the Mind, and as applied to Things in Nature and Art.*".

SYNOPSIS,

OR

GENERAL VIEW OF THE PRINCIPLES CONNECTED
WITH THIS WORK.

*Addressed to Enlightened Teachers and Literary Persons, who are
inclined to examine Language on Reasoning Principles.*

———

THE attempt here made to explain the philosophy
and the proper use of grammar, forms part of a system comprehending an outline of rhetoric, logic, and
the science of the mind, in their immediate connection with the structure of speech. As an exposition of language, it may be considered a striking peculiarity of this system, that its rules are not primarily
sought in the mere forms of words. From a labyrinth
without a clew, in which the most enlightened scholars
of Europe have mazed themselves and misguided others, the author ventures to turn aside. Sensibly as he
may feel the want of adequate talents and means, this
undertaking is not the result of hasty conjecture; but of
deliberate conviction that the whole organic formation
of speech may be exhibited on principles of physical
and mental science, and elucidated by the clearest in-
ductive evidence, from obvious facts, and the general
understanding of mankind.

It will readily be seen, by persons competent to
judge, that such a work, if practicable, must lay the
foundation of vast improvement in most other branches
of human knowledge. It brings to the aid of meta-

physical disquisitions a vast body of facts, drawn from natural science; and, to the philosophic investigator in the material world, on the other hand, written language supplies the common sense testimony of all people by whom it is employed. Here is the center where nature and art, literature and science, unite; where, beyond all other means, we may examine, not only what nations, through ages, have done, but what they knew; how they obtained and expressed that knowledge; and, higher, than all, in what manner they thought.

To obviate, at the outset, the seeming extravagance of such an attempt, it may be proper to observe that rhetoric is but an extension of grammar to elegance and taste, adding very little which is really distinctive, and nothing which is not founded on the same elementary laws. The complex systems of logic and mental science treat in common, of one set of topics, and by similar means of investigation, so that these two names are, in reality, but different appellations for the same thing. It is difficult to conceive wherein the difference between them is supposed to consist, or on what principle a division is to be made. The vagueness and complexity of these systems, as they at present exist, afford strong presumptive evidence that they are wide departures from those strikingly harmonious laws which pervade the physical and intellectual world, so far as these are known.

It is the excellence of speech, as the means of personal and national intercourse, that, instead of depending chiefly on mistaken learning, for the simple grandeur of its plan, the same Divine Wisdom which gave the faculty of its utterance, has guarded it from destructive perversion, by those invariable principles of matter and mind, which determine the elements and the boundaries of thought, and the guiding cast of every known tongue.

All language, then, is to be considered under two points of view :

First; as regulated, in its general structure, by established laws.

Second; as depending, in its minor adjustments, on the conventional regulations of men.

Under the first and most important of these considerations, the principles of language are common to the human family, in every age. They cannot be the subject, either of exception, or of contradiction ; for, in all science so founded in the nature of things, one truth never controverts an other truth ; and, not only each department is consistent with itself, but all the parts agree with each other. Neither are the principles of language, in this point of view, liable to doubt, or difference of opinion ; for, when once properly explained, they coincide with each one's consciousness, and are corroborated, by uniform experience, from surrounding objects. It is owing to these principles, as thus infixed with the native logic of the mind, and not to any thing resembling the arbitrary systems called grammar, that any set of human beings have been able to frame a speech, and use it, intelligibly among themselves, or transmit it to a succeding age.

In examining this essential formation of language, we are struck with wonder, to see how few, uniform, and sublime, are its rules ; and find our admiration still

2*

increased, in contemplating the limitless operations which these few rules can perform.

Language, in its arbitrary modifications of words, or its mere conventional character, is subject to so many and various changes, depending on no certain principles of investigation, that it is chiefly, in this respect, to be learned as matter of fact, in relation to each term, and, in some degree also, to each special case. Difficulties which arise under this head are seldom to be removed by formal rules ; but, with limited conformity to broader principles, resolve themselves into questions of fashion and good taste. They are like the privileges of a city, free in their special enactments, but limited in their validity, by the predominant laws of the state.

It appears to have long been a prevailing misconception, that grammar is to multiply its prescriptive mandates and exceptions, for every form of utterance, instead of giving a clear understanding of principles by which all doubtful points may be tested. A thousand rules of syntax, if they could be learned, remembered, and formally applied, in rapid speaking, could not, of themselves, teach the elegant use of language. On the other hand, the pupil will require very little time to understand, in a practical way, the reason why the writers have supposed that " *adjectives* of likeness or unlikeness *govern* the *dative case*," or to see how a future tense, in any language, must be explained, when he is shown the barrier which the Creator has opposed, to every real deviation by human skill.

The essential construction of every language depends on the following principles :

Distinctive objects of perception, in nature, are presented to the mind, through the medium of one or more of the *five senses.*

Each object of *direct* and *original* perception,* is a *material substance*, as, for instance, an *orange.*

The perception of this object is more or less vivid, in proportion to the nature of the *thing*, and the manner of its presentation to the organs of sense. The *idea*, in the mind, is the retained *impression, transcript,* or *inwrought image*, of this object; and, in its clearest form, true to the original, to such degree, that the person, having competent skill in painting, might copy the object from his own *mental picture,*† so as to exhibit a correct *resemblance* to the *orange*, if it should be brought again, to compare.

The *spoken word*, in language, is the conventional *sign* or *representative*, of the *idea*, and also, by necessary consequence, of the *object* of perception from which that mental *image* is derived : for the one being a proper resemblance of the other, the third *likeness* must represent either of them, according to the self-evident law of mathematics, that two things mutually equal to a third are equal to each other.

The *alphabetic written word*, is the *type* or *sign* of the *vocal utterance.* It also represents both the *idea,*

---

* An attempt will be made in an other place, to show that mere sensations do not become the means of definite ideas.

† It is not expected here to explain how the idea is infixed in the mind, nor to say what is the best term to denote it, but merely to explain the leading fact.

and the *original object*, on the same principle as before.

The proper *idea* of an *orange* must include, not only its appearance to the eye, but also its taste, smell, feeling, weight, and other qualities, as known to the person.

This *idea* of the orange must become varied, more or less, in its extended application, from the incidental fact that all oranges are not alike. Precisely the same variation must attend the meaning of the term in language, where its adaptation to the thing is accurately known. The clear and exact knowledge of words, then, depends on the two fold circumstance, that, as signs, their proper connection with the things signified is duly preserved; and that the objects denoted are, according to their own distinctive forms and included parts, well understood.

This immediate connection between *words*, *ideas*, and *things*, necessarily existing in their elementary presentment, the same conformity must be *relatively* preserved, through all their ulterior combinations.

Alphabetic words differ widely in their character, from *symbolic* writing, or from mere arbitrary signs, as in the figures used in algebra and arithmetic. *A picture*, as of an *orange*, *bird*, or other object, calls up the *idea* of the *thing* by obvious similitude, and its qualities by association; but the written *word* has no such direct resemblance to an original object. Its meaning, as an adopted *sign*, depends on learning its connection with the *thing signified*. A few imitative sounds, in spoken words, form a very limited modification of this principle, in its vocal application.

All which can be properly understood by *general*, or *abstract*, *terms*, in language, must depend on the simple fact, that a word beginning in specific application to a single thing is extended to all others of a class, under the general distinctive appearance, or descriptive character. Such a general *idea*, and its *verbal sign*, become very extensive, when the included individuals of the class are numerous, and much varied in their secondary characteristics ; for the nature of the case requires either that a new term should be invented for each modified perception which can take place, or that a single word should apply to a whole set of *things, relations,* or *actions,* included under a prevailing idea.

From a cautious investigation of physical and intellectual principles, it will probably appear that all *entities* which the mind contemplates as *things,* or which *names* can denote, are either material objects, capable of being directly perceived by the organs of sense, or they are inferential deductions from them, on the grounds of analogy, cause, and effect: for these relations stand so connected with the reasoning powers, that no other secondary conception of the mind can precede them.

Names of things are, therefore, inevitably the primeval words, as parts of speech ; and all other terms, apparently different, are but *derivative forms,* and *new applications of nouns.* There is no need of *description,* till there is some *thing* to *describe : quality,* without a previous *receptacle,* could not exist ; nor could its distinctive sign be known, but by reference to a previous standard perception, with which it is compared ; and every *action* presupposes an efficient *agent,* and *means,* as *things* necessary to its taking place.

A small number of *nouns,* of early and very extensive use, have acquired, in the progress of literature, a modified and convenient application under the name of *pronouns.*

The English word *he* is of this kind, signifying *breath, vitality, light, life, being;* an *animal;* a *being* who *possesses* and *exercises* the *vital functions,* who *breathes* and *lives.*

In its present use, it denotes a *single being* of the *masculine* class. From common consent, also, it receives a farther restriction in modern practice, by being employed, in construction, as *agent* and not *object* of the verb. *I, thou, she, her,* and all the other words belonging to the class of *pronouns,* are to be explained in the same manner, as so many supernumerary terms, serving the purpose of variety and relief in the use of names.

On philosophic principle, each of these *pronouns* takes the same *adaptation* to the *thing,* and the same *relations* to other words, as the immediately appropriate name would do in the same place. As a single *person* may be *son, father, brother,* and *citizen,* which are different names of the same *man,* so each *masculine animal* is designated by *he,* as an appellation common to them all.

He who speaks little is wise.

The *single male being* who speaks little is wise. From necessary association, we understand *that breather* who can speak much or little, and who may be wise ; that is, a human being.

The use of adjectives is founded entirely on the *com-*

parisons of things with each other. They are words of description, or of specific relation.

Every *adjective*, however disguised in form, is either a *noun* or a *participle*; that is, a *primary* word, employed in a *modified*, or *secondary* use : for it is not within the compass of the intellectual powers to *define* or *describe* any *thing* in nature, but by its *relation* to some *other thing*, or to a *verbal action*. When the *noun* is made an *adjective by use*, it describes one thing as placed in some condition of being, or partaking of some character, in relation to an other; and commonly such as is essential to the thing described; as, an *orange grove*, a *marble column*.

Here the *column* is *primarily* and *essentially* a *marble* one, and will be so, as long as it is a *column:* but if we speak of an *upright*, *erect*, or *erected*, column, it is, for the time being, such as these *participles* describe it; be-cause the *act* of *erecting* made it so.

Without such virtual meaning of the *noun* or *verb* included, this *adjected word*, as a *sign*, could not sig-nify any known property of bodies, or any object of distinctive perception, on which the mind could rest, to acquire the idea : or, even, if the thought could pos-sibly arise in the mind of one person, he could not transmit it to an other; for, without such known stand-ard *sign*, they could have no common medium of in-tercommunication.

Various presentations, which, according to modern conception, are called qualities, consist either of some portion of matter united with other bodies, or changed condition of things effected by action.

The adjective, *one, ane, an,* or *a*, is a past participle, signifying *joined, added, aggregated, united, aned,* and,

oned, made *one*. In other languages, ancient and modern, it appears in the different forms, *an, aan, aen, ain,*
ayn, ana, ae, en, een, ein, eine, on, ona, un, une, unus,
una, uno, hun, huna, huno, hum, and many wider departures from what was probably its original form, as,
through the ever varying circumstances of human utterance, it has, in passing from nation to nation, down
the long train of ages, undergone its gradual, and singly imperceptible changes. The adjective *one, an,* or *a,*
under whatever *fashion* the word may appear, refers to,
and defines, so much of any portion of matter, as, according to ordinary understanding, is, or belongs, *to-*
gether. It is the *individual* thing, not to be divided.
Erase this idea from the mind, and let the learned
scholar range through his stores to find its equivalent,
with the same definite meaning affixed, in any other way.
Myriads of single objects are seen ; but which of them
is distinctively and essentially so ? The *universe* is *one*
as an aggregated whole : each *globule*, or separate *part*,
of which it is composed, is equally *one*. The *tree* is
one ; each of its branches, or leaves, is *one ;* the *trunk*
is *one ;* and so is *each chip* into which it becomes divided. Any thing is *one*, or *oned*, while it is *united*, and
no longer.

Two is a *participle, di-vided, se-parated, se-vered*. It
is the same with *twa, twae, twee, twi, tvo, tva, tu, tau,*
duo, duae, dwa, dwo, dvo, dva, du, due, di, de, deux, dos,
dois, and others, as they have been, or now are, written
among different nations. *D* and *T* are nearly approxi-
mating *sounds* and habitually interchanging *letters*, as
most foreigners who speak broken English will satisfy
any one who attends to the subject. *U, V,* and *W,* as
they pass from one age, or country to an other, are not

to be depended on for precision of utterance, and hardly to be considered otherwise than as different forms of the same vowel.

The *twi*-light is so called as *dis*-tinguished from the *prime* light of day, and *secondary* to it. *Twain* is a compound, *twa-ane*, *ain*, or *an.*

First is a participial adjective in the superlative degree; *Fir-est*, *fur-est*, *far-est*, *fore-est*, fore-mo-est; most advanced, in distance, time, or order; farthest gone.

Second is an active participle, *di-viding*, *seco*, *secare*, *sécans*, *secant*, *secand*, *second*, *secando*, *secend.* The *secant* of a circle is so called because it *bi-sects*, *dis-unites*, or *se-parates* the *arc* and *tangent*, or *se-vers* them into *di-vided* parts.

Two or *second* is restricted, by common consent, to the first division of the *integral* body, and thus acquires its fixed meaning as a numeral word. It is of no importance, as a rule, how or when the things became *divided.*

The main difficulty, on this point, and others of like nature, is for the examiner to devest himself of the habits acquired by long familiar use, and arrive at the simple philosophy of the subject. So accumulated and perplexing, too, is the body of mere learning, under the name of philology, grammar, and their kindred arts, that there is constant danger of being mazed in the wilderness of words, and losing the essential principle, in the multiplicity of conflicting authorities, of incidental facts and associations.

The class of words called *nouns*, then, include all

entities, material or inferential, which *names* can denote, or the mind conceive.

Adjectives comprehend the ideas of *comparison;* whether description, state of being, identity, restriction, or direct relation, as such, under every variety, which *things*, not barely in *fact*, but also in *imagination*, ever assume.

There is no employment left for other words, except the sublime one which the verb does perform, in expressing the effective operations of primary and communicated power; whether in the complex being man; in two adjoining particles of dust; in systems of wheeling worlds; or their eternal AUTHOR.

Verbs are all of one kind, in every language, depending on a common and simple principle, for their explanation.

Every verb denotes *action;* because, *First*, There is no other office which it can perform, or by which it could acquire meaning or use; and,

Second, Because the sublime truth that every thing *acts*, at every moment, is a prime law of nature, the experience of human life from the cradle to the grave, the predominating habit of thought; and the ruling principle of construction, in every form of speech.

A real action necessarily supposes, a material substance put into a state of motion, or of relative change; or exerting tendency to change, to which a prevailing resistance is opposed; or employed to resist the action of something else, and which is equally action, whether philosophically or grammatically considered.

In what is deemed the imaginary action there must be, on the simplest principles of reasoning, a cause and a correspondent effect, with the requisite agency and means. Something, by implication at least, must take a new descriptive character, or relative condition, different from what it would have held, independent of such cause: consequently, there can not be, within the bounds of physical, or of intellectual nature, any action, nor in language any verb, without an object, either expressed or irresistibly inferred.

The secret springs of action are not for finite wisdom to explain. No physiologist tells how the thoughts of our minds put our bodies in motion, or what gives the first impulse to thought.

It will not be supposed that the animal frame, barely as an organized mass of matter, can act. There must be some unseen active principle within it: and by what law the incorporeal spirit exists in the body, or directs its locomotion, in all the surprisingly varying modes, is entirely incomprehensible to human skill. According to the habit of thought and of expression, the vital power is the *cause* of animal motions ; but within the province of science, properly so called, neither this cause, nor any other, is understood, except as inferred from its effects. The principle is the same through the whole range of created things, as far as they are known ; and there is no clear line of demarcation between beings possessed of *animal vitality*, and those imbued, as all are, with other *living*, or inherently *active qualities*. Men of science, in character as such, do not appear to recognize, under any name, a distinctive sort of things which can not spontaneously act. Even in the Linnean classification of the three kingdoms of nature, no characteristic principle of this kind is at all contemplated ; for, according to the prime oracle in natural history, the prerogative which distinguishes the animal class is not the exclusive power to *act*, but to *suffer*.

" Minerals grow.

Vegetables grow and live.

Animals grow, and live, and *feel*."

The distinction, again, in reference to the principles of action, admitting it to be well founded in theory, could not be consistently followed in speech or in thought; for, if Buffon was unable to draw the division line between the three primary classes of existences, by any known means of judging, how could a refinement which aims at distinguishing things, not by obvious appearance, but by their inscrutable springs of action, have been generally adhered to in practice, from the earliest ages to the present day? Aristotle's ontology, or division of things in the known world, under the ten categories, with the extensive school systems built upon it, will be examined in another place. Happily for language and the means of improvement, the mass of people followed a more rational philosophy than the expounders who attempted to develop the mental operations. They who were not enlisted under any conjectural theory, ascribed action to all things, according to those manifestations which Nature constantly presented before them; and that luminous teacher had no wrong theory to maintain.

Where can modern science begin with better effect, than in coming back to the same elementary laws, and acknowledging the proofs which they every where exhibit. The zoophyte, the mountain ebony, or grain of fulminating powder, acts according to the aptitudes which, as imparted by Divine wisdom, it possesses, and man, with his highest attainments, and hopes of immortal bliss, can do no more. It is not the essential question whether the machine is moved by ten or ten thousand wheels, but simply whether it goes at all. The operations of *will*, under all the random definitions of that term, have no concern with any fundamental distinction in science, language, or thought; and to assert that man himself, the most complex of all agents, does not perform numerous actions independent of free choice and contrary to it, is to reject the lessons of every day's experience. Equally, fallacious is every system which would refer its votaries to *consciousness* as an original principle, instead of a mere concomitant of action; and one too, which, even in its highest earthly subject, is very limited in its extent. Must the colleges still teach as a principle of language, that a person in an ague fit does not shake, unless he does so by design, nor the chime clock either *uphold itself*, *keep time*, or *play a tune*, because it has no rational understanding of its own movements? How long are the nations called civilized to believe in the doctrine of words void of meaning, and of things without power to act? What is the piece of *steel* which forms the *needle* in the mariner's compass; and what does it *do ?* While the pilot, in the midnight storm, stands watching at the binnacle, this *dead matter*, trembling with each surge which rocks the ship, *graduates itself*, with unerring *skill*, to its fixed points, and *teaches* practised seamen, when human tongues are mute. Is this expression a mere figure of speech, or is it literal fact? Is it action? Does the Divine Wisdom act in this needle? Yes: and in what created thing does that Wisdom not act?

The precise nature of *action*, and of its verbal expression, has long been a deep and mysterious ques-

tion, in philosophy, and its attempted elucidation has
drawn forth a vast extent of talent and learning, with
little seeming utility in proportion to the means employed. The following evidences appear to be offered,.
in the natural order of things, to guide our investiga-
tions on this subject.

The action which a verb denotes includes the correlative ideas of *power, cause, means, agency,* and *effect.*

All POWER is resolved into two kinds, *physical energy,* and *mental skill.* Neither of these two kinds of
power can, in its essential character, be known, but by
its effects; for it is not as mere matter, apparent to the
senses, that any substance can act.

The CAUSE of action is simply that subject, which, in
the consecutive order of things, either by volition, inherent tendency, or communicated impulse, regularly precedes, or tends to, the renewed condition of some *thing;*
which new condition of the thing affected, would not,
independent of such cause, take place, at the same time,
in the same way.

There must be a FIRST CAUSE of action, and may be
as many intermediate ones, as links in the chain of variant things.

The AGENCY or ACTING can have no distinctive or
absolute existence; but is the mere temporary attendant
circumstance of some body of matter which moves or
acts. It must therefore be an error to suppose, that
any specific *action,* as such, is ever perceived. In the
precise statement of the fact, it is not the *acting,* or.

change, but the *acting substance*, in its *changing state*, which is obvious to the sense.

The EFFECT of action exists in the altered condition, absolute or relative, of some *object*, which the *acting body* has, by its operation, *modified*, or *produced*.

The important question remains, what is the *action* in its precise distinctive character, and what the single *rule* which, in philosophy and in practice, every where explains the *verb*.

On natural principles, the first efforts towards the formation of language, must be irregular utterances, which, by repeated use, become distinct in their articulation. By degrees they acquire acknowledged meaning, in their application to familiar objects. While such terms are used *singly*, they denote whatever manifestly belongs to the object of perception, whether *substance*, *quality*, or *action;* but as soon as these *ideas* are separated, and their *signs* constructively arranged, it must be under the guidance of reason. It being easily understood that no action can take place, nor be supposed to take place, without efficient cause and means, we are to inquire what indication is exhibited to the perceptive organs, to impress the *definite idea* of the change : for no *action* affords a single touch for the limner's pencil, independent of the *thing* which acts.

A comparative examination of the operations in *material bodies*, of the *faculties* of the *mind*, and the *structure* of *speech*, each serving to rectify mistakes in the others, will, it is believed, when made with competent learning and skill, lead to the development of the following principles :

The *distinctive perception*, which characterizes each action, is that *obvious* portion of *matter*, in a state of *change*, which, as *instant means*, produces a resulting *effect*.

The *Verb* is the *name* of this *acting substance*, so used, that, by its bearing as a *word*, it implies a *characteristic change*, effected *by means of* the *thing* it denotes.

Such a change in an acting body ends in the *changed condition* of its own substance, or of some other thing which it affects.

This renewed *condition* of an *object* may be *absolute* or *relative:* and, if the expressions refer to imaginary or figurative actions, or to such as, in the particular case, are not manifest to common observation, the *ideas* which they inferentially represent are founded on the uniform laws of construction; and so far as any broad principle of language is concerned, are true to the scientific fact ; for there is no lucid grammar of *words* aside from their interesting connection with *things*, and it is not in human power to speak or think, but in conformity with these exceptionless rules.

When any prepared material called *paint* is used as the *means* of changing the color of a house, the workmen are said to *paint that house;* or, in reference to the *instrumental means*, they brush it over with paint ; or, as *final effective means*, they *coat it* over, with a *coat* of their own making.

So, in succession, at the same building, they *plow*, *hoe*, *spade*, and *shovel*, the ground ; *stone* the cellar ; *brace* and *pin* the frame ; *board*, *spike*, *nail*, *slate*, *tile*, or *shingle* the roof; *lath, plaster, white-wash*, or *paper*, the walls; and *carpet, mat*, or *sand*, the floor.

It is the *characteristic action* of a *wheel* to turn on an axle. Any thing which suitably performs that operation is a *wheel;* and whatever is moved by such *means* is *wheeled*.

The slight changes which take place in *verbs*, for the sake of euphony, or perspicuity, do not vary the principle. To *glaze* the house is to *glass* it; and to " *clothe* a person," means to *cloth* him, or supply him with *cloths*, or *clothes*.

When the cold weather *glazes* or *covers* the river with ice, it *creates*, at the time, the *glass cover*, as the *means*, to produce this effect. It is the same when the spring *buds, leaves*, and *blossoms*, the trees: but, through the ever varying conditions of things, neither the *effect*, nor the *action*, can, in fact, or in supposition, be in advance of the *means* on which it depends.

The word *step*, is the name of the *foot*, become obsolete, as a *noun*, except in its compound, *in-step*, the *in* or *inner foot*.

Hot water *breaks*, or *cracks*, or *fractures* a tumbler. By an unseen agency it creates a *fracture*, which, as *manifest appearance*, is the first resting place for the organs of sense.

The makers of speech did not see *caloric* in water; and the *fracture* itself is the only *visible means* of lessening the beauty or use of the tumbler.

The mistakes respecting *general* or *abstract* terms in language are mischievous in practice. If a verb could

signify every thing, it, of course, would mean no thing
distinctive : but words are not so made; though they
may be loosely used, by not being understood.   Every
verb begins where the *characteristic action* is in some
way distinguishable by the organs of sense; for the strong
reason that this is the only manner in which it possibly
can begin : because it does not appear to be within the
compass of the intellectual powers to make a verb to
distinguish any one kind of action from any other kind,
but by taking a pre-existing noun, and making it verb by
use: Such verb takes an after application, more or less
extensive, to other things, on the ordinary principles of
analogy or resemblance. To *carry* any *object*, is to move
it, on a *car*, or *cart*, or *car-riage*, of some kind or other.
That the trillion-form bodies in nature require carriages
of different fashions for their conveyance, is an incidental circumstance, growing out of the necessity of the
case, from the importance of the action in its primary
character, and the vast extent in which it is applied.

It becomes necessary, from the nature of the case,
either to make a new word for each special modification, required in use, or to give an extended application
to a single term under one prevailing idea. The millions of books in the world are countlessly varied in
their minor points of difference, while they agree in a
general character which makes them all books.   It is
the same with carriages ; and this variety which *things*
present is unavoidably transferred to *relations* and *actions*. The idea of a relation is made of the ideas of
the related things in their proper bearing to each other ;
and the import conveyed to the mind by a verb is full
and clear in proportion as the *agent, instrumentality*,
and *result*, on an object, are well understood. The es-

sential meaning of the verb *to carry*, is to use some
kind of support or vehicle of conveyance, to move some
thing from one place to an other. All supposed deviation from this is incidental, growing out of the difference in agents, transported objects, and means employed. As to the intrinsic conception of the action *to carry*,
it is of no importance whether the carriage is made of
iron, gold, or wood ; with one wheel, two, or four, or
without any ; whether composed of flesh and bone,
water, earth, air, or electric fire. There is no end to
the perplexing technicality which, knowing nothing of
the true principle, would multiply distinctions for every
discoverable modification in terms, as applied to carry-
ing things. If there is a word in any language which
has forty different significations, it might as well not
have any : for that which means every thing, can not,
of course, have any definite import, and such a term
would need an explanatory key, as often as it was used,
to show in which of its senses it is to be taken.

The distinctive principle of verbal actions here hinted at, may be exemplified through all the forms of
words ; but the limits assigned preclude farther detail
in this place.

To explain the sublime springs of action which pervade the system of nature, is not the purpose of this attempt. The influence of gravitation is known to exist
in all bodies ; but if this potent energy operated alone,
all matter would rapidly fall into one mass. It is coun-
terpoised by the complicate projectile forces, in a universe of intervolving spheres.

These are subjects for deep science, with its ample
aids, to exhibit to view. The more familiar laws of
elective affinity, of corpuscular and magnetic attraction,

of glutinous cohesion, and others, are to be sought in
their proper place. Similar principles apply to all combinations of mechanic powers, whether in the Archime-
dian engines, or in animal frames. Civilized man may
learn the *activity* of *matter*, from every scientific book.
The savage reads it alike in the *roaring* cataract, the
murmuring rill, and the vine, with its tendril fingers,
creeping over his bower : the genius-gifted admirer of
nature, *delighted*, views its *quickening* glow, in " the
whole surface of *enlivened* earth ; or in the ' *rejoicing*,'
' *powerful king*,' "

> Who " sheds the shining day, that burnish'd plays,
> On rocks, and hills, and tow'rs, and wandering streams ;
> High gleaming from afar !"

By what process should the intellect frame words to
stupify its own powers, and create that inertness which,
except by misguided credulity, is no where found?

The true exposition of speech, in its connection with
matter, and with the faculties of the mind, affords that
reciprocity in subject, and in corroborating proof, which
may in vain be sought in any thing else. In every
tongue this reciprocity exists, and points to a new use
of language, of incalculable benefit to the progress of
knowledge.

In most branches of science, there are some truths
more clear in their simple proposition, than any means
of elucidation which can be brought to explain them.
The plain philosophy of language furnishes instances
of this kind. Such philosophy is not founded on the
conjectures of individuals, nor the musings of a clois-
ter. It is the slow growth of ages, from the practical

observations of practical men; and the corrector of those wanderings from which no single mind can be free. It is the store-house where, for thousands of years, the plain common sense of mankind has reposited its enduring treasures; and where the investigator, who would learn the distinguishing faculties of men as they are, must repair for his choicest means of induction.

It will not always seem a paradox that the deep secrets of nature are chiefly to be sought in words; for the inquirer in this department of knowledge, will find that, after devoting years to the subject, and trying to understand the best authors on natural science, he can have no definite and extensive views of the divisions between *substances*, *properties*, and *actions*, but in coming back upon language, to see how the terms which, according to general experience, denote them, assume their relations with regard to each other.

In every appropriate subject of inquiry, the plain understanding of mankind, reasoning upon facts, from practical observation, forms all science truly so called. It was the singular felicity of Newton to place the general cause of learning in a different situation from what he found it, to a greater degree than any other human being has ever done: yet all which his resplendent mind performed, will be found, on strict scrutiny, to consist in a vigorously extended application of the principles of sound common sense.

" By their fruits ye shall know them," is applied to minds, as well as trees; and whether taken as a maxim in morals, or in science, it is equally true. The perceptible fruits of intellect are either language or conduct: but the induction of mental character, from human actions, is to be drawn chiefly from facts recorded in words. Neither is any individual able to read the consciousness within himself, but by an instrumentality equivalent to the use of speech; for, however the votary of abstract ideal systems, may try to separate his mind from its means of expression, the thoughts which his frameless hypothesis would thus confine and analyze, had their elements shaped, and the laws of their combination established, before he heared the names of Epicurus, Berkeley, or Malebranche.

The positions thus faintly sketched being admitted as tenable, it follows that all language, and the reasoning connected with it, rest primarily on the evidence of the senses. If, from slight inspection, it should appear to any, that such reasoning leads to that degrading, comfortless doctrine of materialism, into which some theorists have fallen, nothing is farther from such a tendency: for if any scientific research could bring the philosopher to feel the swelling soul within, and prostrate him in adoration before his God, it is when, from ranging through the world of matter, he surveys the ascending scale of intellect, to that Source of *Light* and *Life*, where vision and thought are absorbed, in splendor opening beyond human view.

These propositions, as crudely advanced, belong to a system too extensive, even in its outline, to be submitted entire, in this place. From the manner in which they are suggested, without the proper connection and accompanying proof, they are probably liable to be misunderstood. On the other hand, it seemed necessary to make some allusion to them, in their relation to the grammatical principles contained in the present work.

ELEMENTS

OF THE

ENGLISH LANGUAGE.

———

THIS work is divided into two parts :

First ; Grammatical Principles.

Second ; Criticism and Practical Exercises.

PART I.

———

CHAPTER I.

NATURE AND DESIGN OF LANGUAGE.

1. The term *language* is derived from the French words, *langue,* the *tongue,* and *agir, to do.* It means, in literal English, *tongue-work,* or that which is performed with the tongue. In its extended meaning, *language* is any system of signs by which intelligent beings make their thoughts known to each other.

2. Language is of two kinds, *spoken* and *written.* The first transmits thoughts by regular sounds of the voice ; and the second by suitable letters, or characters, presented to the sight.

Example.

In speaking the English word *earth,* the sound which is uttered, signifies, by common consent, the *globe* we inhabit, or the fine *dirt* of which its surface is composed. The five *letters* as placed to spell the *word,* represent both the *sound,* and the *thing* which it denotes, wherever the same language is used.

General Definitions and Divisions of Grammar.

3. *Grammar* is an explanation of the principles of speech.

Its *design* is to teach the right understanding and use of words.

It is intended to make this volume, as far as possible, a work of practical utility, in plain English. The origin of the word *grammar,* the principles and historic circumstances with which it stands connected, and the numerous modifications which it exhibits in its transmission through different ages, though very interesting to those who appreciate them, do not fall within the plan of the present attempt.

4. *Grammar* is divided into *four* principal parts; *Orthography, Etymology, Syntax,* and *Prosody.*

This is the long standing division in grammar, and it is substantially correct; but there is no complete separating line between these parts, nor is it necessary that there should be. A proper knowledge of Etymology is necessary to Orthography; and the contrary. Syntax depends on what Etymology explains; and Prosody is to be adjusted according to the understanding acquired under the other three heads.

5. *Orthography* is *right spelling.*

It explains the *letters,* with their *sounds,* and the proper *joining* of them, in syllables and words.

6. *Etymology* teaches the derivation, meaning, changes, and classing of words.

7. *Syntax* is the just arrangement of words in a sentence.

8. *Prosody* shows the best placing of accents to produce harmony, and applies chiefly to poetry.

ORTHOGRAPHY.

9. The *letters* of the alphabet are intended to *repre-sent* the different *sounds* of the human voice.

In a perfect system of alphabetic writing, each character should represent one uniform sound, and no more ; but many accidental variations take place, from time to time, to prevent such regularity in practice. The typical characters used in writing assume great interest in reference to the changes they have undergone since their invention. Among different nations, the number of letters has varied, from sixteen to two hundred and fifty-six, which is the present number in the *Sanscrit*, as used in India: but this is an alphabet chiefly of syllables, rather than single letters.

10. A *Syllable* is the sound, of one letter, or of as many as may be pronounced by gliding into each other, without breaking the voice.

11. One, two, or more *syllables* make a *word*, which is the *sign* of an *idea* in the mind, and of a distinctive *thing* from which that *idea* was derived.

12. The English alphabet has twenty-six written letters. Seven of these stand for *vowel sounds*, and nineteen for *consonants*.

13. The *vowel sounds* are expressed by *a*, *e*, *i* or *y*, *o*, and *u* or *w*.

A true *vowel* is a perfectly *simple sound*, and can be distinctly uttered by itself. From the time it is begun till it is finished, the organs of speech are kept in the same position.

Five sounds denoted by *a; two* by *e;* the *short i; o* in *note,* and in *move; u* in *mute, but,* and *full,* all are pure vowels.

14. *Two vowel* sounds, running into each other in *one* syllable, form a *dipthong;* as, *ou* in *round, oi* in *coin.*

Long i in *five,* though represented by a single letter, is a dipthongal sound. It is the same in English with the letter *u,* pronounced like *iu,* or *yu,* when sounded by itself.

4*

15. The consonant sounds cannot be pronounced without the vowels.

NOTE. An extended illustration of Orthography, with the meaning of syllables found in modern words, is to be given in an other work.

Enlightened instructors are aware of the importance of convenient reference in class exercises. To facilitate such reference, this work is divided into short chapters, with sections and questions numbered to correspond with each other.

The portion in large type is intended to be committed to memory. The remainder to be read with attention under the guidance of a teacher. The system, however, is chiefly designed for schools where instruction is conducted on reasoning principles; and not those numerous ones where forms of words, right or wrong, as found in books, are merely taught by rote.

Questions to Chapter I.

1. What is the meaning of *language?*
2. What kinds of language are there?
3. What is grammar? What is its design or intention?
4. How is grammar divided?
5. What is orthography?
6. What does etymology teach?
7. What is syntax?
8. Of what use is prosody?
9. For what purpose are letters used?
10. What is a syllable?
11. What makes a word, and what is it?
12. What letters has the English alphabet?
13. By what letters are vowel sounds expressed?
14. What forms a dipthong?
15. How are consonant sounds pronounced?

CHAPTER II.

ETYMOLOGY.

1. IT belongs to this part of grammar to show what each word means ; to what part of speech it belongs ; and what changes it may admit, while it is considered the same word.

The principles which properly belong to the department of ety- mology, and the extent in which they are to be treated in a system of grammar, do not appear to be laid down with any tolerable accu- racy in the books. If it is only to include the present modifications of what is considered the same word, then its extent is very limited, and its importance comparatively trifling : but, if, as seems to be its true province, it is made to comprehend the origin and history of words; their philosophic applications to things, according to the laws of nature and of thought ; and to show either that this original meaning has been preserved, or the fact, and the reason why, if a change has taken place, it presents the subject in a very different light, and as one of exceding interest. Etymology, so understood, of course does not belong to an elementary work ; but this kind of research is absolutely necessary to the development of language on any thing like scientific principles. No one can suitably explain grammatical relations without knowing the meaning of words; this meaning is not to be guessed at, or judged of by a superficial view, but to be ascertained; and the research for such purpose is etymology. It is as necessary to a correct and scientific exposition of language, as physiology or anatomy is to the knowledge of the human system. There is, in the minds of superficial observers, a blind prejudice on this subject, arising in part, perhaps, from the manner in which attempts in etymology, as deduced from the mere forms of words, have been conducted. The studying of language at all is either to acquire an extended knowledge of facts, or, by a clearer understanding of governing principles, to rectify the occa- sional errors in practice. The short way to judge of any irregular- ity, is to compare it with the standard from which it deviates ; and the appropriate use of etymology is to ascertain that standard. Each unknown or disputed word is, by enlightened, scientific etymology, to be referred, as a *sign*, to the distinctive *thing*, *relation*, or *action*, which it *signifies*. Such etymology will explain the enigmas in grammar, and settle many disputes which have long puzzled the world in a very unprofitable manner.

Grammarians have, in their practical treatises, generally confined their etymology to the modern use of the same word in the same language.

Example.

To walk, walk, walkest, walks, walketh, walked, are all called the verb *to walk.*

2. The different ways in which words are applied to things is called their *manner of meaning*.

3. By such manner of meaning they are divided into the different parts of speech. Words *name* things, *compare* them with each other, or *express action*.

Thus *water* is the *name* of a well known liquid ; a *water* plant grows in or near the *water*; a *water* prospect is a view which includes a body of *water*; *to water* a plant, is to pour *water* upon it; *to water* a horse, is to give him *water* to drink. In all these expressions, we employ the same word, and mean the same thing; but we apply that meaning in different ways.

John bought some *buttons* at a *button* factory, to *button* his clothes. Here the word *buttons* is first used to name the articles which John bought; next to *describe* the place where he obtained them; and thirdly to *express the action* which he did with them.

4. Words are either *primitive* or *derivative*, *simple* or *compound*. This division depends on the *manner in which they are formed from other syllables or words*.

5. Primitive words are not derived from any other in the same language ; as *love*, *book*, *pen*, *glass*.

6. Derivative words are formed by adding letters or syllables to primitives ; as *love-li-ness*, *book-ish*, *glass-es*.

7. Compound words consist of two or more single ones joined; as *pen-knife*, *ink-stand*, *day-book*, *candle-stick*.

Derivative words are, in reality, the same as compounds, though, to unlearned persons, they assume a different appearance. The syllables added are distinct original *nouns* and *verbs*, in a contracted form. The old words now commonly used as added syllables are, *an, en, ence, ant, ent, al, el, age, ar, er, or, ble, ed, es, ess, est, dom, hood, ic, ing, ion, ish, ate, ite, ive, fy, ly, ty,* and *ous.*

To understand the derivations of syllables in the same language, or from a different one, is very important, in order to get a clear idea of their meaning.

Fans in *Latin,* is a participle, and signifies *speaking: In-fans* is *not speaking.* The English word *infant,* derived from this, properly means *a child too young to talk.* In law, an infant is any one under the age at which he can come into court *to speak,* and act for himself in a civil suit.

It has been before stated, that all objects of distinctive perception which the field of nature ever offers to our organs of sense, are *things,* their *relations* to each other, and their *changes.* No transmissible thought can exist, but in conformity to one of these three classes of obvious presentations; and words are not devised in language to denote ideas which never had existence in the mind.

By dividing all words into these three primary classes as thus conformed to the nature of things, the subdivisions are lessened in number, and rendered far more simple and clear.

The words which have been supposed to form distinct parts of speech, are referred to the explanations under their appropriate heads. Those called pronouns are nouns which have acquired a special and convenient use. Prepositions are participial adjectives showing the specific local relation of one thing to an other: the motley set of terms called *adverbs* will be singly explained; and when any *word* is understood, as a *word,* it will be seen to be *noun, verb,* or *adjective.*

CLASSES OF WORDS,

OR, AS THEY ARE GENERALLY CALLED,

PARTS OF SPEECH.

There are three sorts of words, *nouns*, *adjectives*, and *verbs*, distinguished from each other by the manner of their use.

9. Nouns are names of things ; as *man, lynx, Boston, Neptune*.

Man is the name of a human being ; *lynx*, of a quadruped ; *Boston*, of a particular city ; and *Neptune*, of the imaginary god of the sea.

10. Pronouns are a kind of nouns used instead of others, and serve to vary or shorten expressions ; as *John Smith* is good ; *he* learns well ; *we* must reward *him*.

The pronouns *he* and *him* stand for John Smith, and the pronoun *we* stands for the names of the speaker, and of all the persons in whose behalf he speaks.

11. Adjectives are words used with nouns to *define* and *describe* them : as, *Her second* and *third* daughters are *amiable* and *dutiful* children.

The first three of these adjectives point out what persons are meant, and the last two describe them.

12. A verb signifies *to do some action;* as, boys *fly* their kites ; millers *grind* corn.

13. Compound or contracted words, so disguised in use that their true character is not generally understood, are by some writers called *Adverbs ;* as, *al-ready, other-wise, yester-day*. *Contractions* is a better name for them where they can not be explained according to their real meaning.

14. A preposition is a particular adjective describing one thing by its specific relation to an other; as, He found the parrot *under* the tree, and put her *in* the cage, *over* the window, *before* the house.

The preposition or adjective *under* describes the condition of being in which the parrot was found. That *state of being* is one of direct local relation to the tree.

Attempts are sometimes made, to represent by letters the indistinct utterances which break forth under some excitement, and which are not capable of being subjected to the regular forms of language. The sounds thus, without connection or rule, thrown into a sentence, are called interjections. They are not words; and, consequently, not a part of speech; for, if they are capable of being used and understood, with a definite form and meaning, as words, they assume their proper dependence in construction, according to that meaning, and are no longer interjections.

Questions to Chapter II.

1. What belongs to Etymology?
2. What application of words is called their manner of meaning?
3. How are words divided by their manner of meaning?
4. How are they divided by the manner of their formation?
5. What are primitive words?
6. What are derivative?
7. What are compound words?
8. What are the sorts or classes of words?
9. What are nouns?
10. Define pronouns.
11. How are adjectives used?
12. What does a verb denote?
13. What is said of adverbs?
14. What is a preposition?

CHAPTER III.

NOUNS;[*]

sometimes improperly called substantives.

1. Nouns are names of things;[†] as *Troy, tree;* the *Ismus of Darien;* a *student* of *grammar.*

The name used to denote the absence or destitution, as well as the reality of a thing, is a noun; as *nonentity, vacuity, invisibility, gap, nought, not, naught, nothing.*

2. Nouns are either common or proper.

Beside these there is the set of supernumerary and special *names* called *pronouns,* alluded to in the Synopsis, page 22.

These will be more particularly explained in the proper place.

3. *Common nouns* are names of sorts or classes of things, according to their descriptive character ; as *boy, city, dog, chair.*

4. A *proper noun* is the name *individually* applied to a thing or person, to distinguish him from others of his kind ; as, *George Barnwell, Springfield, Hylax.*

5. *Boy* is the *common name* of all young males of the human species, and *George Barnwell* is a proper name of one *boy* to distinguish him from others.

---

[*] Latin *nomen,* French *nom,* a name.

[†] The word *thing* is derived from the old Saxon verb *thingian,* to think. It includes every *entity,* either affirmative, negative, or suppositive, which can be the subject of *thought ;* and, with this latitude of meaning, it is used in this work. For the philosophic explanation of the classes of *things* which nouns denote, see " Essay on Language."

Sheep is a four legged animal, with split hoofs; covered with wool, and chewing the cud. This description becoming well known, the whole is understood by mentioning the word *sheep;* and the long statement of particulars is avoided.

Persons generally receive *proper names ;* because it is necessary they should be distinguished from each other, and referred to in a way of personal identity. They are morally responsible for their *individual* conduct, and therefore should be distinctly known; but no such principle extends to brutes. If a shepherd could know *each sheep* in his flock, from all the rest, they could not be thus known to his neighbors, and therefore to call them by specific names, would answer no valuable purpose in shortening discourse.

6. Any word becomes a *proper noun* when used as a *specific* and *absolute* name; as, " *Christian Wolf*," a noted German robber. The ships " *Congress*," and " *Fair Trader ;*" The race horse " *Eclipse ;*" " *The United States.*"

7. Individual names become *common nouns* when used as words of general import ; as *dunces;* a *judas*, meaning a betrayer ; *jack tars ;* many *catilines ;* the *solomons* of the city; " this is a deceiver and an *antichrist.*"

8. Names which denote an assemblage of things, are called nouns of multitude ; as *army, flock, a score, herd, a thousand.*

Some nouns denote an aggregation of many different things under one complex idea; as a *landscape*, a *city*, the *universe*, the *Copernican system.*

The word *God* is a common noun: because it is not applied to the Supreme Being peculiarly, or as an individual name ; but in reference to his attributes and relations, as the Ruler of the World. The word applies in language to many imaginary beings, or false gods, conceived of, as existing under a similar character. If there was but one national sovereign in the world, the word *king* would still possess the nature of a common noun; for it would not then be the specific name of the individual, but the relative appellation of his office and station, as chief magistrate of the realm.

9. To nouns belong *person, number, gender,* and *position,* or *case.*

The persons are *first, second,* and *third;* or the ones speaking, *spoken to,* and *spoken of.*

Most nouns are of the *third* person. They are of the *second* person when directly addressed. A name is sometimes used to designate the *speaker,* and is then in the *first* person; as, "Now I, *Paul,* myself, beseech you."

NUMBER.

10. Number is the difference which is made in words, to denote either a single thing, or more than one.

11. The *numbers,* or *numeral forms,* are two; *singular* and *plural.*

12. The *singular* noun represents one thing, as *bandit;* the plural, two or more, as *bandits.*

13. Some nouns have no plural, either in idea, or in form; as *fitness, chaos, universe;* others have no singular; as *tongs, shears, vitals.*

Sheep and *deer* are of both numbers; as, *a sheep, ten sheep: twenty deer.*

The word *people* stands alone, in its character. Without changing its form, it is either a noun of multitude, having no plural: or, referring to individuals, it has no singular; as, "*A* united *people :*" *Many people are* of that opinion."

" The word *cattle* is without change; singular in form, with a plural meaning.

14. The plural is commonly formed by adding *s* to the singular. This practice has some variations.

When the singular ends in *ch, sh, ss, x,* or *z,* the plural is formed by adding *es ;* as, bunch, bunch*es;* dish, dish*es ;* mass, mass*es ;* box, box*es.* Distinctness of pronunciation, in this case, requires an ad-

ditional syllable to be sounded. The words also which end with
the sound of *s*, *z*, or soft *g*, require a final *s* to be pronounced; as
rose*s*, place*s*, maze*s*, wage*s*.

15. A small number of nouns, derived from Saxon,
retain the old plural forms. Some of these add *en* to
the singular; as ox, ox*en*; child, child*ren*.

Other words, formerly of this kind, have changed their forms, and
superadded new plural endings, for want of being properly understood. Of this kind are chick, chick*en*; kit, kitt*en*; stock, stock*en*;
now written stock*ings*; bat, batt*en*; and others.

16. The chief nouns which make irregular plurals,
are the following :

First, Those which, with the addition of *es*, change
f into *v*; as,

beef beeves,	leaf leaves,	wolf wolves,
calf calves,	elf elves,	life lives,
half halves,	self selves,	knife knives,
thief thieves,	shelf shelves,	wife wives,
staff staves,	sheaf sheaves,	loaf loaves.

17. Singulars ending in *y*, form the plural in *ies*; as
cherry, cherr*ies*: but if the *y* is preceded by a *vowel*,
the plural is regular; as, day, day*s*; attorney, attorney*s*;
money, money*s*; and not mon*ies*.

The following nouns from the Saxon, do not come
under any particular rule; but are familiarly understood :

man men	woman women	penny pence
louse lice	tooth teeth	mouse mice,
foot feet	goose geese	die dice.

Cherubs and seraphs are proper English plurals; but there is a
strange awkwardness in using the Hebrew plural termination *im* to
these words, and still adding *s*.

Some other words are used to a considerable extent with foreign,
obsolete, or barbarous plurals. These are omitted here, as it is

hoped they may soon be submitted to the public in a proper English form.

18. *Proper* nouns, as well as *common*, admit the plural number : as, forty *John Smiths* ; the twelve *Cesars* ; both the lord *Littletons* ; all the *Howards*.

The plurals of nouns frequently signify different sorts of things, instead of mere increase of number; as, *drugs, medicines, cloths, wares, joys,* and *griefs,* mean different kinds or modifications of the things which the nouns denote.

GENDER.

19. Gender is the difference in words as applied to the sexes, male and female.

Names of males are *masculine* ; those of females are *feminine* gender ; and the technical word *neuter*, signifies those which are of neither sex.

Many nouns are of both genders ; as *person, scholar;* others may be of either of the three kinds : as, *one, ones; subject* and *others.*

By a figure of rhetoric, personal qualities are often ascribed to inanimate things. This practice depends on fancy and taste, and not on grammatical rule.

Mistakes are often made in capriciously applying *masculine* and *feminine* terms to things without life ; as, in saying of the ship *Jupiter, Hercules,* or *John Wells, she* sails well.

20. In the forms of language, there are three ways of making the distinction of the sexes.

1st. By words essentially different ; as, *brother, sister* ; *uncle, aunt* ; *lord, lady.*

2d. By a different ending of the same word ; as adding to the masculine *ess*, which is a contraction of the Hebrew word *essa*, a female.

3d. By prefixing a descriptive word ; as, *man* servant, *woman* servant ; a *male* pigeon, *female* philosophers; *gentlemen* visiters, *lady* boarders; a *ewe* lamb, a *she* goat.

In many languages, all nouns are, in grammatical construction, made masculine or feminine, according as the words, in their early use, happened to take the form, or become associated with the idea, of one or the other.

21. The following are the principal terms employed in English to distinguish the sexes by different words.

mas.	*fem.*
bachelor,	maid.
boy,	girl.
buck,	doe.
bull,	cow.
cock,	hen.
drake,	duck.
father,	mother.
friar,	nun.
gander,	goose.
hart,	roe.
horse,	mare.
husband,	wife.
king,	queen.
lad,	lass.
man,	woman.
milter,	spawner.
nephew,	niece.
ram,	ewe.
sloven,	slut.
son,	daughter.
stag,	hind.
steer,	heifer.
wisard,	witch.

A considerable number of nouns have *er* or *or* for the masculine, and *ess* for the feminine of the same word; as, sorcerer, sorcer*ess*; embassador, embassadr*ess*; and a few others admit variations of different kinds; as, *widower*, *widow*; *marquis*, *marchioness*; *master*, *mistress*.

5*

POSITION, OR CASE.

22. Nouns stand in different relations to other words ; as, Henry conquered *Richard;* Richard conquered *Henry.* The first noun denotes the *agent* or *actor*, and the second the *object* whom the action affects.

23. The difference between *agent* and *object* is *called position* or *case.*

Several languages express these different relations by varying the endings of the same word. The forms called cases in Latin are six : thus,

Nominative	dominus,	a lord.
Genitive	domini,	of a lord.
Dative	domino,	to a lord.
Accusative	dominum,	a lord.
Vocative	domine,	O, lord.
Ablative	domino,	from, with, or by a lord.

The nominative case denotes the performer of an action ; and the accusative the object which receives its effect.

Nouns have no such different endings in English ; and therefore it is more easy and proper, instead of asserting that a noun is in the nominative case, to say, according to the plain fact, that it is the *agent* which performs an action ; or that it is the *object* which is influenced by a *verb* or a *preposition.*

> *They* sent a *letter* to *him.*
> *He* sent an *answer* to *them.*

Whichever did the *action* of sending to the other, is the *agent* or *actor ;* the other is the *object.*

(It will be found a very useful practice in schools, for pupils to adduce examples for themselves, in addition to those which their lessons may contain. This will not only show their knowledge of the subject ; but by exercising their inventive faculties, will increase their interest for ulterior progress.)

Questions to Chapter III.

1. What are nouns?
2. What are the kinds of nouns?
3. Define common nouns.
4. What is a proper noun?
5. Explain the difference.
6. What word becomes a proper noun?
7. Do proper nouns become common?
8. What are nouns of multitude?
9. What circumstances belong to nouns?
10. What is number in grammar?
11. Explain the numeral forms.
12. What does the noun singular represent?
13. Do all nouns have plural forms?
14. How is the plural formed in English?
15. What forms have Saxon nouns?
16. Singulars ending in y?
17. Have proper nouns a plural number?
18. Explain the meaning of *gender*.
19. What forms in words distinguish sex?
20. What different words?
21. Explain the relations of nouns.
22. What is position or case?

CHAPTER IV.

PRONOUNS,

OR

NOUNS OF SPECIAL APPLICATION.

Pro is the Latin adjective or preposition *for*.

1. *Pronouns* are nouns used instead of others to prevent their tiresome frequency ; as, *Fulton* was an eminent engineer : *he* invented steam boats : *we* owe much to *him*.

Fulton was an eminent engineer: *Fulton* invented steam boats : *Americans* owe much to *Fulton*. The last sentence means the same thing as the one before: but is more inelegant, by inserting the noun *Fulton* three times, instead of relieving it by the pronouns *he* and *him*.

2. There is but one kind of pronouns.

These words take the same relations, positions, or cases, in a sentence, as the nouns for which they stand ; as, in the lawsuit concerning the *bull* in the *boat*,

either *it* ran away with *him*,
or *he* ran away with *it*.

Whichever did the action of running away with the other, is the agent, or nominative word ; and the one run away with, is the object, suffering or affected by the action.

3. The following is the whole list of English pronouns, divided into *agents* and *objects*, or *actors* and *things acted upon*.

Agents or actors.			*Objects or recipients.*
1st person		*I,*	*me,*
2d		*thou,*	*thee,*
	mas.	*he,*	*him,*
3d	fem.	*she,*	*her,*
	neut.	*it,*	*it.*

Agents.	*Objects.*
we,	*us,*
ye or *you,**	*you,*
they,	*them,*

Both numbers, both genders, and all the three persons;

Agent.	*Object.*
who	whom.

In this list of pronouns, it will be seen that these words, by various forms, preserve, more clearly than the other nouns, the relations of *number, gender,* and *position* or *case.*

4. Pronouns are of three persons ; *first, second,* and *third.* The first is the person who *speaks ;* the second is *spoken to ;* and the third is *spoken of :* or the first person speaks to the second about the third.

The *first* and *second* persons being present, are, of course, supposed to be *known,* and the distinction of gender in relation to them is therefore useless.

5. Examples of pronouns in the two cases or positions,

---

* The plural pronoun *you* was applied to a single person of distinction, at first as a mark of politeness and respect. Its use has now become general, and *thou* is scarcely heared in familiar discourse. This magnifying of the single person in the plural form by way of courtesy, is adopted by many nations. It is becoming the established practice, for an individual monarch, reviewer, or editor of a newspaper, in the exercise of his prerogatives, to say *we* instead of *I.*

Agent.	*Object.*	*Agent.*	*Object.*
We teach *them,*		*who* believes *it ?*	
they heared *us,*		*you* see *her.*	
he honors *them,*		*it* affects *whom ?*	
she feared *him,*		*thou* hearest *him.*	
I know *thee,*		*ye* love *me.*	

6. The pronoun *ye* was formerly much used, especially in the solemn style, instead of *you :* but it rarely occurs in modern writings.

Who and *whom* are considered as belonging strictly to *persons,* and are not applied to *brutes* or *inanimate things,* except by personification. The pronouns of the *first* and *second* persons, are necessarily confined to intelligent beings ; because these only can enter into social conversation.

The pronoun *it* often stands for a sentence, circumstance, or general idea.: as, " *It* is desirable that grammar should be truly explained." Here the pronoun *it* represents the whole idea which the sentence conveys ; and *for which whole sentence,* a single noun might readily be substituted, tho it is not. Other pronouns also stand for ideas equivalent to nouns.

That special application which nouns acquire, under the name of pronouns, involves a very important principle, not only in the history of language, but in the science of the mind. The following hints may give some idea of this principle, the more full explanation of which belongs to an other work.

The early names of most importance, and frequency of use, were necessarily such as had direct application to man himself; and if, as in almost every instance, such name was significant, instead of being entirely arbitrary, then some of the few words which might exist would be employed, to denote the man and the functions which he characteristically performed. *To breathe* is one of the most striking and distinctive manifestations of animal life. It is that perception which would obviously present itself to any portion of mankind who might have occasion to form a new language. The word, *noun* and *verb,* for *breath,* and *to breathe,* would be in some degree imitative of that animal exercise, and equivalent to *he, hai, ho, hah, heh,* as written by different nations, or to the sound of our letter *h* or *he,* the " mark of aspiration or strong breathing." In all languages in which-letter writing can be traced, this word appears to be in common and important use, and, in all, to denote the same idea, whether called noun, pronoun, or verb.*

The primary meaning of the word *her* is light. From the necessity of the case it included *air,* the existence of which, as a distinct substance, was unknown to the early nations, as well as to the modern ones who have not made some considerable progress in science; for *air,* at rest, is not obvious to the sense. *Light* and *life,* and *live,* are one word, as modified in the progress and refinement of language. To *light,* or *life,* or *liven,* or *enliven,* one's self, was the verb; and the secondary or inferential use of the noun was the *possessor* of *light* and *life,* and the *enlivened being,* which is now the exact meaning of *her.*

Nouns of so great use would need to be relieved by some variety, to obviate monotonous repetitions, and to express the shades of modification required. The same people might soon form more than one; and those of different languages and dialects who are brought into contact with each other, are always prone to interchange words of this character, each adding the terms of the other to his own, by which each tongue is enriched.

When different words, meaning substantially the same thing, are brought into a language, they are not long used in the same manner of application. The noun *he* is by degrees used to denote the *male part* of the animal creation, instead of referring to the whole; and at last receives that exclusive application. By an other gradual conventional understanding, *he* becomes the *single being,* while some other noun is used to denote the plural; and, again, it is agent, while an other ancient noun has obtained a correlative employment, as the object of a verb. The pronoun *her* has come by a similar train of gradation to its present conventional use in English.

These pronouns have not in reality changed their meaning. It is only the employment of that meaning within a limited sphere of application, by which variety and convenience in language are promoted.

---

* See page 22.

The word beast, be-est, from *be*, is any thing which has life or be-ing, and if applied in its full meaning, would include the higher as well as lower orders of being. It is difficult to say what is its present extent of application. In some local districts it is exclusively horses, in others neat cattle. Till lately, it included all insects and reptiles, as it now does in French.

Hen is the Danish pronoun *she*. It is the *single female* animal of any kind, instead of being, as now applied in English, the *she* of birds in general. The noun *cow* is originally, noun and verb, *life* and *to live;* but it is used to denote one kind of animal instead of all kinds. *Man* is a pronoun in several languages, and in English is acquiring a conventional appropriation. It is said "*man* is mortal;" but we can not say, *ox* is stout, *horse* is swift, *dog* is mortal ; because elegant usage will not warrant these expressions. All the words called pro-nouns are, according to the principles here alluded to, very signifi-cant original nouns, not with their meanings destroyed, or essential-ly altered, but with those meanings applied to a part, instead of the whole, of what they formerly denoted.

Questions on Pronouns, Chapter IV.

1. What are pronouns?
2. How many kinds of pronouns?
3. Give the list of the eighteen pronouns.
4. How many, and what persons have pronouns?
5. Give examples of their position or case.
6. What is said of the pronoun *ye* ?
7. *Who* and *whom* ?

CHAPTER V.

ADJECTIVES.

1. *Adjectives* are words used with nouns to *define* or *describe* them: as, an *able* man; two *sensible young* ladies; *ripe* fruit; *fine silk* velvet; *our daily* bread.

This part of speech is of very extensive use in distinguishing *different* things, and *different* sorts of things, coming under the same general name. If it is asked, concerning a man, *what kind* of person he is, it is answered he is *old* or *young, wise, ignorant, silly, fleshy, lean, short, tall, pleasant, morose, dull,* or *active;* or he is *described* by any one of a hundred other *adjectives,* designating his general qualities, appearance, or traits of character.

Other adjectives, instead of describing things in sorts or kinds, *define, point out,* or *specify* directly *which,* or *what* things, *how many,* or *how much.*

2. Adjectives are of two kinds, *defining* and *describing* adjectives: but the difference between the two is not great, and they run into each other in various ways; as, when we say, " The *northern* hemisphere;" *northern, defines* which half of the globe we mean, and *describes* its local relation to the other half.

The chief *defining* adjectives are, *an, a, one,*[*] *two, twain, three,* and all the *cardinal numbers; last, first, second,* and all the *ordinal numbers; many, much, few, little, several, this, that, the, these, those, which, what, my, thy, his, her, its, our, your, their, whose, other, each, every, either, some, no, any,* and *all.*

---

[*] The word *one* is often used as a *noun* of very extensive application; as, " The knowing *ones;*" " The evil *One;*" " Pick out the good *ones,* and leave the *others.*"

Most adjectives partake of both these two characters. In saying *all quarto* books, though the leading intention is to describe the kind, we necessarily limit the noun *books* to those only which are of quarto size.

3. *Examples of Defining Adjectives.*

an ox,	the *five* senses,	our *twelve* tribes.
some birds,	every *four* weeks,	her *seven* sons,
two books,	these *forty* days,	which *several* acts,
all regions,	this, my *last* will,	his *much* speaking,
no noise,	the *twelve* tables,	your *first* letter,
one pencil,	those *two* witnesses,	whose *whole* fortune,
many people,	all *which* things,	each *tenth* man.

4. *Defining* adjectives answer to the specific question, *which* or *what* things, *how many,* or *how much.*

5. Many nouns become adjectives by use, and serve either to define or describe other nouns : as,

window glass,	*bonnet* paper,
glass window,	*paper* bonnets,
beef cattle,	*silk* hats,
ox beef,	*horse skin* gloves,
smyrna figs,	*gun powder* plot.

6. Other nouns, in being turned into adjectives, receive slight modifications of different kinds; as, a *wooden* dish, a *gloomy* prospect, a *national* concern.

7. One kind of these *adjectives,* formed from *nouns,* is of extensive use in defining or pointing out things by their individual relations to each other.

These are commonly formed by adding *s*, with an *apostrophy* prefixed : as,

The *slave's* master,	*Cesar's* funeral,
Hamlet's father's ghost,	*Cicero's* banishment,
Wat Tyler's sedition,	*Maria's* likeness,
Montgomery's monument at *St. Paul's church.*	

The least definite of all the defining adjectives is the word *the*. This word can hardly be said to *define* at all of itself; as it does not confine the noun to either number, gender, person, or case; but refers alike to all. It is of general use where it is not necessary to be very *specific*, or where a sufficient idea of the thing exists to answer the purpose of ordinary communication; as a person at evening says, "*The stars* appear to night." *How many* or *what* stars appear, must depend on something more definite to explain.

"*The wind* blows." "*The camel* is a beast of burden."

"*The wolves* were heared howling in *the woods*."

"New-York was evacuated by *the British army*, and re-occupied by *the Americans*, Nov. 25, 1783."

A particular aukwardness prevails in the employment of the nouns *few* and *many* as defining adjectives. "*A* great many *horses*." If the words *great* and *many* were to be considered as adjectives, leaving them out would not alter the construction; and there would then remain *a horses*. As we never, at present, hear the phrases "*a few many*," "*little many*," or "*bad many*," it seems quite unnecessary to speak of "*a good many*," as if it added something distinctive to the word *many*. "*Many floods*," "*The rushing of many waters*," would be rendered less expressive by the clumsy addition so often heared in modern conversation. Those who, in point of taste, prefer these redundant words, it is readily admitted, can find sufficient *authority* for the practice.

Several analogous expressions prevail in using nouns of number; as, "*a dozen*, or *a hundred men*:" The word *of* is understood after the collective noun, as in the phrase "*a score of sheep*;" but the other phrases being more familiar, omit *of*, for the shortening of discourse.

There is a set of *defining adjectives* showing the relations between the *three* grammatical *persons*, employed in discourse, and the various things with which they may stand in some kind of connection.

These words, in the existing systems of grammar, are called personal-pronouns in the possessive case. These words are *mine, thine, his, hers, its, ours, yours, theirs*, and *whose*.

Four of these five books *are thine*, and *one is ours*; but *ours* alone *is* worth more than all *thine are*.

The word *ours*, shows that the single book mentioned stands in some kind of relation to the speaker and others, who, together, represent the *first person* plural. In the same manner, the adjective *thine* specifies an existing relation between the person spoken to, and the remaining four books.

The words *mine*, *thine*, and others of this class, are used when the nouns which they *specify* are not expressed in their place after them, out understood. When the following nouns are inserted, the adjectives defining the same relation, are changed to *my*, *thy*, *his*, *her*, *its*, *our*, *your*, *their*, and *whose*.

Example.

my children,	the injuries are *mine*,
thy parents,	the benefits were *thine*,
his friends,	her debts become *his*,
our father,	the evil designs were *hers*,
your country,	the day is *yours*,
their king,	liberty will be *ours*,
whose death,	the prize is *theirs*.

The injuries are *mine*, implies that the injuries specified are those which the individual making the assertion, either gives or receives, or with which he stands in some way connected.

An extensive mistake has prevailed respecting the class of words called possessives.

" Samuel Badger, hatter, makes and sells all kinds of *boys'* hats."

If the hats belong to the boys, it is improper for Mr. Badger to sell them; but the boys have the right to go and take them when they please.

8. Adjectives in English never vary for number, gender, or position; but describing adjectives are varied to express the qualities and conditions of things in different degrees.

9. The degrees of comparison are three, called the *positive*, *comparative*, and *superlative*.

The *comparative* commonly is formed by adding *er*, and the *superlative* by *est*; as,

Pos.	Com.	Super.
clear,	clearer,	clearest.
happy,	happier,	happiest.

10. Many adjectives also take the termination *ish*,[*]
to express quality in a slight degree; as, *greenish*. This
ending is often used to form new adjectives, especially
in familiar language; as *waspish, sheepish ;* inclining
to the qualities of a *wasp,* or a *sheep.*

11. Besides what are called the regular comparative
and superlative degrees of adjectives, they are compared by each other, under a great variety of circumstances.

12. When one adjective is used to define or describe
an other, instead of referring directly to the nouns, it
may be called a *secondary* adjective.

13. Secondary adjectives refer to the different species of things which come under one general quality;
as a *sheet iron,* or *wrought iron,* stove; a *seemingly
good,* or *real good* man.

A *Russia iron* bar.

Russia and iron are both adjectives : the first describes the second,
and both refer to the noun bar. There are not only different
kinds of bars, but also different kinds of iron of which bars are made.

A shawl may be *cotton,* or *worsted,* or *silk.* A *silk* shawl may be a
China, French, or *Italian* one : and this again may be any one of a
dozen colors; as, *blue, red,* or *green.* The color takes various subdivisions, *sea green, grass green, pea green ;* and these again may be
pale, dull, bright, or *deep.*

---

[*] This syllable *ish,* is from an old verb, traced through many ancient tongues, and will be explained in an other work.

Many secondary adjectives are formed by adding *ly* or *like* to other words.

An *orange* grove is a grove of *orange* trees. An *orange-like* grove is one which resembles an orange grove. A *gentlemanly*, or *gentle-man-like*, person is one who conducts in character as a gentleman.

The adjective *like* with some others has been a source of difficulty in parsing, as it requires an objective word after it, without any apparent reason under the existing explanations of adjectives. *Like* is a past participle contracted for *likened*. The thing which is *like* an other, is made like it, or *likened to* it. It is the same with *similar* and many other words.

A considerable number of adjectives are compounded of two or more simple ones. The word *what* is *which that*, or *that which*, and may refer to the agent of one verb and the object of an other.

The youngest scholars who engage in the study of grammar, should endeavor to understand the meaning of the words in their parsing lessons: then, to distinguish nouns from adjectives, they should come directly to the fact, whether they are used merely to *name* things, or to *point out* and *describe* other things.

Examples for practice.

Older men,	some China ships,
large trees,	Solon the wise philosopher,
a silver cup,	Alfred the Great,
an iron wedge,	John's Camel's hair girdle,
men, wise and good,	that beggar's humble request,
fresh Smyrna figs,	ladies' best morocco shoes,
many canal boats,	fine British ink powder,
dry walnut wood,	most elegant marble chimneys.

Pittsburg cut flint decanters,
Warranted cast steel cradle sithes,
Very old Holland gin, *warranted pure,*
Genuine old Madeira wine,
A gold mounted sword,
An honest meaning person,
A snow white linen neck cloth,
The chief city gate keeper.

A fiery red East India silk bonnet.

a,   defining adjective, referring to bonnet,
fiery,   secondary adjective, describing the kind of red,
red,   adjective, describing silk,
East,   adjective, describing India,
India,   adjective, describing silk,
silk,   describing adjective, referring to bonnet to denote the kind.

The adjectives in this phrase come under a broad principle founded on the minor divisions in the sorts, qualities, and degrees, included in the extended application of a primary descriptive word.

Secondary adjectives admit the different comparative forms, either of a single or a duplicate kind, according to the nature of the relations which they are employed to denote ; as,

A *dearly* beloved, *more* beloved, *best* beloved child.
A *bright* purple, *brighter* purple, *brightest* purple robe.
Little known, *less* known, *least* known truths.
Ill devised, *worse* devised, *worst* devised schemes.
Very well finished, *far better* finished, *much the best finished* houses.

Adjectives of more than two syllables, and commonly those exceeding one, make their various degrees by secondary adjectives prefixed.

Instead of adding *er* and *est* to *atrocious*, to mark its degrees, we use the expressions *very, horridly,* or *shockingly* atrocious deeds.

The chief practical direction which can be given for the use of adjectives to modify each other, is that no two, in a single phrase, shall be employed to express the same idea ; nor more than one in what is called the comparative, or superlative form ; as, *more whiter,* or any similar expression.

For an exercise, let the scholar distinguish the secondary adjectives in the preceding examples ; and then show the words to which all the adjectives refer. In the phrase, *"fresh Smyrna figs,"* ask the question, *fresh what ?* or *what is fresh ?* answer, *figs.*

There are two sets of words called *numeral adjectives.* The cardinal numbers which denote the amount, numerically taken ; and the ordinal numbers, showing the relative succession in the order of things.

cardinal numbers.	*ordinal numbers.*
one,	first,
two,	second,
three,	third,
four, and others.	fourth, and the rest.

The words *dozen, hundred,* and *thousand,* are collective nouns. A thousand men is that aggregate number taken as an entire body. The word *of,* which is understood in the singular, must be used in the plural; as, "*hundreds* of persons."

The other cardinal numbers are *adjectives* or *nouns,* according to their use; as, *five* dollars and *ten* cents; or, a *five* and two *tens :* by *fifties,* by *twenties,* and *twelves.*

Numeral adjectives, like others, may be secondary; as, " a *five* dollar bank note."

The single and essential idea on which all adjectives depend is that of *comparison,* or the relations of things to each other.

It is said, in the existing grammars, that " *an adjective is a word added to a substantive, and generally expresses its quality.*"

This kind of *definition,* if it can be so called, leaves three very important questions for the learner to settle for himself.

1. What is this quality in its precise meaning, as depending on some known principle.
2. By what medium or instrumentality is that meaning expressed.
3. What office does an adjective perform, when it does not " express quality ?"

If there was, among the objects in nature, no difference to be expressed, there would be no need of adjectives: but these variations every where exist in what are called *qualities.* The use of adjectives is to distinguish things coming under the same name. The idea of a quality, as a some thing essential, appears to be a total mistake.

It was said before, that all adjectives are either *nouns* or *participles,* made adjectives by use.

Whatever has substance or body, must have form, extension, and color, and local relations to other things; with those also of resemblance and contrast.

After naming a substance, the design of an adjective, is to give the idea of its distinctive character to the person who does not know it before. To effect this, it becomes necessary either to show him the thing which you would have him understand, or tell him its relation to some thing which he does know. This standard relation to which he is so referred, for the idea of quality, must be some obvious appearance in nature, capable of being mutually and definitely understood, and therefore not liable to deceive.

Suppose, for instance, we enter the field of nature to examine the principle which explains those striking "*qualities*" of objects, included under the term *color*.

The following *standards of color*, among others, will be found, as referred to familiarly, in modern English, without disguise of the words.

amber,	fox,	peach blow,
ash,	fustic,	pearl,
blood,	gold,	pink,
bottle,	grass,	plum,
brick,	hazel,	raven,
butternut,	ink,	rose,
carmine,	indigo,	ruby,
carnation,	iron,	saffron,
carrot,	ivory,	sea,
sherry,	jet,	silver,
chesnut,	lead,	sky,
chrome,	leek,	smoke,
coal,	lily,	snow,
cream,	logwood,	snuff,
dove,	mahogany,	steel,
ebony,	milk,	stone,
fawn,	mouse,	straw,
fire,	mud,	verdigris,
flax,	olive,	vermilion,
flesh,	orange,	violet.

The predominating *quality*, coming under the idea of color, is *green*, a term slightly modified in its present use. Milton employs it without disguise.

> " All in a robe of darkest *grain*,
> Flowing with majestic train,"

Green is green colored; *grain* colored, the color of the spring-
ing blades of *grain.* This term is too general to answer, of itself, all
the purposes to be subserved. It therefore takes a number of secondary adjectives to express the minor differences, in things which
are *green ;* as *bottle* green ; *sea, pea, olive, grass, verdigris, leek,* or
emerald green. In all these instances, it is seen that this quality of
green is denoted by a *noun,* made secondary adjective by use. To
describe the *green* thing, it is referred to some standard sign, which
is *green ;* that is, *grain, grain* colored, or *grain* like.

Thus it appears that these " *names of qualities,*" are names of
material objects, affording the definite perception of what, for want
of understanding the principle, is erroneously imagined to be a
mere inherent property of something else. So far as language is,
or can be, concerned, this mere relation of a thing to an other thing,
affording some standing resemblance, is the unavoidable necessity
of the case.

In other adjectives, the reference is directly, to the effect produced by an action, and thus, indirectly, to the thing which is the
means of producing that effect ; that is, in the language of grammar,
the word is a *participle.*

The adjective *red* is *rayed,* a participle in a modified form. It
is, the appearance of objects, produced by the *raying* or *reddening*
of the morning beams, or other *radiating* cause.

White is the substitution of *wh* for *qu,* formerly used in a large
proportion of the words with this beginning. It is *quite, quited,
quitted, clear, cleared,* from all *color, spot,* or *stain.*

Blue is the participle from the verb *to blow.* It is the sky where
clouds and vapors are *blown* away: the *clearing* up, or *fair* weather. The poet Thomson, drawing his lessons from nature, is
true to these principles of language.

" He, from the *whitening undistinguished* blaze,
Collecting every ray into its kind,
To the charmed eye educed the gorgeous train
Of *parent colors.* First, the *flaming red*
Sprung *vivid* forth ; the tawny *orange* next ;
And next delicious *yellow ;* by whose side
Fell the kind beams of all refreshing *green ;*
Then the *pure blue,* that swells autumnal skies,
Ethereal played ; and then, of sadder hue,

Emerged the deepened *indigo* ; as when
The heavy skirted evening drops with frost :
While the last gleaming of refracted light
Died in the fainting *violet* away."   Thompson,
                    Poem to the memory of Sir Isaac Newton.

The special adjectives of local relation, under the name of *prepositions*, also receive the secondary adjectives, in various ways of modification; as, *beyond*, far *beyond*, very *far* beyond Jordan; *entirely through*, or *half way* through the plank; *exactly over* our heads.

The words called *prepositions*, are all participial adjectives. They express the local relation of one thing to an other. That relation is, in fact, and in the contemplation of the mind, a produced relation, and produced by action. The explanation of this principle, however, in its requisite extent; will best be understood after the exposition of verbs, and the participles formed from them.

To say that adjectives express the qualities of things, far from being a true elucidation of this important class of words, is chiefly calculated to mislead.

A *hot* brick is not the quality of the brick. It may be alternately *hot* and *cold*. A *line* may be *horizontal* one moment, and *vertical* the next. The *burned* brick conveys incidentally, the idea of quality, because the burning of this article produces an effect which is lasting : but if we say "a slightly *burned* finger," we do not mean that the quality of the finger is permanently changed. So, if we say a *sick*, or a *well* man, we allude merely to the condition, in which, for the time being, the man may be placed. That the *burning* of clay gives it the *quality* of hardness is an incidental fact, and does vary in principle, from the phrase a *full* or an *empty* cup ; a *horizontal* or *vertical* line.

The adjectives *like* and *own*, have caused much difficulty.

Like is the participle *likened*, in a contracted form. Whatever is *like*, is so, because it is *likened*, or made *like* ; and it must be *likened to something else*, as a matter of course, or it would not be *like*. It has an object before it, and an other object after it; and expresses the *relation* of *likeness*, or *resemblance*, between them.

Own is a past participle, from a verb signifying *to work.* All property which can be *owned* is the produce of labor. Any spot of ground which a man *worked* originally was his *worked* ground, and the crop it yielded, was what his work had produced. In the contemplation of law, and of the essential fact, it is the same principle thro all the modern forms of a commercial state. A man may work one kind of property and exchange it for an other, or may receive his father's *worked* property by inheritance.

Questions to Chapter V.

1. What are adjectives?
2. How many kinds of adjectives?
3. Give examples of defining adjectives.
4. What questions do defining adjectives answer?
5. What words become adjectives by use?
6. How are other nouns made adjectives?
7. What is said of an other kind of adjectives?
8. How do adjectives vary?
9. What are the degrees of comparison?
10. What other termination has adjectives?
11. What comparisons have adjectives besides the regular degrees?
12. When one adjective refers to an other, what is it called?
13. What is the use of secondary adjectives?
14. What are cardinal numbers?
15. What are ordinal numbers?

CHAPTER VI.

———

VERBS.

The term *verb, verbum,* or *word,* is very appropriate, as used to denote this part of speech. It signifies the essential principle of activity or of life, and, in language, the distinctive expression of its exercise.

1. A VERB signifies to do some action, as, " Farmers *plow* their fields ; Clouds *shed* rain *to wet* the ground; the miser *dies,* and *leaves* his gold.

2. All verbs which form their past tense, and past participle, by adding *d* or *ed,** are called regular ; as I rule, I rul*ed,* I have my paper rul*ed.*

3. Those which differ from this ending, are about two hundred, in English, and are called irregular. They generally consist of such as are, or have been, in most frequent use ; as, I *write,* I *wrote,* I have *written* a letter.

4. Three things are to be considered in the use of verbs :

I. An agent or moving cause which produces an action.

II. The *motion, change,* or *acting,* which the verb denotes.

———

* The ending *ed* is a contraction from the old verb *dede, did. Aunciente* *custome blend-dede* these words for convenience. Their contraction afterwards was according to the general practice in language.

7

III. The *object* which that action effects.

5. David *killed* Goliah.

I. *David*, the *agent* or *actor*, moved, changed, or affected some thing, or caused it to be done.

II. *Killed* denotes the *movement, acting,* or *operation,*
which took place.

III. *Goliah,* is the *object* which that action changed
from a *living man* to a *dead body.*

Remarks on the Laws of Motion.

The primary laws of action, as they exist in nature, are intimately
connected with those subjects which form the chief amount of
scholastic learning; and the want of suitable regard to their principles must be an essential defect in any work on language.

In submitting a few remarks under this head, it is proposed barely
to offer, in a brief form, such explanations as have direct reference
to purposes of utility: not to multiply distinctions, but to inquire
whether the distinctions which have been supposed to exist, are
not alike destitute of foundation in fact, and of possible application
in practice.

It has been said by eminent writers that the word *motion* can not
be defined. Let it be so; and if, without a definition, it can be ascertained what the thing is, it will be easy afterwards to find the
meaning of the term.

To avoid being lost in the regions of conjecture, it is necessary
to keep in view those obvious facts which are generally acknowledged by the plain sense of mankind.

It will be recollected that, as before explained, the presentations
of material objects, and the perceptions drawn from them, are naturally divided into three classes.

1. *Entities,* or *things,* individually considered, and to which nouns
   are applied.

2. *Comparisons,* or the *relations* which things, as such, bear to each
   other. This class of perceptions is the foundation for words of
   description and *specification,* called *adjectives.*

3. *Actions*, *motions*, or *changes*, expressed in language by *verbs*.

These three classes, alike in nature, in thought, and in speech, inseparably depend on each other, and it is needless to say which is least or most important. The third class is to be explained, and is, from the principles which it embraces, by far the most extensive, varied, and sublime, in its means of elucidation.

Every portion of matter is influenced by different active principles, more or less complex, tending to produce change, existing both within itself and without. All the perceivable operations in nature are a succession of effects, which, as they are followed by other effects, become, in turn, apparent causes. The knowledge of their laws is derived from repeated observation; and all active principles, alike inscrutable in their own essential character, are inferred from the aggregate results which they are seen to produce.

Beams of light and heat are emitted from the sun; the air, unequally warmed, is put in motion; a tree is blown down; and, in its fall, an elephant is killed. In other cases, thick vapors are produced, hail and rain descend, the edifice is struck by lightning, and shattered in ruins. A series of actions run successively thro all material objects, each effect converted into the proximate cause of the next in order; while the real active principle remains for ever unseen. Whether we speak of *cohesion*, in glue, *elasticity* in India rubber, the *gravitation* of a stone, or *vitality* in the roe buck, all these springs of action, however variant in operation, are alike untangible by the sense.

Semper causa latet; vis est notissima.

To show that the fact, as well as the principle, of change, is often to be learned from its effects, instead of being directly manifest to the senses, we may place a red hot brick upon a cold one. In a short time it is found that one has lost, and the other has gained heat, and that an equilibrium is produced. The warmth, in passing from one body to the other, of course is not seen; but the fact is inferred from the different state of things which has taken place, and which, according to the plainest dictates of reason, could not happen without the requisite means. The perception by which the action in this case is ascertained and asserted, is the contact of the two bodies, under the influence of a general law, by the necessary *operation* of which, as learned from experience, the heat is actually known *to pass* from one body to the other. The man who never heared of such a word as *caloric* perceives, equally with the best philosopher, the material fact that one brick gains, and the other loses, heat. The distinctive manifestation that two bodies, of unequal temperature, are placed together, with the tendencies they are known to possess, enables any one of ordinary intelligence to determine, without seeing a stream of fire in its passage, that one is cooling, and the other growing warmer than before.

If a powerful loadstone is let down, over a piece of iron, to a near approach, the weight of the metal is overcome by the attraction; the mass is drawn up with considerable force to meet the suspended magnet. When these two bodies come in contact, the first being fixed in its place, they are both, in appearance, entirely at rest: yet, according to the ablest scientific writers, other things being equal, the force of this attraction is inversely as the square of the distance; and there is twenty times as much exertion of the attractive power, when no motion is apparent, as there was when, by its force, the body was plainly seen to move.

No *motion* as such, is, of itself, ever obvious to the senses. A single instance will illustrate this principle, as it runs thro all manifestly changing bodies. If the swinging pendulum of a clock is perceived, it is common to say, that its vibrations are seen. It is most certain, however, that, in this, or any other instance, the *motion* is not exhibited to our senses, as having any separate, independent, or absolute existence. The only real perception is that of the pendulum itself, under the circumstances in which, for the time being, it is placed.

Actions are in principle the same, thro all possible modifications under which they ever take place. The object of perception can be no other than some portion of matter, which may be obviously in a state of motion, or in a state of apparent rest; but a substance in the condition of real quiescence does not exist.

The principles of activity may be effectually exerted, to *produce*, to *continue*, or to *prevent* motion. These modifications of action are of very little importance, as philosophic distinctions, and of none at all, in the ordinary employment of language, or of thought. They would hardly deserve to be mentioned, if it was not for the perplexing systems growing out of misconception of their nature.

Under one or the other of these modifications, *action* and *re-action*, reciprocal and equal, pervade the whole creation. This is alike the uniform experience of plain men, and the induction from the deepest scientific research. If Newton had not stated the fact that the trace rope pulls the horse back, as much as he draws that forward, any teamster might try the experiment, by stopping his cart, in ascending a hill. On the supposition that the traces make no resistance to the horse, he would need no strength to draw the load. But in this, as in every other mechanical operation, the force requisite to produce the effect, is in exact proportion to the resistance opposed. The seeming preponderance in moving the load does not destroy the equality ; it only overcomes the resistance which the weight could oppose, and lie still ; the equilibrium is preserved thro all changes ; for, by every accumulation of force, to increase the rapidity, the resistance is increased, precisely in the same degree.

No movement which takes place, is ever perfectly free : because, no substance can be in motion without some obstacle directly opposed, nor without counteracting principles of motivity more or less complex. The pebble, thrown from a sling, would continue indefinitely to go forward in a straight line ; but the air impedes its progress, gravitation diverts it from its course, and the solid wall not only stops it, but throws it back.

Actions, in reference to their operative principles, are never simple. Different active influences are exerted, in every portion of matter, at every instant of time. The motion of a cannon ball thro the air depends, in the first instance, on the impulse given by the gun powder ; it afterwards remains with the ball itself to continue that effect, to a greater or less extent. A ball of lead, of iron, and of cork, successively discharged from the same gun, would go to unequal distances, and might produce extremely different consequences, on the objects exposed to their shock. In the three cases supposed, the action commences with the same projectile force, and whatever difference afterwards takes place in the momentums of the balls, depends on their *comparative power* to *continue their own movements.*

So, if a playing ball should be vigorously thrown on a firm platform, it would rebound to a considerable distance : but a ball of wax would stick fast where it was thrown. The action of throwing is the same in the two cases. They strike the floor nearly alike; and the rebounding of the elastic ball is the exertion of a *principle of activity*, in the substance itself, to *extend the effect* of the first impulse. This *co-operating principle of activity*, the mass of wax does not possess. The difference in the results supposed certainly does not depend on the bare *act of throwing*, which is in both instances the same; but the compound actions of the hand and the ball, in each case. If it depended simply on the act of throwing, performed in the same way, then, by every just rule of reasoning, there should be no difference of result; for if like causes do not produce like effects, then the world has a new philosophy to learn.

Action may be *absolute, relative,* or a *mixture* of the two.

When a ship sails from the land, it is said, " The hills gradually *sink* from the sight:" and the assertion is true, tho the action is only a relative one. If two persons are travelling the same way, at an unequal rate, one is said to *fall* behind the other. So in saying the sun rises, it is no matter whether that orb really moves upward, or the eastern part of the horizon is depressed.* The sun does acquire an additional elevation above the plane of vision; and, as to the substantial fact, it is entirely immaterial by what means. In language, as following the general principles of thought, the speaker seizes upon the direct and obvious presentation, and uses his words accordingly.

With regard to the inverted position of objects, as exhibited according to the laws of optics, it is only to observe that they are seen

---

* To show how fallacious and unprofitable are all disputes on questions like this, it is only necessary to observe that the ideas of *up* and *down, high* and *low*, with others of the kind, are mere *relations*, and have no absolute existence. The futility of the objection that the sun, in point of fact, does not rise, becomes more striking, on recurring to the acknowledged law of optics, that all objects within the scope of vision are seen inverted, and that it is only by familiar observation, that this illusion of the sense is corrected. If the scales are balanced with a pound weight in each, then taking the weight out of one side, or putting an additional pound into the other, will, as a plain matter of fact, produce the same result, that is, one scale rises while the other sinks: and every mathematician knows that, in a comparison of two algebraic quantities, a plus or a minus number, on either side, will equally vary the difference.

in their proper relations to each other, and if there is in the first instance any illusion in the view of these objects, it is corrected by early habit. The modern improvements in the science of astronomy create no necessity for new phraseology in speaking of the same motions. The sun continues to rise and set, and the tables of Dr. Maskaline and others, with the present knowledge of the solar system, are governed by the same laws of language and thought that formerly prevailed.

On the same principle that we contemplate in numerous instances mere relative *things*, we also witness *actions* under a prodigious variety of modifications, in reference to different *agents*, *means*, and *objects*. The words *cause, instrument,* and *effect*, are themselves mere relative terms; and it is so with a large portion of the words employed in speaking of actions. All the mechanic powers are merely such by the offices which they actively perform. It is not as a bar of iron or wood that an article can be called a lever; but only by application to its appropriate use. The same holds good of the *wedge*, the *wheel, pulley,* and *screw*; and thro the whole range of nature, or of rational conception, power inert is a contradiction in fact, and no power at all.

So far as scientific research extends, *action* is the exertion of some operative principle to produce change, and motion is the effective* operation of such principle in the real alteration of some portion of matter.

The attempted distinctions between things animate and inanimate, in motion or apparently at rest, in reference to any differential principle of action, or of expression, appear to be altogether unfounded and impracticable, in every point of view in which they can be considered.

Time, in its simple principle, is the set of relations which things bear to each other, in the successive order of their movements. In

---

* It is not intended by this explanation to say that any causal principle is ever exerted without instrumental activity, and real motion: but the bodies *moved, interchanged,* or *transfused,* are often too subtile for observation. When the magnet draws iron, we do not see any cords, but there may be machinery, as well as completely organized animals, beyond the powers of human sight: but a farther examination of this subject is not necessary to the present attempt.

its practical application, it is the computation of periodical changes, in bodies whose movements are most regular or best understood.

Manner of action is either the mind, intention, or plan by which an action is directed, or the means or instrumentality with which it is performed ; or the effect which it produces on an object; inasmuch as all possible modifications of action, and all which the mind can ever contemplate concerning them, must be divided between the three. The explanation in detail of these principles of action, in their relation to language, belongs more properly to an after part of this work.

We come next to consider these laws of action, as they flow into the habits of thought and the forms of verbal expression ; and here, it will be recollected that the leading position to be borne in mind, throughout this work, is that there is no important rule in any language, which has not its foundation in some established principle, in the mind of man, and the nature of things. To say that speech depends chiefly on capricious custom, and attempt to explain it by rules primarily deduced from the beginnings, endings, or collocation of words, is to describe the temple by its finishing ornaments, instead of the proper drawing of its plan and elevation.

The verb is the part of speech, without which no sentence can be formed, and on which other terms, in construction, mainly depend. Any system which misinterprets this essential class of words must, in its chief remaining parts, necessarily be wrong.

In reference to any philosophic or grammatical principle, capable of being understood or applied, in theory or practice, all verbs, in in all languages, are precisely of one kind, with the single miraculous exception of the burning bush.* This proposition will seem very extravagant to a very large majority of readers, who, on this subject, are accustomed tamely to follow authoritative opinions, instead of employing their reasoning powers. It becomes necessary

---

* The observations which follow, respecting the transitive action expressed by every verb, it will be perceived, are not addressed to mere learners ; but to able teachers and others, who can investigate the principles submitted, and take a more comprehensive and philosophic view of their application than could be formally given in the course of ordinary school lessons. If learning is worth learning, it should be learned according to rational principles, founded in truth, and addressed to the understanding.

then to examine, somewhat in detail, the principles on which this proposition depends.

It is the received opinion, among writers on language, that there are three or more kinds of verbs essentially differing from each other. This is considered the predominating, and most extensive principle of speech. It is truly and eminently so, if the doctrine is founded in fact.

No one, for slight reasons, should presume to question a rule so excedingly important, as it runs thro the whole system of language and of instruction, and which has received the general assent of the great leaders in talent and learning hitherto known. Strong arguments, however, present themselves in favor of a different theory ; and such theory, if it should prove just, will not only have the intrinsic merit of truth, but will be found far more simple and useful, in all its practical applications.

The three sorts of verbs, according to the most distinguished expounders of language, are,

1. *Active* or *transitive,* implying an *agent,* an *action,* and an *object* acted upon ; as I *love* Penelope.

2. *Passive,* signifying the *suffering* or *receiving* the effect of an action; as, " *To be loved ;*" " *Penelope is loved by me.*"

3. *Neuter,* which express "neither *action,* nor *passion,* but *being,* or a *state of being ;* as, I *am,* I *sleep,* I *sit.*"

Some writers make four or more kinds, with different names; but the variance is of no importance : the objection is alike to all. In all, the attempted division does not depend on any philosophic principle whatever; but results wholly from misconception or mere accident.

1. *Active or transitive verbs.* This class presents, in many instances, the greatest apparent contradictions, and is, of all the kinds, the most difficult to reconcile with the very principles laid down to explain it,

" Bonaparte *lost the battle* of Waterloo."

This sentence, according to all the teachers, is the direct and literal assertion that Bonaparte performed the *action* of *losing* that *battle*. How stands the fact? Until after the battle was irretrievably lost, he exerted his utmost energy of body and mind to *win* the *battle* and *prevent* the *loss*. He never did the least act with intention to produce such a result, but skilfully strove, with all his talents and means, to guard against it. How then did he perform the action which the sentence directly affirms?

If it was proper to say that a verb is *neuter*, because, in some instances, it does not denote *movement*, *directly obvious to our senses*, there would be a double objection to *manifest activity*, exerted in opposition to what the affirmation asserts. No philosophy like this has, in either case, any bearing on the question.

The verb *lost*, as above quoted, and most others, depend on different principles from any which have probably been explained, from the days of Aristotle and Ennius to the present time.

Some radical errors of a similar nature, appear to run through the general systems of grammar, rhetoric, logic, and mental philosophy, in all countries where these studies are pursued. The propositions laid down as axioms in the structure of speech, being grossly wrong, the complex systems founded upon them, of course, could not be right.

With respect to the *agent* which produces an action, it is no matter by what *motive*, *fatality*, *inherent principle*, or *communicated impulse*, it may operate; what name it bears; how inert it may appear; nor what secondary means it may employ. These moving springs of action are precisely as numerous, convolved, and minute, as the train of causes and consequences throughout the Creator's works. The short sighted philosophy which attempts to draw division lines between them, leads to endless perplexity, without any beneficial result; and has misdirected the systems of instruction in language, ever since a college existed in Europe.

Sir Christopher Wren *erected* St. Paul's *Church* in thirty-seven years.

Solomon *built* the *temple*.

It is not necessary to the correctness of this assertion that he should have raised a gavel or hammer on the building, or any of its materials, or even made a line on the trestle board. He did something, or caused it to be performed, which, but for him, would have remained undone, or not done in the same way. The least possible difference is that it must have been independent of him as an effective cause.

The geese, by their gabbling, *saved Rome* from destruction.

They performed an action which, in its train of consequences, waked the soldiers, roused them to arms; led them to battle; slaughtered many of the Gauls, and drove the rest from the city.

Mr. Smith of Boston *raises* a large *crop* on his farm in New-Hampshire. The King of England *made a treaty* in Pekin. The admiral *sunk five* of the enemy's ships. The Emperor of Russia *builds forts* on the North West coast of America.

David did not *touch Goliah* when he killed him. He threw a stone with a sling, and that stone *produced a wound* which *caused* his *death*. The succession of intermediate causes, whether explained in grammar books or not, must be recognized in most indictments for murder, or, by well established rules of law, the manslayer would be cleared.

The infant, in America, *inherits a farm* in England.

How does he *perform* that *action?* He, as a cause, *gives* to the chain of legal title, a *different direction* from what it would otherwise *take*, and *prevents an other person* from *holding the farm* as rightful owner.

How does the *miser perform the transitive action* of *leaving his gold?* By the *action* of *dying.*

The pier *supports* the *bridge.*
The roof *shelters* the *family.*
The walls *enclose them.*
Windows *admit light* and *exclude cold.*
Chains and fetters *bind* the *man.*
The cord *sustains* the *weight.*
Strong boilers *hold steam.*
The ague fit *shakes* the *person.*
The falling beam *killed* the *workmen.*

Hot iron *burns* the *fingers*.
"Neuter verbs *express* a *state of being*."

John *lost* his *money*, while he was asleep.
How did John *perform* this *transitive action* of losing his money?
A thief *did it* for him, by *stealing* his *purse*.

The next class of verbs, as explained in the systems of instruction, are those called *neuter*, implying *neither action* nor *passion*;
but *being*, or a *state of being ;* as, I *am*, I *sleep*, I *sit*. *Cesar stood*.

The objections which have been or can be offered against the
activity of four thousand English verbs, appear, when brought down
to their specific statement, to be reduced to three. It may be farther observed, that these objections all depend chiefly on a common
principle.

1. The *subjects* of the verbal affirmations are *inanimate matter*,
and therefore can not *act*.
2. The ideas denoted by the verbs do not amount to *action*, perceivable, real, or fairly implied.
3. The verbs have no recipient *objects*, expressed, or necessarily
understood, and are not capable of being explained, as signifying
any resulting *effects*.

The fallacy of the above propositions and the theory founded
upon them, with their consequent errors in practice, it is hoped
may be satisfactorily explained. The causes of these errors are in-
attention, either to the definite meaning of terms; to the science of
physical and intellectual nature, as connected with speech; or, to
the proper application of words to things, in the special case.

Instead of beginning with disputes growing out of the casual
omission or expression of objective words, it is proper to come at
once to those principles, on which, according to the laws of matter
and mind, all verbal affirmations depend. These affirmations denote, not merely *implied*, but always *real action*, in every form of
their utterance. For something, to do something, with something,
to something; or, *cause*, *means*, *action*, and *effect* is the rule in the
use of every verb. It is the Creator's rule, which man may mis-
conceive, but can not change ; and is alike extensive, simple, and
sublime.

The strong arguments of the Schools seem directed chiefly against the activity of the verbs *to be* and *to live:* but how fallacious is the objection, that man has no independent power to sustain and preserve himself in life, and that, at every moment, he relies on his God to enable him to live. It was, of course, only by the same Divine sustenance, that Moses wrought all the wonders in Egypt ; led the Israelites through the Red Sea ; smote the rock, and drew forth a refreshing stream, in the parching desert. Without the same upholding aid, how is any action of man to be performed, at any period of his being ? So far as language, or any distinguishable principle of philosophy, is concerned, man *supports, upholds,* and *continues, himself* in life, by his own free will, as much as he *quenches* his *thirst* with a drink of water. The rule which would refer the verbs *be* and *live,* to the direct agency of the Creator, would also make the name of the living God the agent of every verb, in all tongues, which dependent beings could frame.

It is no way inconsistent, in philosophy, language, or fact, to say, either " The storm *destroyed* the armada," or that it was " He who rides on the whirlwind and directs the storm ;" nor in saying the lightning *strikes* the tower, do we contradict, in the least degree, the all-including thought, that the power, and the immediate providence of God, *directs* the bolt.

Language applies to all *agents,* and all *objects,* on one common principle ; for the plain reason that it could not be applied on any other.

A *beaver,* a *clam,* and a *log,* as well as the *man,* are, in the structure of speech, considered independent, *self acting,* and *self sustained; holding* their several *places* and *relations,* as links in the boundless chain; each, according to its nature, *preserving* the *organization,* and *consistency* of its parts ; *exercising* its proper *qualities* and *functions ;* and *producing* such *effects* on surrounding objects, as belong to its absolute and relative power to act.

The *log,* unobstructed by its blocking, *rolls itself* on the man, and *crushes him* to death. The " *thin ayre,*" invisible, impalpable, and the most unsubstantial portion of matter, yet tolerably known to science, *converts itself* into the hurricane, *prostrates* the *forest,* and *spreads destruction* in its course. The same *thin air,* confined in the deep recesses of the earth, by causes beyond the reach of human ken, *rocks kingdoms, heaves* up new *islands* through the sea, *shakes* down the time tried *walls,* and *sinks* the frightened *tenants* of the palace and the dungeon, in one common grave.

Preparations of phosphor, sulphuric acid, and potash, brought in contact, under water, *set themselves* on fire, and *burn* till one or all are consumed. With the million forms of commotion; constantly *taking place,* in all the constituents of the material world, shall we still continue to learn as a rule of speech, the absurd lesson that *matter* can neither *cause* an *action,* nor *produce* any *effect?* The lump of gold which still *keeps* its *place* at the bottom of the mine, *retains* at least its *cohesion, gravitation,* and *repulsion,* if it could *exert its action* in no other way ; and the cubic foot of matter which *occupies* the *center* of the globe *has* its proportional *influence* on the circumvolving spheres. Could we suppose such mass destitute of all possible *tendency to move,* it would then *possess* what the colleges have happily named " *vis inertiæ,*" or the *power to lie still.*

It is impossible for the imagination to conceive any thing, even in the grammatical creation, more *inanimate* than a " *neuter verb ;*" yet this illusive representative of quiescence, *positively, actively,* and *transitively,* " *expresses being, or a state of being.*" The *passive verb,* too, the next tame thing in the verbal world, includes a *transitive action,* with its governed *object,* in every attempt to define it. What other verbal *subject,* or *nominative word,* then, can possibly typify a thing *too dead to act?*

When we say of the Deity, " *He was,* and *is,* and *is to be,*" we express more and higher action, than in affirming that *he created,* and constantly *upholds, a myriad of worlds.* The first expression *signifies,* that the Divine Being *sustains himself,* in the unchanging per-fection of all excellence, through an eternal round of ages. This is by far the loftier *action* of the two ; inasmuch as the potter is more than the clay, and the Sovereign Lord high over all the works he has made.

So, in saying, " The *man is* alive," we imply, according to the plain import of the word *is,* he *sustains* and *preserves himself* alive ; he *inspires, continues, vivifies, inspirits,* and *upholds, himself,* with all the requisites, and in the exercise of all the functions, essential to vitality. In order to *be,* as this *verb asserts, he must,* by continual alternations, *inhale* and *respire the air ; inflate* his *lungs,* and by their instrumentality, *impart oxygen* to chyle and blood : he must *eat* and *drink*, *sleep* and *wake*, *feel sensations* of pleasure and pain, *perceive* external objects, and *exert himself* in various ways : he must *repeat* the *pulsations* of his heart, through the numerous arteries and veins; and *maintain* all his complex vital *organs* in their proper tone of action. It is for the physiologist to say, whether the human machine, of frame work, cords, pivots, tubes, valves, cylinders, and retorts, *can retain its* own *vitality*, without *performing*, at each instant, ten thousand *actions*, beyond what the *microscope can display*, or the united *skill* of the philosopher, chemist, engineer, and optician *can explain*.

So far as verbal affirmations *have* any *concern* with the *action* of *living*, it is not of the least importance whether its complex movements are regulated by consciousness and will, or by the necessary constitution of the corporeal frame. The continual *performance* of these *actions* is one indispensable condition, by which the living "tenant at will," *must* "*have, hold, possess, and enjoy*," his *being* on earth.

It is far more absurd to deny the high *action of living*, because, from habit, *it is*, in part, unconsciously *performed*, than to *re-assert* the exploded *belief*, that the *earth has* no *motion*, because its rapid progress is not felt.

When it is asserted "The *man is* dead," we still mean, the body *retains its personal identity*, and its corporeal *organization :* it *occupies* a *place* in the Creator's works, which, but for this monitory remnant of humanity, *would be replaced* by some other portion of matter ; for even the monastic schools, whether they knew what they meant or not, said that "*Nature abhors vacuity*."

The dead *body* at the least which, as matter, it can do, *retains its* corpuscular attraction, and *causes* a different *disposition* of surrounding substances from what *would* otherwise *take place*. This organized *mass continues to be* the dead *man*, so long as a predominant *portion remains* to which personal identity can be affixed : and when the crumbling *dust mingles itself* with its kindred earth, it can no longer be said the dead *man is ;* but only that *he was : "Fuit Ilium*," Troy is no more.

This application of words, in their endless use, by one plain rule, to all things which nouns can name, instead of being the fit subject of cavil, is the most sublime theme presented to the intellect on earth. It is the practical intercourse of the soul, at once with its God, and with all parts of his works.

"An undevout astronomer is mad," is the sentiment which even a partial and mistaken view of the heavenly orbs has often extorted from pagan lips. If such aspirations arise, in contemplating the world of matter, what would the same man feel, could he trace its connection with the brighter world of mind, and justly contemplate that WISDOM which, beyond the comet's track, or the astronomer's thought, pervades the whole.

The declaration, "I can do all things through the Deity strength-ening me," is the universal proposition, in language as well as religion. "By him, *we live, move*, and *have* our *being*." For the plainest reason, such qualification applies ♭ every *action* which dependent creatures could assert, or the mind conceive. It would be preposterous to impute *independent agency* to all other operations, and deny it to the highest of all, without which no other can take place.

It has been the misfortune of this branch of science, to misemploy the rich treasures of learning, in superficial and endless disputes, concerning forms of words, instead of ascertaining those laws in the physical and mental creation which govern all forms. The philosophy of the dark ages has strangely misinterpreted the simple, beautiful, and limitless rule of speech, which ascribes verbal actions, on a common principle, to all things; from the unchanging AM, down the countless gradations of being in the amazing system of his works.

. The *archangel*, or the *insect*, *lives a dependent life:* a *hero*, a *city*, or a *pebble, sinks:* The *Eternal is ;* and the same is affirmed of each particle of dust, through all the worlds he has made: for, between which two links, in the inconceivable chain, of *spirits, men*, and . *minor things*, could speech makers on earth draw the division line?

Let the believer in the doctrine of *unacting subjects* turn from the lessening degrees of animal being, to the vegetable productions around him. Here he sees each tree and plant, "from the cedar of Lebanon, to the hysop on the wall," *sprouting its germ ; shooting its stock ; drawing nutriment* from the earth and the air; *putting forth leaves and flowers*; and *maturing its fruit.* The shamrock, mistleto, and Iceland moss, *propagate themselves*, with all their distinctive qualities, through the whole range of time.

In the mineral kingdom we find each mountain and hill, *decomposing* and *re-indurating its rocks; corroding* and again *forming metals;* each acid *combining itself* with its kindred base, in crystals *assuming* their appropriate *forms :* every portion of the solid globe *producing* its manifold *actions*, and those *actions* their *effects*.

These principles, it will be seen, do not depend on vague metaphysical deductions. The man of science, who chooses to scrutinize, rather than trust, will find the whole field of nature, the stores of learning, and the conscious record of his own intellect, full of converging proofs to establish their truth.

If there was any word answering the description of a *neuter verb*, it certainly could not be used in the *imperative mood;* for it would be the height of folly to exhort a man to *stand* firm, *rise* up, *sit* down, or *be* what he is not, if no *action* was ever *signified, understood,* or *complied with,* by the expression. A little girl, in play, may use these commands to her doll, as the *representative* of a *being* who can *will* and *act :* but children know that the imperatives of *miscalled neuter* verbs demand both *volition* and *change;* for one boy habitually says to an other, " *Be* there quick :" " *Stand* out of my way," " *Sit* or *lie* farther ;" expecting him to *act,* according to the request : but no boy of common sense would soberly use the same address, to a bar post, chair, or billet of wood.

Again, no neuter verb, if such a word was created, could ever form a past participle, which, in every possible case, denotes the resulting effect of action or change. If the verb *go* had po *object,* nothing could ever be *gone.* The thing which *one moves,* or that *moves itself,* till it *ceases to move,* is then *moved.*

It is no objection to this statement, that some actions take place with a fixed point of completion, and others in successive degrees. The ship is *lanched,* when the lanching is *done.* The flag may be *lowered,* by every gradation, from the topmast head to the deck.

An other strong absurdity is connected with the doctrine of neuter verbs. These words all take the " *auxiliaries*" before them, with all the motives, the conditions, and obligations of action. How can a man promise *to be* what he *is not,* if *to be* has no connection with his own power to *will* or *act?* And how absurd to say, a man *ought to do, can do, must,* and *shall do,* and be punished if he *does not do,* that which is doing nothing at all.

That we may not be entirely ignorant what a neuter or intransitive verb is, one sublime example is given, in Exod. III.; and it is believed that all the stores of human learning can produce no other. This example is the miracle which Moses beheld in a flame of fire out of the midst of the bush. The astonished lawgiver, deep skilled in all the philosophy which scientific Egypt taught, saw the laws of nature overruled by the Author of Nature. " He looked, and behold the bush burned with fire, and the bush was not consumed."

Well might the wondering naturalist cry out, "I will now turn aside, to see this *great sight,* why the bush is not burned;" for, from the beginning to the end of the world, the leader of the Hebrews must doubtless remain the only man of whom it can be truly said, " He looked, and behold the bush burned with fire, and the bush was not consumed;" or who is ever to see any other action take place, without affecting its object, according to those unerring laws which Divine Wisdom has ordained.

Having attempted to show that great errors prevail in the existing systems of inculcation in language, it may seem proper to develop, if possible, the causes by which so many celebrated writers have been misled.

Those who, during many centuries in succession, devoted their lives to this study, were, in too great a degree, mere linguists, and not persons of accurate scientific pursuits. The most distinguished, with few exceptions, confined their attention to language as a kind of exclusive theme, and not as necessarily connected with every other department of human knowledge. Even as philologists, they did not rise on one hand to the strong, crude models of early expression, nor on the other to the skill in science, which would have explained its practical adaptation. On the middle ground between the two, men expert in the inflections of words reasoned in a circle, adopting, as first principles, their own views of speech, in its scholastic forms, instead of attempting the analysis of its primeval cast. They learnedly expatiated on declension, mood, and tense, according to their unguided fancy. They exhibited the expanding conjugations of Greek and Latin verbs, through all their varying forms; but these plants in bloom were not traced back to their germ; nor forward to their ripened fruit and reproduction.

In this limited way of examination, words were found in use, applied to things which, according to the philosophy of these expounders, did not act; and hence they adopted the strange theory of *neuter* and *passive* verbs; a mistake which either the simplicity of ancient times, or the real science of the present, would at once have set right.

In such modes of hypothesis, and such wretched systems of exposition, too many lives have already been spent; and false principles, authorized by imposing universities, and royal academies, ought no longer to be received, from age to age, on trust.

Instead of theorizing upon the dress of language, in its classic finishing, let us take a new view of its primitive state, and see how different it will appear.

Proofs drawn from different tongues, in their earliest written forms, are referred to an other work. A few hints will here be offered, as directly presented by plain sense.

All verbs must have been originally used to denote visible activity, and generally in its highest forms of manifestation. It was not the *post* or *tree, sustaining itself* in an erect posture, which gave rise to the verb *stand;* nor were other verbs first applied to apparently motionless things. They all had their origin in obvious actions; and in the progress of language, extended their meaning, through lessening degrees of analogous appearance. In this unconscious manner, the nations of unlettered men, so adapted their language to philosophic truth, that all physical and intellectual research can find no essential rule to reject or change. What the simple fathers of mankind did, from first impulse, was exactly accordant with those laws of nature which industrious genius may admire, but can never fully explore.

Having, in some degree, examined these principles as they exist in nature, we may procede to trace them, in their extension to thought, and to practice in language.

1. With regard to those *verbs* which are supposed not to denote *action*, but to be used for the distinctive purpose of expressing " *state or condition of being*."

It is well known without the *helpless aid* of *neuter verbs*, that

every thing which has *being*, must have that *being* in some *condition* or *state*: and the only way in which the mind can contemplate
the *state* or *condition* of any *being*, is either in reference to its own
changes, which are *action*, or in its *relations* to other things, which
are *description*, and expressed by *adjectives ;* for there can be no
such thing as *absolute condition* or *state ;* these terms themselves
contradict such a supposition; nor can words be employed to represent those ideas, except as mere relations : consequently, it does
not belong to a verb to express a *difference* between one *state of
being* and an other.

Every expression to be used for any valid purpose, must convey
some *distinctive idea*, some information which the hearer does not
know, independent of such assertion. It must not mean *every
thing*, nor *all states of being*, because that would be, in other words,
to mean nothing at all. To communicate any useful intelligence it
must communicate some fact, no matter whether in the form of assertion or inquiry ; and certainly every one who knows what fact
means, knows that it must include action, or it would not be fact :
and this position is not taken barely in reference to the unavoidable
meaning of the word, but also in regard to any principle of logic
which can be applied to the case.

Again, every thing which acts, must be in some state or condition
of being while it acts; and this proposition, which is evident without the use of *nugatory verbs*, holds equally true of all agents or
subjects concerning which any affirmation can be made. The only
valid reason for setting apart a set of verbs, under the name of neuter, is by showing that they perform some office which other verbs
do not.

> The ship *rides* at anchor.
> The ship *lies* at anchor.
> The cable *holds* the ship.
> John *saws* wood.
> The mill *grinds* the corn.

The first two of these verbs are said to be *neuter*, and to be used
merely to show the state of being in which a subject is placed. It
certainly, however, is not the verb *rides*, which, of itself, tells us
whether the ship is on the water, or the ridge of a house ; in the
air, on horseback, or in a coach. Any distinction of this kind must
be known, by the nature of a ship and its relation to an anchor.

The man *sits* in his chair.
He *keeps his seat*, very quietly.
He *keeps himself* quietly *seated*.
He *is seated* quietly in his chair.

What difference is there in the man's condition of being in these four instances, including the *active*, *passive* and *neuter* verb, with the *self action*, and the *action passing over to an object :* and, if there is no difference, then how is this supposed *neuter verb*, more than any verb, used merely to express the *state of being ?*

So in the expression "the *cable holds the ship*," tho the *transitive* action, in the imaginary grammatical distinction, yet the necessary *state of being* is as well expressed here, as in the other examples : that is, the cable is attached to the ship, at one end, and to the anchor, or some other fastening, at the other.

The man *saws* wood.

In this example, better than in either of the others, the *" state of being"* is very exactly understood; for the relations of the *actor*, *instrument*, and *object*, are necessary and familiar.

Let us take an other instance of the *same agent*, and the *same verb*, and see if any *difference* is made in either, to express all the differences between one *" state of being"* and an other ; or whether this difference, as to every *expression* of it, and every thing which the *mind contemplates* respecting it, is made entirely by *adjectives*.

A prince is *born*.
He is *sleeping in his cradle.*
He is *playing in the nursery.*
He is *very sick.*
He is *perfectly recovered.*
He is *taking a walk.*
He is *riding in the park.*
He is *fighting the enemy.*
He is *sitting on his throne.*
He is *laid up with sickness.*
He is *prostrate on his couch.*
He is *bowed down with age.*
He is *dead and buried.*
He is *forgotten on earth.*

This verb *is*, certainly, can not be *habitually used* for a purpose which it *never, in any case, performs* ; and nothing is clearer than that this verb, applying, *without change*, to all *conditions of being*, indicates no one distinctively ; and, therefore, that this can not be its *essential office* in language.

Much is said, by learned writers, respecting *general* and *abstract terms ;* of the *arbitrary, conventional,* and *artificial* nature of speech. We are wisely told that " *custom* in language governs every thing." This is such verbiage as men *accustom themselves* to employ, when not aware of the import of their own terms. *Custom* does not govern those who make *custom*, any more than the *cut, make, fashion, habit, costume,* or *form* of dress governs the fashionables, and their tailors, who direct these *fashions* or *makings*, at their will.

This *custom*, in language, so much talked about, and so little understood, is like the Grecian philosopher's metaphoric cob-web. It catches small flies; but if the large ones did not break thro it, the custom would never change.

Language is *conventional* only in its slighter modifications ; no convention can change its elementary laws. People did not, in early times, call a town meeting, and agree to employ certain words to denote certain specific ideas. They had the words first, or they could not have passed their vote.

To avoid a vast extent of bewildering technicality on this subject, it is proper to begin by asking ourselves a plain question of common sense, and trying to remember the answer which plain sense readily affords.

By what *conventional* rule can men form *signs*, and make them practically *significant*, without any *characteristic thing* for them to *signify?*

Every verb is employed to denote some *obviously distinctive* fact, without which, the assertion would be nugatory. Such fact has a necessary connection with some material instrumentality, or means of action ; not an *abstract, artificial, inconceivable, neuter, something, any thing, every thing, and nothing ;* but a standard substantial object, tangible by the organs of perception. Without such *distinctive manifestation*, the *idea* could not exist, nor the *word* be wanted.

It could neither acquire an origin, nor, by any possibility, be understood : and, if a verb should cease to denote a matter of fact perception, it would cease to convey any meaning ; for the expression
of action is the *distinctive, exclusive,* and *only* office which a *verb* can
perform.

The man *lives.*

This expression either means nothing, or, according to its only
practical use, it asserts a *fact* which the speaker does know, and
the hearer does not. If the speaker knows the fact, he knows it,
of course, by some means of knowledge ; some sensible indication,
or real *action,* which this man must perform, in order to manifest the
fact that he lives. The *action* which a living man performs, to show
that he lives, is necessarily expressed by this assertion, however
stupidly the speaker himself, misled by an absurd theory, may talk
about his supposed *neuter verbs.*

In all ages, these laws of action and thought have formed the basis of every language ; and, if it should be asserted that words, in
their modern use, have acquired a conventional acceptation, independent of these principles, and contrary to them, it remains to
inquire of such theorists, how *words* came to be employed to denote
ideas which cannot possibly exist ; or when, and by what means,
the technical rules of grammar obtained the ascendancy over those
laws of nature, which unerring Wisdom has ordained ?

At every patriarchal home, it was, of course, seen that adult persons could support themselves in an erect posture, and the infants
could not ; that the revered parent, at one time, *stood* firm, sur-
rounded by the family circle, and at an other, lay prostrate on a
bed of sickness, while they were anxiously bending over him ; for
these things are common to human life : one man was seen to *stand*
faithfully by his friend, or stedfastly at his post, in the hour of danger, while an other fainted with fear, or basely deserted, to extri-
cate himself from the peril : an other stood in a slippery place,
where his companion was seen to fall ; all these, and a thousand
others, were instances of manifest action ; and a word to express it
became of important use.

When the verb *stand* was established to denote what the man did, from united volition, energy, and skill, it was easily extended to the post and tree, *sustaining themselves* in the same position, without stopping to inquire by what unknown cause their action was performed. In this extension, the continuity remains unbroken, and the application just; for where obvious movement ceases, action on scientific principles always exists; and so inevitable is this rule, in its adaptation to things, that not only no neuter verb ever was employed, but it is beyond all human power to form one, to give it either meaning or use.

If the "*wonderful activity*" of the rope dancer, who *stands* on his head, upon a swinging cord, at an elevation of fifteen feet in the air, is no action, then what is action? and who shall dare to name the feats of the mountebank, in comparison with what the *oak*, by Divine Wisdom, *performs* in *standing*, and *renewing its verdure*, for ages, against all the tempests which howl around it?

Concerning the *objects* of verbs, the errors in grammatical inculcation appear to be of a remarkable cast.

The few specimens which follow will give some idea of the reciprocity of verbal *actors*, *actions*, and *objects*. These examples are clumsy indeed; but not therefore the less instructive. It belongs to the art of an able writer to conceal this structure, and obviate its monotony, or alliteration. The enlightened linguist, on the contrary, instead of being deceived by this disguise, should make it a most efficient instrument in the elucidation of his principles; for it should not be forgotten, that, in the construction of language, the first process is the formation of single words, with definite meanings, and not the practice of elegant brevity in their combinations.

A very large class of verbal *objects* are the *productions*, or *effects*, *resulting* from *actions*. Many others denote the *performance* itself, taken as a *circumstance*, *fact*, or *thing*.

Agent,	Verb,	Object.
Builders	build	buildings..
Pinmakers	make	pins.
Dreamers	dream	dreams.
Laughers	laugh	laughter or laugh.
Singers	sing	singing, or songs.
Breathers	breathe	breathing, breath.
Speakers	speak or make	speeches.
Actors	act or perform	actions or parts.
Sleepers	sleep	sleep, or naps.
Drinkers	drink	drink.
Walkers	walk or take	walks.
Producers	produce	products or results.
Workers	work or execute	work.
Sitters	sit, or hold	sittings or sessions.
Profligate livers	live	profligate lives.
The dying	die or encounter	dying or death.
Pleaders	plead or make	pleadings or pleas.
A coiner	coins	coin.
Sufferers	suffer	sufferings.
A player	plays	plays.
Thinkers	think or employ	thoughts.
A person	personates	a personage.
Casters	cast	casts or castings.
Fishers	fish or catch	fish.
Twisters	twist	twists.
An equal	equals	an equal.
Light	lights or sheds	light.
The glow	glows or diffuses	a glowing or glow.
The taste	tastes	the taste.
The feeling	feels	the feeling.
Rain	rains	rain
Frost	frosts or freezes	frost.
The sight	sees	the sight.

All languages are full of this construction. The veil which covers it is more thin than would be at first supposed. This tabular explanation will serve to explain it, instead of explaining any other explanation which can be explained respecting it. The student has only to study the study of nature, around him and within him, to know the knowledge of those principles which chiefly govern all human speech.

The next mystery, in verbal *objects*, appears to be the extensive class of self actions, commonly included under the name of reflected verbs. These imply actions which recur upon the agents, or in which the actor does something to himself.

An other set of verbs called reciprocal, denote actions in which two or more agents act on each other.

None of these distinctions amount to any real difference in the character of verbs, which are substantially alike. No rational division line can be drawn between them.

Dr. Sangrado often bled his *patients*, and occasionally *bled himself*: he sometimes *opened their veins*, and sometimes *his own*.

The doctor, in both cases, performed the operation of bleeding, with the same lancet, in the same way. Whether he opened his own, or his patients' veins, appears not to vary the nature of the action, or the character of the verb, any more than the difference between bleeding the same person in the arm, on the foot.

After attempting to show that all verbs are active; that they all denoted, in their origin, manifest action; in what manner they act; and what that action produces; it remains to *think* some farther brief *thoughts*, concerning the nature of verbal objects.

" To Sleep."

The action signified by this verb always affects two objects at the same time; and both are inevitably understood as the objects of the verb, whether either is expressed or not.

The noun *sleeping* is the *name* of the *act* which the verb denotes, as, "His *sleeping* was quiet." "They were kept from *sleeping*."

The noun *sleep* is the resulting effect of the action of *sleeping*, or the thing which *sleeping produces*, as *breath* is only what is *breathed*. The way to *have, get*, or *take sleep*, is to *sleep it*.

"The stout hearted *have slept their sleep.*" "They shall *sleep* a perpetual *sleep* and shall not awake," means that they "shall *sleep* the *sleep* of death," or, "*Sleep* the long *sleep*," and not merely *sleep* a short *nap*, or *sleep* the ordinary *sleep* of the night.

That the noun *sleep* is always the *object* of the verb *sleep*, is, on the clearest principles of philosophic demonstration, as certain as that very simply proving must afford very simple proof, or bleeding produce blood.

Sleeping also, as a self action, infallibly produces its effect on the sleeper as its object.

This action, like most others performed by man, depends partly on necessity, and partly on reason and choice.

"For this cause many sleep:" 1 Cor. xi. 30.

"I will not give sleep to my eyes, nor slumber to my eyelids, until I have found out a place for the Lord."—Ps. "Awake thou that sleepest, and arise."

Every human being, at short intervals, resorts to "tired Nature's sweet restorer, balmy sleep;" to *sleep himself* into new vigor, after the exhaustion of his waking hours. A mother, because her child was peevish, rocked it to sleep, and "it *slept itself quiet.*"

"A young lady, in great distress of mind, took a strong opiate, and *slept herself* to death." "Many idle persons *sleep themselves* into a kind of unnatural stupidity," as topers *drink themselves drunk.*

The acetous fermentation of wine is one of the moderate kind of actions. A moment's attention will show something of its nature.

1. The wine *converts itself* to vinegar.

2. It *imbibes oxigen*, or the acidifying principle, from the air.

3. It *changes* the surrounding *atmosphere* by changing the proportions of its constituents.

f This liquid then, apparently motionless in the cask, *performs* its direct *actions* on *three objects* at the same time.

To shine.

The original and strict meaning of the verb to shine is to *brighten objects*; to make them *sheen, sheeny, shining, glossy,* or *bright*.

"The Sun shines."

This verb, during the last four hundred years, very seldom has an object directly expressed; not because it has no object, or because the sun, in shining, *produces* no *effect*: but for more consistent reasons, which may be clearly explained.

On philosophic principles, and likewise according to popular conception, the sun, in shining, either produces some effect on its own body; or it throws out something from itself; or it influences bodies *on* which its shining falls. It does all the three. It *exhibits itself* in brightness, "in peerless majesty:" "It *sheds* its dazzling *radiance* through the world:" and it *brightens* all *objects* on which this radiance falls.

The *brilliancy* which the sun *displays* on its own disk, is *sun shine*. It *diffuses* or *sheds* this *brilliancy* by *shining it :* and the light with which it *shines, enlightens,* or *irradiates* the *world*, is *sun shine*.

The reason, then, why this verb has no object expressed, is, in the first place, because it has so many objects, that it is impossible to enumerate them; and secondly, because its action is so uniform and familiar that it is unnecessary to particularize for the sake of perspicuity.

To smile.

To smile is necessarily to *smile smiles*.

The sycophant "*bowed* and *smiled himself* into favor at court."

"To *smile* our *cares* away."

"And *smile* the *wrinkles* from the brow of age."

No action in the order of nature can effect less than two objects at the same time, nor can any verb ever have less than two objec-

tive words inevitably depending on it in construction, whether either is expressed or not. This statement may be exemplified by
the following anecdote, in which duplicate objects, to each verb,
are alternated with each other.

A foreigner, hired to an American farmer, *wrote writing* on a *sheet*
of paper, or *wrote* a *sheet* of paper with *writing*, to *inform* the *information* to his *mother*, or *inform* his *mother* by the *information*, that
the man who *employed him* in *employment*, or *employed employment*
for *him*, *fed him* with *meat*, or *fed meat* to *him*, twice a week. His
fellow laborer, struck with the singularity of such a letter, *asked*
the *question* of *him*, or *asked him* by the *question*, how he *could* the
cunning of *himself*, or *could himself* with the *cunning*, to *communicate* such a *communication* to his *friends*, or *communicate* his *friends*
and *himself* by such a communication, and whether he *did not himself*
in the *deed*, or *did not* the *deed* for *himself*, to *eat* the *eating* of *meat*,
or *eat meat* for his *eating*, every day in the week ?

The foreigner *answered* the *answer* to his *companion*, or *answered*
his *companion* with the *answer*, " Poh! *would* you the *will* in *yourself*,
or *would you yourself* by the *will*, to *have me* with the *having*, or
have the *having* of *me*, to *tell* the *telling* of such a *tale*, or *tell* the
tale by such *telling*, that my friends in Europe would never *believe*
the *belief* of *it*, or *believe it* with their *belief?*"

Such a letter, of course, is not given as a specimen of fashionable
elegance in modern practice ; but, if any one, on perusing this kind
of composition, should think it whimsically new, far fetched, or
overdone, let him take a little time to examine it, and try the most
doubtful words, by the substitution of others, of similar meaning,
as, instead of " *employing* a man in *employment*," to employ him in
business, or *furnish* him with employment. When this is done, let
the expressions here used be compared with their prevailing contractions, which doubtless sound better, and perhaps, may at first
seem more correct, because they are more familiar.

" A man communicates, by letter, with his friend."

Communicates *what* with his friend? The communication which
communicates, without the community of more *objects* than one, is
much worse grammar, rhetoric, and logic, than any thing in the
foreigner's letter, however singular that may appear: yet this communication of *nothing* with *some thing else*, has become the estab-

9*

lished diction, and is one of the most trifling absurdities in the doctrine of unoperative actions, and neuter affirmations.

It is the purpose of grammar, properly conducted, to explain language, on rational principles; to show the reciprocal dependence
and connection of words; ascertain what is vague; and supply what,
for the sake of common sense, must necessarily be understood: for,
if the scholarship of the civilized world is to be confined merely to
teaching set forms or words, by rote, then it aims at nothing higher
than children in all savage countries may learn from their grand-
mothers.

No other word is of so extensive use as the verb *to be*; and consequently none has so much need of relieving its monotonous
repetitions by making its inflections irregular. No less than five
verbs therefore are blended to make the parts of this one: for *be*,
am, *is*, *are*, and *were*, are so many distinct radical terms. They
have different shades of original meaning; as *to live*, or *preserve
one's self* in being ; *to assume* or *take* some *position, appearance*, or
form; *to exist, stand* forth, or *exhibit one's self*; to *breathe air, enjoy it*,
or *appear* in it; and to *exercise* vital *powers* of body or mind. Most
of the applications of the verb *to be* are the inferential meanings
from the original ideas.

This verb is not of a different nature from others. The frequency
of its use depends on its specific importance, and not on any thing
distinctive in its verbal character. It expresses transitive action
in every form of its use; but that action belongs to itself, and is
not employed to conjugate other verbs; nor to make them either
active or passive.

On the same principles which have already been explained, the
verb *to be*, always has two objective words irresistibly inferred.

They *are*, or *breathe* air.
They *are*, or *air* themselves.

This verb has its first-application in the manifest and highest
qualities of living beings, and then, like other verbs, descends to
inferior things, till the analogy can hardly be traced. No one can
doubt that the verb *to be*, with its governed objects expressed, must

appear remarkably new to those who never thought of such a thing before, and who take it for granted, that, if a word is not explained in their grammar or dictionary, it can only be because it never had any meaning. If, from unconscious and familiar use of the verb *to be*,* we are inclined to overlook its important signification, the reflections of common sense ought to set us right; for while we see so strong a tendency to omit all words which can be spared, how should this one be retained in more than half the sentences through the language? The verb *are*, with its governed objects, has, indeed, a clumsy appearance in practice, because so little known; but this cannot alter its nature, nor the truth of its principle. Let the objector read the account of the English prisoners in the Blackhole dungeon at Calcutta; suffocating for want of air; climbing over their dead and dying companions, and gasping for breath, at the scanty aperture; and he will have a better idea of the verb *are*, as connected with the question of life and death. The twenty-three persons who survived that scene of horror, would easily have understood and felt the explanation of this word, and would not have considered it either aukward, unmeaning, or entirely new.

In the practical use of verbs, the variations are often very great. From one original and strict meaning, they pass, by easy transitions, to very diversified, analogous, and figurative uses. One striking circumstance in the employment of verbs, is the number of different agents to which the same verbal action may be referred.

Mr. Jones has a new grate in his front parlor, in which he burns Liverpool coal.

His new *grate burns coal* very well.
The *coal burns* handsomely.—(burns itself.)
The *fire burns* well.—(burns the coal.)
The *servant burns* too much *coal*.
Mr. *Jones burns coal* in preference to wood.

The same kind of action frequently assumes very great variety in its relations, both to *agents* and *objects*.

---

* For the comparative etymology and definitions of the different parts of the verb *to be*, see Essay on Language.

All verbs have objects alike; but, as it happens with other words, it becomes an elegant practice to omit these objects, when they are sufficiently understood to answer the purposes of discourse without them. Whether they are to be used, or omitted, does not belong to any possible rule to explain; but is entirely a question of fashion and good taste.

The verb *to feed*, to supply with *feed* or *food*, is in very familiar use. A moment's attention will show how differently the same action in its literal and strict sense is performed in relation to different objects, as applied to their nature and wants. *To feed a babe*, is to put feed into its mouth : to *feed a horse*, is to fill the rack or manger before him : a man, who carries on large business, and employs a hundred workmen, *feeds them* and their *families* effectually, by sitting in his office, and signing a bank check, for the amount of their wages, when it becomes due.

To run, is one of the verbs which frequently, by custom, has its object omitted. This is particularly the case, when the fact is, that the agent *runs himself*, and the accompanying circumstances are such, that no other object is likely to be understood. Any necessary distinction, or particularity, requires the objective word, in this self action, to be expressed, and this is to be determined by the sense, and not by arbitrary rule.

Two men were engaged in argument. The believer in intransitive verbs, sat out to *run his opponent* into an evident absurdity, and, contrary to his expectation, he *ran himself* into one. Leave out the objects of this verb, *run*, and the sense is totally changed. He sat out to *run* into an *evident absurdity*, and he *ran* into one : that is, he did the very absurd thing which he intended to do.

To run signifies to advance some thing by continued progress from one place to an other, and generally includes the idea of rapidity.

In general, a word has only one meaning, and all apparent varieties in its use, are but extensions, not perversions, of the original and strict import.

" The man soon *ran himself* into discredit by his mismanagement." " We chased the deer till we *ran ourselves* out of breath."

" The horse *ran himself* to death." " The pirates *ran* their *vessel* into a small creek." " We determined to *run* our *ship* ashore, and *betake ourselves* to the boats." " The profligate *runs* a dreadful *career*." " They were compelled *to run the gantlet*." " He *ran* the *spear* through him." " He *ran him* through the body." " The captain *ran* his *men*, to *rescue them* from the enemy." " The whale ran out fifty *fathoms* of line." " The glass has but a few more *sands to run*." " He *ran* a godly *race*." " The company *run* their *steam boat* every day." " They *run* three *lines* of stages." " The drivers *run* their *horses, trot*, or *walk them*, according to circumstances." " He *ran* his *head* against a post." " He *ran* a *sliver* into his finger." " The still *runs* a *puncheon* of whiskey a day." " The distance was seven miles, and he *ran it* in twenty minutes." " The barrel *runs emptyings*." " We *ran* the *squirrel* up a tree, and *ran* the *rabbit* into his burrow." " The wheel and reel *ran* off forty *runs* of yarn, and which yarn *runs* forty *knots* to the pound." " *Run* that *calico* off, and see if it holds out measure." " *Run* the *account* over, and see if it is right." " The brokers *run* the *bank* severely." " The note *overran* its *time*." " He *out ran* all his *competitors*."

6. Verbs are to be considered in relation to *mood*, *tense*, *person*, and *number*.

MOOD.

7. Mood is the difference in the manner of expressing actions, with regard to the agents or causes by which they are produced.

8. There are three moods, divided by *personal relation*. They are perfectly distinct from each other, and under one or the other, every verbal action is to be expressed.

9. These moods are the *indicative*, or assertive ; the *imperative*, or commanding ; and the *infinitive*, or unlimited.

10. In the *indicative* mood, the verb has *one* direct *personal relation* to the agent who performs the action : as, *John studies* Latin.

11. The *imperative* mood relates to the *will* of a first person, addressed to the *agency* of a second person, to do, or not to do, an action ; as, *study* your lessons ; *bring* me a book.

12. The *infinitive* mood has no direct connection with a personal actor ; but grows out of some stated condition of things ; as, the fire is kindled *to warm* the room. They are collecting a subscription *to build* a school-house.

Here it is not said directly that any actor warms the room; but *that fire being kindled,* the consequent action, *to warm* the room, grows out of that pre-existing circumstance. This is the nature of the infinitive mood, wherever it is found, though it is sometimes disguised in its appearance, by the contracted forms, or inverted order of expression.

It is not necessary that the person who is said *to perform* an action, should *be* the direct and immediate actor. It is enough that he causes something *to be* done, which, without such causing, would not *take* place; as, the postmaster-general *established* a post office in Louisiana. He sent a written order which *required* it *to be* done.

The indicative statement may be affirmative or negative, suppositive or interrogative; but in either case, it is equally the single personal relation to the actor. The difference between the *positive, negative,* and *interrogative* statements, in any case, has nothing to do with the character of a verb; but is a mere question of fact.

TENSE OR TIME.

13. *Tense* denotes the verbal forms to distinguish the different periods of time.

14. There are three tenses, *past*, *present*, and *future*.

15. The action begun and not finished, is expressed by the verb in the present tense ; as, I *go* to school. George *studies* Latin. I *have* a letter now written.

16. Completed action is expressed by the verb in the past tense ; as, I *wrote* a letter and *sent* it away.

17. The present and past tenses belong to the indicative mood.

18. Verbs in the imperative and infinitive moods, are always future. *ei d*

No person requests an other to do an action yesterday ; and no one can obey a command till after he receives it.

Imperative Mood.

Harry, *go* and *fetch* in some wood.
Meet me to-morrow, and *fail* not.

Infinitive Mood.

I *intend to go* immediately.

Intend is a verb in the indicative mood, present tense, and declares a purpose of the mind, to perform the future action denoted by the verb to go.

To go is a verb in the infinitive mood, signifying an action *intended* by the speaker, but *not commenced ;* and therefore necessarily future.

I *intended* yesterday *to go* before this time.

Here the verb *intended*, is in the past tense, and the infinitive following is future in relation to it, though it is not so in reference to the present time.

19. The following verbs, on account of the frequency of their use, drop the word *to* before the succeding verb in the infinitive mood: *Bid, can, do, dare, feel, hear, let, may, must, see, shall*, and *will;* as, they can *read*, and not they can *to read;* I heared you *sing*, and not *to sing*.

So we say I *must, shall*, or *can* have a new book, next week; and not, I *must, shall*, or *can, to have* a new book.

This is a mere contraction for convenience in the use of words, which by their important meaning are so often repeated. The omission does not alter the grammatical construction. The second verb is alike dependent on the proposition which contains the first, and is in the infinitive mood.

PERSON AND NUMBER.

20. Verbs in the indicative mood, through their changes of form, take the agreement of person and number with those of their agents ; as, the *horse runs*, the *horses run; he is* gone, *we are* ready.

21. *Imperative* and *infinitive* verbs are not varied in form, by *person* or *number*, tho the imperative mood may be addressed to a single person, or to more than one.

PARTICIPLES.

22. A verb forms two derivative, or compound words, called participles ; one always ending in *ing*, called the present or active ; the other, commonly in *d*, called the past or perfect.

From the verb *rule* are formed *rul-ing rul-ed ;* from *go* are formed *go-ing gone.*

23. The participle in *ing*, if not taken as a noun, retains its character as a verb, and has its governed object expressed, or necessarily understood.

At the same time it is an adjective, by use, describing something by its condition, employment, or situation.

The man is *riding** his horse.

Here the participle *riding*, retaining its *action* as a *verb*, has the noun *horse* as its objective word.

Riding, as an *adjective*, describes the man, by the circumstances in which he is placed.

24. The past participle denotes the resulting effect produced by verbal action. It, as an *adjective*, always *describes* some thing as being in the state or condition of being, in which the *terminated action* has placed it.

The glass *is broken.*

It is in that *condition*, in which the *finished action* of breaking has left it.

The book is *printed.*

The act of printing is finished, and the book is as the *effect* of that *action* has made it.

"My son was *lost*, and now is *found*."
He was *well*, but now is *sick.*

---

* The syllable *ing*, is a part of the verb *to be*, and signifies the *acting*, or *life-giving* principle.

25. The irregular verb *to be* is thus conjugated thro the different *moods* and *tenses*, *persons* and *numbers*.

Indicative Mood.

Present Tense.

Singular.   Plural.

I *am*, thou *art*, he *is*.   We *are*, you *are*, they *are*.

Past Tense.

I *was*, thou *wast*, he *was*.   We *were*, you *were*, they *were*.

Imperative Mood.

be,

with *thou,* or *you,* understood.

Infinitive Mood.

to be.

Participles.

Present, or active.   Past, or descriptive.
being.   *been.*

26. The assertion of the future can only be made by placing an *infinitive verb* after its proper *indicative statement;* as

I am *to be*   we are *to be*
thou art *to be*   you are *to be*
he is *to be*   they are *to be*

"Man never *is*, but always *to be* blest."

Any other verb in the indicative mood admits of the same construction ; as,

I can, shall, must, wish, will, or intend *to be.*

Next to the verb *to be,* which stands in importance before all others, the verb *to have,* is one of the most extensive meaning and use. In its present acceptation it signifies to *retain, claim,* or *owe,* some *possession, relation,* or *duty,* and may have its object expressed or implied ; as, a man *has* an arduous *journey* to perform, *next year.* He *has* his *arm* shot off.

27. The verb *to have,* is thus conjugated.

Indicative Mood.

Present Tense.

I *have,* thou *hast,* he *has.* We *have,* you *have,* they *have.*

Past Tense.

I *had,* thou *hadst,* he *had.* We *had,* you *had,* they *had.*

Imperative Mood.

have.

Infinitive.

to have.

Participles.

Present, or active.	Past, or descriptive.
having.	*had.*

Indicative and infinitive moods together, to make a future tense.

I *have* to be.	I am *to have.*

28. The regular verb to love, has its object either expressed or implied. It is thus conjugated:

Indicative Mood.

Present Tense.

Singular.	Plural.
I *love,* thou *lovest,* he *loves.*	We *love,* you *love,* they *love.*

Past Tense.

I *loved,* thou *lovedst,* he *loved.*	We *loved,* you *loved,* they *loved.*

Imperative Mood.

love.

with *thou* or *you* understood.

Infinitive.

to love.

Participles.

Present, or active.   Past, or descriptive.
loving.   *loved.*

Indicative and infinitive.

" We exhort you *to love* one an other."

Two species of composition may be equally correct, and yet differ very much in elegance. This depends on a happy choice of
words, so varied, as to prevent the appearance of repetition, or monotony. The following sentence shows in how many ways the same
word, with its slight changes, may be used. Such composition
would be very clumsy in practice; but it exhibits a better view of
the principles of construction, and of the classing of words, than
would be done by a more varied style.

29. The *writer writes* a *writing*, on *writing* paper ;
when he has done *writing* the *writing*, or done the
writing of the *writing*, the *writing* paper is *written*,
or becomes *written* paper.

This sentence is thus parsed :

The	defining adjective, referring to writer.
writer	common noun, singular, agent of the verb *writes*.
writes	irregular verb, indicative mood, present tense, agreeing with its agent *writer*, which is third person singular.
a	defining adjective, referring to the noun writing, to show how far its signification extends, or that it extends to one writing and no more.
writing,	common noun, name of the thing written, or produced by writing, singular number, and object of the verb *writes*.
on	preposition, or adjective of specific local relation, de- scribing the condition in which the writing is placed, with reference to the paper.
writing	describing adjective, referring to paper.

10*

It describes the paper by denoting the kind of paper, and the use to which it is applied.

paper;   common noun, singular number, object after the preposition *on.**

when   contraction of two words, meaning *what time,* with a preposition understood before it.   *At what time.*

he   pronoun, third person, singular number, masculine gender, agent of the verb *has.*

has   irregular verb, indicative mood, present tense, agreeing with its agent *he,* which is third person singular.

done   describing adjective, referring to *writing;* has the writing done, or *finished;* has it in the state of finished or done writing.

writing   common noun, name of the *act* of writing; singular number, and object of the verb *has.*

the   defining adjective, referring to *writing.*

writing,   common noun, name of the *thing* written, object after the preposition *of* understood; done the *writing* or *performance* of the *writing.*

the   defining adjective, referring to *paper.*

writing   describing adjective, referring to *paper.*

paper   common noun, singular, agent to the verb *is.*

is   irregular verb, indicative mood, present tense, agreeing with its agent *paper,* which is third person, singular.

written,   describing adjective, referring to *paper,* to show the quality, *condition,* or *state* of *being,* in which it is placed by the *finished act* of *writing.*

or   contraction for other, defining adjective ; in *other* words.

becomes   irregular verb, indicative mood, present tense, agreeing with its agent *paper,* which is third person singular.

written   describing adjective, referring to *paper.*

paper.   common noun, singular number, object of the verb becomes.

The same construction is preserved in the following sentence, though the monotony is in part relieved by substituting other terms.

----

* A particular explanation of the character and use of prepositions, will come more properly under that class of words.

The *scrivener draws* a marriage *contract*, on *writing* paper ; when he has done *writing* the *contract*, or finished the *draft* of the *agreement*, it is a *contract written* on *written* paper.

A man bought some *buttons*, at a *button* store, to *button* his cloak; and an *iron* bar, of Vermont bar *iron*, to *iron* a yoke, and bar his door.

30. In the indicative mood there are four ways of expressing verbal actions. These are *affirmative*, *negative*, *interrogative*, and *suppositive*; as, *I go; I go not; Does he go ?* If *I go*, I will give you timely notice.

31. The different moods are often combined in the same compound sentence; as in the last one given, which contains the three moods.

32. The difference. between the positive and negative assertion, consists in the terms added to express the negation, and makes no difference in the character of the verb.

33. It often happens, that, instead of making an absolute assertion, the statement is offered by way of supposition, in connection with some thing else. This suppositive use of verbs belongs to the indicative mood, and is very frequent in compound sentences.

Example.

If I go, I will give you timely notice.

Imperative demand,	*If, gif, give, admit,* this fact.
Suppositive assertion,	I *go.*
Direct assertion,	I *will* the determination.
Infinitive result,	*to give* you timely notice.

If two yards of cloth cost nine dollars, what is the price of thirteen yards?

Imperative demand,	*if, give,* or *allow* this fact.
Suppositive statement,	two yards *cost* nine dollars.
Indicative question,	what *is* the price of 13 yards?

An other imperative verb may always be substituted for *if*, without altering the sense; as, *Allow*, or *suppose* that 2 yds. of cloth cost nine dollars, what will 13 yds. cost?

BROKEN OR DEFECTIVE VERBS.

34. Several verbs, formerly conjugated through the different moods and tenses, have acquired a specific application in the most contracted form. It is found very convenient in practice to employ them in this way, on account of their appropriate import, and frequent use; but the contractions of these words have not changed either their *meaning* or their *manner of meaning*.

35. The verbs disguised by their contractions, and still retained in very frequent use, in the imperative mood, are *but, else, if, tho* or *though, unless,* and *yet.*

The disguise of these words, in most instances of their present use, is very slight.

36. *But* is composed of two words with directly opposite meanings, accidentally run into the same spelling.

But, contracted of be out, becomes a verb, in the imperative mood, signifying the same as the compounded verbs *ex-clude, ex-cept, out-take, re-ject.*

"All, *but* one *man,* perished."

All, *except* or *leave out* one *man.* In this example, the noun *man* is the direct *object* of the verb *but.*

"When nought *but* the *torrent* is heared on the hill,
And nought *but* the nightingale's *song* in the grove."

Torrent and *song* in this example are direct *objects* of the verb *but*. Nought *save* the *torrent*, would be the same construction.

"None *but* his intimate *friends* were admitted."

"Any thing *but* a *disjunctive conjunctive*." "No thing *but fear* restrains him."

The noun before the verb *but* is often omitted where by necessary association it is sufficiently understood.

"These (seasons) are (nothing) *but* the varied *God*."

"He had (none) *but* only *me*."

"(Nothing) *but* five *loaves* and two *fishes*."

But, to *but*, to *butt*, is to *add*, to *join*, bring into firm contact.
His land *buts* or *butts* mine.

"It is *butted* and *bounded* as follows."

Two fighters *butted* heads, and one killed the other.

A *but*, *butt*, or *butment*, is a joining, or joining part. The *butt* of a tree is the part which *joins* the stump or support. The *but* or *butt* of a farm is the boundary, where it butts or joins an other, or is *butted* by it. The *butt* of ridicule; that against which ridicule is to be thrown.

An animal gives an other a violent *butt* of the head. A man ran with a full or severe *butt* against a post.

Button is a derivative from *but*; and is so called because it *joins*, or *fastens*, one thing to an other.

"Not only saw he all that was,
But much that never came to pass."—*M'Fingal*.

"He is gone; but by a gainful remove."

Add the *fact* or *consideration*, he is gone, by a gainful remove.

But, to *add*, to superadd, to join, to profit, was formerly written, in different ways, *butte*, *bote*, *bot*, *boot*.

"If love had *booted* care or cost,"

that is, *added*, *profited*.

Five dollars *to boot*, between horses, is five dollars to add to the cheapest.

It was evidently the want of knowing the etymology of the word *but* which led Mr. Locke into such confusion in attempting to explain its meaning: for even with his powerful intellect, the question still applies, "What can we reason, *but* from what we know?"

The two meanings of *but* are directly opposed to each other ; *but* (add the fact) there is no difference in their *manner of meaning ;* neither of them can be used, *but* (except) as an imperative verb.

37. *Else* is a verb used at present only in the imperative mood; and, consequently, without change of form.

Unless is the same word in an altered appearance.

Else, elese, elesse, alesse, alaes, alase, onles, onlese, unlesse, lese, lesse, less, and many others, are different forms in which the same word has been spelled, by the best English writers. In all the forms it means the same thing, *less, lessen, loose, loosen, unloose, lose, unlose, release,* relinquish, dismiss, take away. The prefix *un* is some times used, from habit or carelessness, where it is redundant; as to *ravel,* or *un-ravel,* and others. To *lessen* any *thing ;* to *less if,* as twenty *less five, x less y,* in algebra; to *unless a thing,* or to *else it,* if it was fashionably elegant to say so, is to *loosen, detach,* or *take away,* some portion from it. There is no difference of meaning between *else* and *unless ;* but the beautiful and convenient difference, in the modern application of that meaning, gives not only variety, but brevity and clearness, and ought not to have been so long overlooked. This difference is that *else* always *refers back,* and unless *refers forward,* to the *proposition, fact, circumstance,* or *thing,* which is to be *lessened,* or *taken away.* (*Else* is *less,* except, or obviate, some thing *previously specified;* and *unless* is, take out or remove some thing *to be specified* after the use of this word.

> He will be punished, *unless he repents.*
> *Unless (the fact) he repents,* he will be punished.
> *He must repent; else* he will be punished.

From this use of these words, it unavoidably happens that *unless* may come at the beginning, or middle, but never at the end of a sentence ; and *else* can never begin one. The condition to be dismissed or obviated, must in one case be actually asserted before, and in the other, after, the verb. There are two opposite statements brought before the mind : one is to be withdrawn, or relinquished, that the other may stand good.

This principle is right : it can not mean any thing *else* (this condition).

This principle is right : *else* (the preceding statement, then) I mistake.

This principle is right; unless (the following position) I mistake. Unless (the supposition) I mistake, (then) this principle stands good.

To *lessen* any thing, is, in its philosophic principle, to take some part of its bulk, or substance, from it; and to take one thing from another, is to lessen the aggregate made by the two.

Else and *unless* are called, in the existing grammars and dictionaries, *pronouns, adverbs,* and *conjunctions.* They certainly are not *pronouns;* unless, as *names,* or at least as *substitutes for names,* they represent *persons* or *things.* The *connection, opposition, circumstance,* or *manner,* denoted by these words, under the imaginary character of *adverbs* and *conjunctions,* can be no other than what *nouns* generally, and *verbs* and *adjectives* always convey. The nouns *debt* and *credit,* as referred to a merchant's leger, denote both *connection* and *opposition.* Every possible *relation* of one thing to an other, includes the ideas of *opposite sides,* with a connecting medium: consequently, every *adjective* is both *conjunction* and *adverb,* for the same reason that *else* and *unless* are so. The verb to *weigh* must suppose bodies *opposed* to each other, and *connected* with one pivot. In the phrase, "to *subtract* one thing from an other," this *verb,* by its necessary meaning as a verb, includes all the " *opposition,*" " *connection,*" " *modifying,*" " *time,*" " *place,*" " *manner,*" and " *circumstance,*' which *unless* and *else,* under any name, can possibly denote; and it has the same specific meaning, as a word.

Lest, in reference to its formation, as a word, is a past participle, from the verb to *lessen, less, loose, release;* and is an *adjective,* as a part of speech. It relates to a *fact, condition,* or *circumstance,* as being *rejected,* that the whole force may be concentrated on what remains, after such *relinquishment.*

"Help him, *lest* (the circumstance) he die."

That *supposition,* "he (should) die," being *lessed, lest, unlessed, dismissed, rejected, determined* against, "help him," accordingly, with undivided purpose. The adjective *lest* refers to the noun *circumstance,* or equivalent word, of which the after phrase, " *he should or might die,*" is only the extended proposition. The participial adjective *lest* is idiomatically confined to this form of use; and this necessary order, in the collocation, is the only peculiarity or disguise in the employment of the word. Other adjectives often take the same construction, but are not confined to it.

Fruitful the soil, "*inviting* the clime," "*serene* the sky."

"No torturing ills can find admittance there,
Supplied each want, and *banish'd* every care."

38. *If,* formerly written yif, yef, yeve, gif, giff, gyff, geve, give, and in various other spellings, is a verb, in the imperative mood. It is an altered form of the modern verb *to give,* with the same meaning. In its use, it requires the person addressed to grant, suppose, or allow, a *fact, condition,* or *statement,* made, as the foundation of another proposition or question. The *direct object* of the verb is the noun *fact, proposition,* or other equivalent word, and of which the proposition expressed is the exemplification.

If four yards cost eight dollars, five yards will cost ten dollars.
Give or suppose (the statement) four yards cost eight dollars.
If (it is true) (that) four yards cost eight dollars.
If, give, grant the fact: what fact ? *that* fact, *the* fact, "*it is true.*"

"Ye must come unto my master deare,
"*Giff that* your name be Barbara Allen."

39. *Tho,* or *though,* or, as the same word appears in various forms in the old books, *thoh, thof, thoff, dof,* and others, is nearly synonimous with the verb grant. Like other verbs of this restricted use, it has for its direct object a noun understood; but which is a substitute for a whole proposition repeating the same idea in an amplified form.

Yet is *get.* The Saxons had one letter for *y* and *g,* and the interchanges between the two are very frequent in later times. *Yet* is a verb, in the imperative mood, and like the rest has a noun understood for its direct object. It is also followed, like the rest, by a proposition, of which the direct object is the summary name.

"Tho he slay me,.yet will I trust in him."
"Tho (the fact) he slay me, yet (the opposite fact) I will trust in him."
Tho or grant the fact: what fact ? the fact, "he (may or should) slay me," yet or get, or retain this fact: what fact ? the fact that *I will trust in him.*

Yes is an other form of the same word.

When a proposition is stated by way of question, it is very seldom necessary to repeat the whole in the answer. The contractions are various, in different countries and ages; but, among polite modern nations, a single emphatic term, with the associations familiarly understood, is deemed sufficient.

Those who can reason on this word, with its necessarily associated facts and principles, will perceive that *yes* is a proper answer to a question, only when simple consent is all that is required. If the answer itself is to explain facts, the word *yes* is not appropriate.

Do thirty-two quarts make a bushel ? *Yes.*
How many quarts make a bushel ? *Yes.*

Why is it that the word *yes* is a proper answer to one of these questions, and not to the other? It will readily be seen that simple assent is all which the first question requires; while the second demands positive information. This second interrogation is answered by saying *thirty-two*, which stands for the whole proposition, thirty-two quarts make a bushel, the connection of the answer with the question necessarily explaining the rest.

Yes, in answer to a question, is *get, take*, my *consent ; have* the *thing* as you suppose or wish.

Tho it is the design of this work to avoid foreign languages, *yet* it may not be improper to mention, that the same practice prevails generally in other tongues. Several nations use the imperative of the verb *to be*. In France the *yes* is the participle of the verb *to hear.* This answer, equivalent to the English word *heared*, is, by implication, favorably *heared ;* that is, *consented to.*

"*Be it unto thee as thou wilt.*"

Ay aye is the old Norman or French verb, *aye, ayes, ayez, have, get, take*. Like *yes*, it is now a verb in the imperative mood, *have* or *take* what you ask ; *take* or *receive* my assent. *Be it* unto thee, or *have the thing*, as thou wilt.

Besides the foregoing irregular or defective verbs, there are several others, which, from a vague conjecture that they have no meaning of their own, are, under the name of *helping verbs*, represented, in existing grammars and dictionaries, as being used *merely* for the purpose of modifying a portion of the words which have significa-

11

tion : and yet, unaccountable as it may appear, these *helping verbs* are employed *to help each other*, where, according to the neuter theory, there is no *action implied*, nor *specific meaning* to be modified. What is the philosophic nature of that *help*, which is either given or required, where there is no *action to be done or* "*expressed?*" To call a set of words *auxiliaries*, and say they are used to conjugate the *moods* and *tenses* of other verbs, is no explanation, and is only calculated to deceive. Which of the colleges is sufficiently expert in the art and mystery of *neutrality*, to interpret what is meant by the *mood* and *tense* of a "*condition of being?*" What do *auxiliaries* denote by their own meaning as words? for, if they have no *absolute meaning*, then certainly there is no *difference of meaning* between one of them and an other, more than between two noughts in arithmetic.

The compilers differ very much from each other, in making out the arbitrary lists of words to call *auxiliaries*. Mr. Harris, in his learned work, has *seven;* Mr. Murray *ten;* some have more, and some less. Which is right? What is the *essential character* of an *auxiliary*, or the difference between that and a *principal verb?* Why is the same word *auxiliary* at one time, and *principal* at an other; *active* and *neuter*, *transitive* and *intransitive*, in the same sentence? and by what evidence shall the learner distinguish these opposite characters in the same verb? Does it vary its *absolute* or its relative meaning, where it has no meaning at all? For a particular example, what is the *difference* in *do, be, have,* or *will*, as *auxiliaries* and as *principal verbs?* What is the *grammatical* or *philosophic* difference between the *neuter principal* verb *to exist* and the *neuter helping* verb *to be*, when, in all the dictionaries, each defines the other, and neither means any thing distinctive, but each expresses *state of being in general,* and not *one condition of existence* more than an other?

Instead of multiplying grammar rules and exceptions, for each phrase which language can employ, it will save much confusion, to begin by finding a meaning for the important words too long represented as having no real signification.

All the believers in helping verbs appear to reckon among the number, *be, can, do, have, may, shall,* and *will.* Some add *let, must,* and *ought.*

It is somewhat curious, that, taking either list, these words neither differ from other verbs, nor agree with each other, in any one principle, assumed as the basis of their *auxiliary* character and classification.

Are they *auxiliaries*, because they are *defective*, or not carried thro all the correlative parts in *mood* and *tense?* then the list should reject *be, do, have,* and *let,* and admit several others. Is it because they do not take the proper *infinitive form* after them? then we must reject *be, have,* and *ought,* which always take the infinitive, with *to,* as its sign; and the verbs *bid, dare, feel, hear, help, make,* and *see,* must be classed, *in part,* with *auxiliaries.*

As an instance of a *defective verb,* and one specifically applied, the word *quoth* is the most remarkable in the language. It is used only in the indicative mood, singular, and the past tense; and, contrary to general practice, it must come before the agent, and only in the first or third person.

Few as the words called *auxiliaries* are in number, so important are their *meanings,* and the *actions* they "express," that no theory which misinterprets them can be otherwise than bad.

An examination of these words, according to rational science, and the most elegant practice, will present them in a light very different from the mysterious technicality in which they have hitherto been involved.

What is called the verb *to be,* is made up of six different radical verbs, taken to make out the correlative parts of mood and tense, and relieve the monotonous repetition of sounds which would attend its employment with that frequency its importance requires.

Am is a compound of *ah, breath,* and to *breathe, life,* and to *live, light,* and to *light;* and *ma,* the *hand,* and *to hand.* In early times, this verb *ma* denoted a large part of the actions done by man, of which the *hand* was the *instrument.* It took the general meaning to *make,* to perform, operate, execute, produce, *manufacture.* The early words in language were few in number, and very extensively applied. The verb *ma* was first to operate with the *hand* as an instrument, and next with any *means* of *effective production* substantially equivalent. Those who have not paid much attention to the subject, might view with great surprise, the prodigious number of words, in every known tongue, which have relation to the human *hands.* All unlettered nations are ignorant of air as a substance at rest. They see the *light, live* in it, and *breathe* it; and that is to *light* or *life* themselves; for *light, life,* and live, are but modified forms of one word. The word *manufacture,* itself, signifying to *perform with hands,* runs into other equivalent operations. So the compound *Ah-ma* was to exercise, or perform, the function of *light-ing*, or *lifing* one's self. The letter *a*, according to the general course in contracting words, was soon dropped, and the letter *h* being sub-sequently omitted, leaves *am*, as now used; but with the same meaning which the word has always had: for no one can use the term without conveying this fact, whether he truly interprets his own expressions or not.

In the practical application of the verb *am*, it can have no varia-tion in its *objects*, and *objective words* are, therefore, unnecessary in use. They could serve no purpose of distinction or perspicuity. One man is not contemplated as inflating the lungs of an other; but each as performing this vital function for himself. It is not neces-sary to say I *breathe breath*, or *vivify myself* with *breath*; for this is unavoidably understood in saying I *am*: and this understanding of the objective words depends, not on any difference in grammatical or philosophic principle, but on the associated facts in the special case. *Am* is confined in its use exclusively to the indicative mood, present tense, first person singular. It has, therefore, no variety in its *manner of meaning*.

Am, as a noun, is *life* or *being*, *spirit*, the *vital principle*; and, in its highest application, *Essential, Self-Existent Being, the Life-giving Power.*

This word may be exhibited in most of the principal languages of the earth, as far back as letter writing can be traced. It is, in its principle, very deeply interesting by its historical and religious associations, and by the manner in which it stands connected with the thoughts and circumstances of men. A volume might be written upon it; but it is not the design of this work to depart from expla-nations confined to the English language, and addressed to English scholars.

   air, are, art, these are the same word, which in modern practice is slightly and conveniently modified in form; but with-out any alteration of meaning. Thou *art* is contracted from thou *arest*.

"*They are*," means first, they *air* or *are themselves*; they *supply themselves* with *air*; they *vivify, inspirit*, and *preserve themselves* by means of *air*; and applied to the lower ranks of creatures, they *continue them-selves* in *air*; or the regions of *air, light*, or *being*. Se-cond. They *are air*; they *inhale* or *imbibe air*; as they *drink drink, sleep sleep,* or *breathe breath;* they enjoy the *enlivening* influence of *air;* and inferior things do some thing as nearly analogous to the same *action* as their various natures and circumstances will admit.

Be   signifies to *live,* to *breathe,* to exercise the qualities and functions of *animal life;* and when applied, by analogy, to matter, to *take, possess,* or *hold,* some state of being, among existing things. It is the same *word,* with one letter altered, as in the first syllable of *bi-ography,* which, if modern fashion allowed, might be written *be-ography,* or *life-ography;* that is, a *graved, engraved, in-scribed,* or *written* account of a person's *life.*

is   signifies to *ex-ist,* being a contraction from the same radical word; to *stand forth;* to *exhibit one's self;* to *take,* or *hold* some *stand,* or *position,* in the universe of *existing things.* *Is,* always denotes *self-action.* One person does not *exist* an other *person,* and the *actor* is one of the *objects.*

     Is, like other verbs, has a verbal noun, or the equivalent idea, necessarily implied; as, It *stands its standing;* it *exists its existence;* it *holds its place,* and *acts its acts,* among the actors, living and dead, throughout the Creator's works.

Were, wert, werth, worth, werde, word, "In the beginning was the *Word,* the *Word* was with God, and the *Word* was God." These are all but the variations of one term, signifying *spirit;* the *enlivening power;* the *vital,* or *life giving principle:* "They *were;*" they *inspirited themselves,* they possessed vitality; and, as applied to the minor gradations of being, they *retained* and *exercised* those *acting powers,* analogous, by receding degrees, to *animal life,* which *acting powers* pervade every portion of the material *world.*

Was   is a modification of *were,* from the same radical term, and with the same meaning.

     To *can,* past tense *could.* To *can a thing* signifies to *perceive* it, to *comprehend,* or *know* it; to possess the requisite *knowledge, ability,* or *skill,* to *manage* it. To *con,* to *cun,* to *ken,* are different spellings and pronunciations of the same word, for different counties of England, and at different times. They all have the same meaning, to *see*, to *understand*, to be *able*, that is *skilful*, by practice, or enlightened comprehension of the subject. "I *can* demonstrate all the problems in Euclid's Elements:" that is, I *can* or *ken* the *way* or *mode*, I *can* the mathematical skill. That can denotes the "*potential mood*," or signifies "to be able," is simply because "*knowledge is power*:" It is for the same reason that "a *wise* man is *strong*: yea, a man of *knowledge* increaseth strength ;" or, that "he scaleth the city of the *mighty* and casteth down the *strength* of the confidence thereof."

> "And ignorance of better things makes man,
> Who *can not much*, rejoice in what he *can*."
>
> COWPER.

> "A famous man,
> Of every *witte* somewhat he *can*,
> *Out take* that *him* lacketh rule
> His own estate to guyde and rule."—GOWER.

> Of every *art* somewhat he *knows*,
> *Ex-cept* that *to him* lacks rule
> To guide his own affairs.

The essential idea of the verbs *can* and *see*, is precisely the same, to *grasp*, *seize*, *per-ceive*, or *com-prehend*, external objects. The word *mind* is itself a *participial* or *derivative* word. It signifies the same as the *per-ceptive* faculty, that is, the power which *catches*, *takes*, and *holds* ideas or objects. No real *operative cause* is ever seen. No name applied to *a cause*, as such, can ever be otherwise than a derivative word. Among the best writers in the language, the use of *can* without a following infinitive, is well established. It is often employed by the earlier writers as synonymous with *see*.

> "Jason, she cried, for ought I *see* or *can*,
> This deed, &c."   CHAUCER.

May ; past tense *might*, signifies to have and exercise *might*, *strength*, or *physical power*. An *ignorant* man *may* lift a great weight; an elephant *may* carry a heavy load; an *orator can* make an eloquent address; a *poet can* elevate our conceptions,

A slight examination will show that all power must be resolved into the two kinds, physical energy and mental skill. The word *may*, immediately denoting one, and *can* the other, renders these verbs of great use; and, as actions take place in consequence of the power to do them, *may* and *can* are generally followed by an other verb, in the infinitive mood. The word *to*, as in other cases of the kind, is commonly dropped in this following infinitive, to shorten the expression, on account of its frequency. May has been represented by learned writers as denoting *liberty* or *permission* merely; but this liberty is delegated *power*. The liberty is the incident, not the essential principle. If one man gives an other a " *power* of attorney," to authorize and *empower* him to do what he was not at *liberty* to do before, it is the same principle. This *permission* which *may* is supposed to express, is but the granting of *power* from a superior.

The word *do* will require very little explanation, as that is not considered in present grammars and dictionaries as absolutely without meaning.

There is no other difference in the use of the word, than that the object is sometimes expressed, and at others only implied; but the same holds good of almost every other verb in the language which is any way frequent in its occurrence.

I *do* write is a mere contraction; and means, in grammar and fact, I *employ* or *exert* my *skill*, I *do* my *endeavor*, to write. It is not common in modern style, to insert the object for the verb *do*, when it precedes an other verb, in what is considered its " *helping*" office; as, " We *do* you *to know*."

Have. The chief difficulty with this word, under the imaginary character of an auxiliary, results from the mistake of its import. It is represented as denoting mere possession. When we say " A man *has* his *leg* broken, or his *arm* shot off, we certainly do not mean that he gets his *leg*, in one case, and his *arm*, in the other, into possession, by these accidents. This shows at once that possession does not belong to the essential meaning of the verb *have*. I *have* lost a *paper*. The argument to show that, in this sentence, the word paper is not the object of *have*, is, that if the paper is *lost*, it is not in possession: but if I *have a paper* in my hand, and say I want to *have* that *paper* burned; my want here, is to *have* the *thing*, from an actual possession, not only out of possession, but out of being. *Have* and *heave* are originally one word, and are nearly synonymous in modern use. To *have* is to sway, controll, dispose of, in any way, to stand so related to a thing as, in any way, to affect its absolute or relative condition. A man has these relations not only to his possessions, but to his actions, duties, moral, social, and other connections. He has important business on his hands: he *has obligations* which must be discharged: he *has* an *uncle* in China: he *has his work* done: he *has it* yet to do.

He *has* a *letter* written.

He *has* a written *letter*.

He *has* written a *letter*.

These three sentences, by familiar and habitual association, convey different ideas to the mind, but that difference does not depend on the verb *has*, either specifically or grammatically. This verb *has*, is, in the three instances, equally active and transitive; equally in the present tense, and the noun *letter* is alike the object of it.

The first sentence imports the man *has* a *letter*, in the *condition* in which the *act of writing has* placed *it:* in the second expression, the letter is in the same relation to the *man*, and to the verb *has*. He *has* the letter, and it is of that kind which the act of writing *has* made *it*, and which the participial adjective written describes. The third sentence, he *has* written a letter, conveys the additional, associated fact, that the written letter *has* become so, by the man's own agency, direct or indirect.

I want you to *have* my *watch* cleaned.

This sentence does not mean that I wish to *have* an other *man* possess my *watch:* but to *have him have it*, heave *it*, put it, or cause it to be, in a new condition.

The reason why the old *perfect tense* of helping verb grammar "always conveys an allusion to the *present time*," is the simple and strong one, that this verb *have*, which makes it, is always *present tense*. The *past participle* connected with it, is, without exception, an *adjective* referring to the *object* of the verb.

It is important to *have* this *verb* well understood. Those who attempt to *have it* explained as an auxiliary, will *have* much *trouble* to little purpose; and it will be fortunate for the rising generation to *have* this absurd traditional neuter *theory* banished from colleges and schools, that they may *have* language taught according to fact and common sense, which would, indeed, be a very different *having* from what they now *have*.

Must, signifies to be in bondage or constraint, to be *bound* or *compelled*. I *must* depart this evening. Some power, or circumstances, to which it is necessary to conform, *require me* to depart. I yield, or acknowledge the obligation to depart.

Shall signifies to *owe*, to lie under constraint, *obligation*, or duty. "The subject *shall* bear true allegiance to his king ;" the citizen *should* be faithful to his country.

To will, past tense *would*, signifies to *wish*, to *exercise volition*. I *will the thing* to be so. I have the will or wish to have it done. In the extension of *will* to objects not having free volition, in its literal sense, it is analogous *inherent principles*, or *tendency*. A bullet in the water *will* sink, and a cork *will* swim ; water *will* run downward, and smoke *will* ascend.

Will, in its essential principle, is an *active* tendency in all things, disposing them to change, and to one kind of *action* or change rather than an other. In verbal expression, the reference is to the sensible indication of such disposition or tendency to change, manifested to the organs of perception, as the means or instrumentality employed, or exhibited in a state of preparation.

The word *will*, as a word, traced thro the principal languages of the earth, from early times, with the physical and mental principles with which it is unavoidably connected, is extremely important and interesting ; but this is not the place for an extended illustration.

The difference, in use, between *shall* and *will*, is very simple, when the words are understood. *Shall*, from its meaning, always relates to external necessity, obligation, or requirement, and *will* to *inherent disposition, aptitude,* or *tendency*.

The *moon will* rise, this night, in its own regular course, and according to the *inherent* laws of its nature : it *shall*, one day, be extinguished, in conformity with a superior law or power to which it *shall* and must yield obedience.

We read in the homilies of the Saxon English church, To Him alone we *shall us* to devote ourselves : Chaucer says, The *faith* we *shall* to God ; that is, the *faith* we *owe*. To *shull* is always to *owe* the *debt, duty, obligation, reasonable service,* and *must* is simple *bondage,* or physical *restraint*.

It would be difficult for any thing under the name of explanation, to excede the perplexity with which the existing grammars are filled, in the vain hope of teaching the use of words, by artificial rules, without knowing their meaning. Having given a slight view of some of these words, which appear to have been the subject of great error, the reader will be better prepared to examine the farther principles, which depend on a clear understanding of the *verb*.

It was before said that a verb forms two *participles*, one always, in English, ending in *ing* ; the other, having its regular ending in *ed* : and, in about two hundred irregular verbs, ending in *d*, *t*, or *n*, which are alterations of *ed*, or the retention of the Saxon terminational syllable *en*.

The participle in *ing* is a compound of the radical *word*, *noun*, or *verb*, and the appended word *ing*, which signifies *be* or *act*, for the ideas are both one. The *active* and the *vital* principle are the same thing. *Lively* and *active*, *liveliness* and *activity*, are synonymous terms. *Ing*, and the equivalent syllable to form the present participle in other languages, is the noun *being*, and the verb to *act*, or to *be*.

This participle, as a word thus compounded, is primarily a noun, and is the name of the *action*, taken as an act, a fact, circumstance, or thing. Like other nouns, it takes a secondary place, as a word of description, or an adjective.

The horse is *running* a race.

He is in the act of running a race : he is in the *running* of a race.

The man is *performing* a piece of work. He is engaged in the *performing* or *performance* of a piece of work. It is the most simple way of explanation in practice to make the participle a mere noun, or an adjective, without regarding its *incidental* character, as expressing action. Where, according to the old grammars, it is said to govern an *objective word*, all difficulty will be removed by putting a defining adjective before it and a preposition after it.

The compound word called the *past participle*, and which in English ends in *ed*, is formed by getting one verb into the past tense, in the way which will be hereafter explained, and then appending that word to other verbs. The syllable *ed* is contracted of the old past tense verb *dede*, *did*, or *done*.

The wall is *paint-ed*. It is a *paint-ed* wall. It is a *paint-done* wall, such as the *done* act of *painting* has made it.

It was said, in the Synopsis, that every adjective is either a *noun* or a *participle*, made adjective by use. A *paint* store is a store which has some relation to the article called *paint*. A *paint-ed* store is made so by the effect of some *action* performed upon it with *paint*. A *trotting* horse, a *spinning* machine, a *writing* desk, are so by some relation which they bear to those several *actions*. It is the common process of language that *participles* turn into nouns by dropping the names which are at first used with them, as when we say the *ground*, instead of the *ground-earth*. In the same way we have *mortals* instead of *mortal beings ;* a *domestic,* a *general.* With a little more of disguise, we have *field* for *felled* land, that is, where the *timber is cut down;* the *road* for the *rode* way, and a vast variety of others. While a past participle is considered in character as such, it is always an adjective by use. The term *participle* is therefore applied to those words in reference to their mode of formation, and the term adjective to designate their classification as belonging to one of the three parts of speech.

Among the participial adjectives which have become most disguised in modern language, are those which *describe* the *specific local* relation of one thing to an other. From what appears to be a total mistake of their character, they have been called *prepositions,* and represented as governing a succeding word. These *adjectives* called *prepositions,* never govern other words, and their immediate reference is always to an *objective word before them.*

The following hints will give a general view of this set of *adjectives,* or *describing words :*

Every *action* which takes place produces some *resulting effect,* both on the *actor,* and on one or more *external objects.* It will not be necessary to repeat what has already been said respecting these general principles of action. The *effect* of every *action* is, first, to throw its *direct object* into some relative *condition, state,* or *character,* in which it was not before, and, independent of such *action,* would not have been placed. Whatever *agent moves* an *object,* necessarily *moves* that *object from* some position, *to* or *towards* some other. A *participial adjective describes* the *object,* as being in such *new, produced* condition ; and the new relation in which the object is so placed may be general, or it may be specific, with reference to some other particular thing.

A man had his house *raised.* In this expression the adjective raised is the general relation. The house was made a *raised house,* in reference to its former condition, as compared with the surface of the earth, or other surrounding things sufficiently understood, by familiar association.

The binder made one *book like.* He placed one *book near.* He laid one *book on.* He sent the *book thro.*

The last words, in these four sentences, are all participial *adjectives* describing the book in its new condition; but the description, in each case is incomplete, because this new condition is one of *specific* relation to some other thing which must be mentioned to finish the description.

Whatever is like, is likened to some thing else; and *near* is the participle neared. *On* is *joined*, and *thro* is *past*, with the associated idea of having *passed* by *traversing* or *perforation*. Each of these four adjectives has the object of a verb before it, to which, as a descriptive word, it immediately refers: it has an other *object* expressed or understood, after it; connecting the two, and showing the *relation* between them.

The following are the chief adjectives of specific local relation, called prepositions, as at present used in English.

About, above, after, against, amidst or *amid, among, around, at, before, behind, below, besides* or *beside, between, beyond, by, down, for, from, in, into, of, on, over, round, thro, to, towards, under, up, upon, with, within, without.*

There is much confusion in what is given for explanation of these words in the books; and the theory of neuter verbs and prepositions, as taught in colleges and schools, will not for one moment bear the test of scrutinizing investigation. The position, however, is assumed that this system must be true, because it has long been believed. The old have grown familiar with the formal routine, and follow it from habit, as their grand fathers did when they were masters of ceremonies in the technical masquerade; the young receive it on trust; and, all together, under the sanction of authority, pass on in throngs, to keep each other in countenance.

A boy fell *into* the river, and got *wet.*

Fell *what* into the river? *Nothing at all;* because, we are learnedly told, by all the colleges and royal academics in the world, that *fell* is a *neuter* or *intransitive* verb. What was *wet?* The *boy.* Certainly not the *boy,* as *agent* of the verb, and *before he fell.* Neither can it be the *boy,* after he *fell,* if this verb has no object, and denotes no *resulting effect.* What is *into?* A preposition. What office does it perform, as a preposition? "It connects other words, and shows the *relation* between them." What *relation* here? The *relation* between the *boy* and the *river.* Surely not the relation between the *dry boy* before he *fell,* and the *river;* that *relation* would be expressed by *out of,* instead of *into.* The *boy* was no more *in* or *into* the river, than he was *wet,* till he was placed in that new "*condition of being,*" by the effect which his fall produced on an *object.*

The boy *fell* (his *person,* his *body,* his *self,* into the river, and got *himself*) *wet.*

If grammar is worth learning, at an expense of so much time and money, it should be stripped of its absurd technical assumptions, and taught according to fact, science, and good sense.

These *effective* instructers will show that, after every *falling*, some *object* must be *fallen*, and that, according to rational probability, the resulting *condition of being* in which such *fallen object* is placed, at the *termination* of the *fall*, is either *in* a fluid substance, or *on* something else.

The implied *object* of this supposed *intransitive* verb, obviates the strange logic of a *one sided relation*, and offers the means for a clear understanding, both of the *essential principle*, and of the *elegant use*.

A *man* ran *against* a post and *was* badly *hurt* by it.

How *against* a post, or badly *hurt*, if the *action* has no *object?* What is the *agent*, or *actor* of an *intransitive action?* Simply an *efficient cause*, without *real* or *implied* connection with an *effect; a parent* independent even of a supposed *relation* to a *child.* How comes this *actively malicious post* to *practise* such an *unprovoked injury* on the *man*, and make him *suffer* this *effect* of *being hurt?* If the man dies by *being* thus *hurt*, the post is guilty of manslaughter, without any other mitigating circumstance, than that it was done without premeditation. It has not the plea of self defence; for the peaceable man confined his *inoperative action* entirely to *himself*, and ran no *object against the post*.

" *Prepositions*," in the ordinary school practice, are called *adverbs*, or *conjunctions*, when the objective word is not *expressed after them.* Dr. Blair, in his Rhetoric, as other learned writers had done before him, calls them *post*-positive *pre*-positions, when apparently depending on a verb, and not followed by an " objective case," as,

" To lift a thing *up*."

If this *up* thing does not happen to be raised *quite enough up*, then it becomes necessary to *raise it higher up*. In this expression, then, of every day use, we have an unquestionable *adjective*, to express the *comparative degree* of the " *quality*," denoted by this rhetorical *foregoing*, *aftercoming* word, called a *post-positive preposition*.

12

Up, upper, upmost, are adjectives in the three degrees of comparison, as much as *high, higher, highest,* and the difference in their meaning is very slight. So we have *in, inner, inmost ; out, outer* or *utter, outmost* or *utmost.* The prepositions are also, like other adjectives, compared by a great number of *secondary adjectives ;* as, *very far above,* or *beyond; directly against, entirely thro, exactly over;* the child was *close by,* or *very near to,* its mother.

Keeping in view the very plain fact that every *relation* must have *two sides;* and also the exposition of *adjectives* as being founded entirely on *comparison,* or the *relations* of things to each other, it will readily be seen. that the partial modification of the more *specific kind,* is, in its principles, very simple. If we use the adjectives, *east* and *south,* the mind instantly suggests the correlative points *west* and *north,* without their being mentioned, in words. We can no sooner say that the sky is *clear,* than the ideas of *clouds* and *storms* are *comparatively* presented ; and if the weather is said to be *cold,* that description is opposed to *warm.* *Up* has its *general comparison* with *down,* and may take a *specific* relative application to a *second object;* as, The squirrel is *up* the *tree;* the person is up *stairs;* the hunter rides *up* a steep *hill.*

We never use the word *above,* without speaking of some thing as being *above,* and it must be above some thing else, as a matter of course, whether it is barely *above* the ground, or " *Above* these heavens, to us invisible, or dimly seen."

After, whether called *preposition,* or *adverb,* has but one meaning, and one application. Some thing must be placed *after,* or *farther aft,* than some thing else. No matter whether that some thing else denotes *position, motion,* or *time,* which are but different names for the same relation. The word *after* describes the first thing by its *relative,* or *comparative* situation : it makes the second thing a connected part of that description; and shows the relation between the two. This preposition is *preceded by an objective word,* depending on a verb, and *followed by an other objective word,* because in the *same grammatical relation.* This is the secret of the *objective case* after a preposition, which becomes a confirmed habit in the use of language, though there is nothing in the meaning of the words themselves, by which they can *govern* a following *object.*

Prepositions, as well as verbs, frequently omit the following word, because it is necessarily understood.

" I told the man who is painting my *house*, to put *on* a good coat of white lead."

Every person of ordinary sense understands that the workman was to put the paint *on* the *house*.

If we speak of a man's taking his hat *off*, or putting his boots *on*, there is no need of being very particular about objective words. Children will readily find them, if not falsely taught, and they are not likely to mistake in supposing that the man takes his hat *off* his feet, or puts his boots *on* his head. There is no need, therefore, of "*adverb conjunctions*," or "*post-positive prepositions*," to explain this prevailing structure in expressing the relation of things. It is the business of grammar, rightly conducted, to teach, first, the complete and undisguised construction of words in a sentence; and second, how far it is allowable to abridge or modify this structure in practice.

As the term *preposition*, though not very appropriate, has become extensive and familiar in practice, there can be no strong objection to the use of the *name*, with the understanding that the words so called are not a separate part of speech, but as a subdivision in the class of *adjectives*, are *partially distinguishable*, by the more specific local relation which they denote.

It is not necessary, here, to explain each of these terms, etymologically, as a word. That will be done in a dictionary. The principle may be exemplified on a single one, and the others, after what has already been said, will not, among intelligent persons, present much difficulty in their use.

The adjective *of* or *off*, is a past participle, signifying *disjoined, separated, broken asunder.*

A fragment *of*, or *off*, a rock.

It is a *fragment*, because *broken;* and *of*, or *off*, for the same reason. The idea of *separation* is one of the most extensive in the operations of thought. Its modifications are necessarily various. The nouns to denote a *part, share, abstract, portion, lot, piece, quarter, scrap*, and others of like kind, are *participial* in their formation. The *noun* is a *relative name;* and the *relation*, like every other, must have its *two sides*. The *share* is the share *of*, or *off*, some thing that is, the *part shared, sheared, cut,* or *divided.* If we speak of a *share,* or *part,* where the separation has not *actually* taken place, it is because the mind, from experience, and familiar habit, runs before the *action,* in the special case. By the same mental operation, also, we may suppose a *division,* where, in practice, it can not be made ; as, for instance, to *extract* all the heat *of* the Sun, or *divide* Saturn's belt into *parts.* The *relative* ideas, belonging to *of,* or *off,* are *connection,* on one side, and *separation,* on the other. The modification of the word *off,* which took place in England about five hundred years ago, is very convenient in practice, and adds to the elegance of language. When the intention is more immediately to describe the *state of being of* the *off,* or *separated,* thing, in reference to the *fact* of *distance,* or *separation,* the word is written *off,* and more emphatically pronounced. When the mind leans rather to the *connection,* present, former, or merely supposed, the recent word is spelled *of,* and lightly articulated, unless contrasted with some other idea, not belonging to its *customary* associations.

The wine is drawn *off.*

He has sawed the piece *off.*

- He has it *separated* by sawing.

The man is well *off.*

He is well *separated,* from poverty, danger, or other evils, idiomatically understood.

The man is far *off.*

He is far *remote, removed, distant, gone, separated,* from his *friends,* or *home,* or from the *speaker.*

" Off! interjection."—Dr. Johnson. *De-part yourself* from me ; take yourself *off, distant,* or *away.*

" Off, preposition, distant from."—Dr. Johnson.

He fell *off* the scaffold ; *distant,* or *separate ;* an adjective describing the object of the verb *fell,* which is *his self ;* or *himself,* to avoid the unpleasant sound of *s* in its immediate repetition.

A true *chip of,* or *off,* the old *block.*

The *chip* is the *chipped* piece, the *part detached,* by *chopping,* or *chipping. Chip* was the original verb, and *chop* was its past tense. Both are now in good use in the present tense.

If the *chip* did not exist, in supposition at least, it could not be named. It could not *ex-ist*, nor rationally be supposed to exist, unless *pro-duced*; nor be produced without the *requisite means*. Where, in point of fact, the *chip* is not *cut* from the block, the *int-el-lect* must perform that operation, before we can talk about it; and the same *dexter-ous* mind which, with its ready ax, brings the *chip* into *separate ex-istence*, as a *thing*, also *describes* it as *of* or *off* the *block*, from which it is so *taken*.

The fragrance *of* a rose.

This expression implies the connection of the fragrance with the rose; but this fragrance could not be mentioned, or conceived, in *dis-tinction* from the rose, if the separation, in *fact*, or in idea, had not taken place. So we say "the brightness *of* the sun," where there is the idea that a portion of its brightness is actually *separated*, or thrown *off*; but the mind, according to the habits of thought, may *separate* from this orb, all, as well as part, of *light, heat, globular form*, or any thing else connected with it.

On the same unavoidable principle the mind must *ex-tract*, or take away the *hardness* of the diamond, or the *six sides of* a cube, in order to make any *distinctive* assertion concerning them. It is to be remembered that the *adjectives* of this class always denote *produced* relation, and necessarily include the *means of production*, whether that is expressed or not. The *chip of* the block, is the *chipped piece*, which *chip* some actor, corporeal or mental, chopped *off* the block. The *means* of production includes an *action* represented by a *verb*. That verb has an *object* coming *before the adjective* which describes its new *relative* character, or state of being. The interposed adjective, when the relation is specific, refers *directly* to the object before it, and incidentally, datively, or ablatively, to the following one. This is the single principle on which all the "*oblique cases*" Latin, Greek, and every other tongue, depend. It is in importance second to no other in the science of language, or of thought. belongs, in construction, to every sentence which verbal utterance can frame. In the hands of those whose learning, talents, and means, can do justice to its exposition, it will throw great light on the course of *physical*, as well as *mental*, researches; and it will correct some of those errors which have misled the men to whose splendid talents human nature is most indebted for its present degree of exaltation.

Over is the *comparative degree* of the *participial* adjective *of* or *off*, spelled as it is pronounced, with the letter *f* softened into *v*. The thing which is *ov-er* some thing else, is *off-er*, more distant, farther off, or projected, from the center of gravity, the position of the speaker, or some other beginning place, from which the *offing*, or *distinct* position, of the *off-set* thing is reckoned.

" *Over* the brook Kedron." *Farther distant* from Jerusalem. *Over* the top of the house ; *farther e-levated*, from the earth. The rounds of a ladder, rise in succession, *over* each other ; farther se-parated from the foundation. The prime associations of *high*, *low*, and *offing* or *distance*, are the relations to the center or surface of the earth. They spontaneously arise in the train of thought ; but may receive a specific modification by the circumstances of the particular case.

The adjective *of* is taken to illustrate, in some degree, the whole set of " *prepositions*," because it is considered the one most liable to objection of any in the list, and most difficult to apply, without a previous exemplification.

After the suggestions here offered respecting the formation of adjectives from verbs, to describe the relative effect, general or specific, produced by action, the reader will be prepared to test the principle by the general list of irregular verbs, as at present used in English.

IRREGULAR VERBS.

1. Such as are not varied for tense.

present	*past*	*participial adjective.*
beat	beat	beat
eat	eat	eat
burst	burst	burst
cast	cast	cast
cost	cost	cost
cut	cut	cut
hurt	hurt	hurt
hit	hit	hit

knit	knit	knit
slit	slit	slit
spit	spit	spit
split	split	split
let	let	let
put	put	put
rid	rid	rid
set	set	set
shed	shed	shed
shred	shred	shred
shut	shut	shut
spread	spread	spread
thrust	thrust	thrust
bid	bid	bid

2. Such as, in the past tense, change *d* to *t*.

bend	bent	bent
lend	lent	lent
rend	rent	rent
send	sent	sent
spend	spent	spent
wend	went	went

3. Others change the final *ed* into *t;* shorten a preceding vowel, or are otherwise modified in the past tense.

creep	crept	crept
keep	kept	kept
sleep	slept	slept
weep	wept	wept
feel	felt	felt
leave	left	left
meet	met	met
hold	held	held
uild	built	built
se	lost	lost
beseech	besought	besought
bring	brought	brought

buy	bought	bought
fight	fought	fought
seek	sought	sought
think	thought	thought
teach	taught	taught
bleed	bled	bled
breed	bred	bred
feed	fed	fed
speed	sped	sped
lead	led	led
read	read	read
flee	fled	fled
hide	hid	hid
have	had	had
cling	clung	clung
fling	flung	flung
sling	slung	slung
sting	stung	stung
string	strung	strung
swing	swung	swung
wring	wrung	wrung
ring	rung rang	rung
sing	sung sang	sung
spring	sprung sprang	sprung
swim	swum swam	swum
shrink	shrunk	shrunk
sink	sunk	sunk
slink	slunk	slunk
stink	stunk	stunk
stick	stuck	stuck
strike	struck	struck
bind	bound	bound
find	found	found
grind	ground	ground
wind	wound	wound
spin	spun	spun
win	won	won
sit	sat	sat
shoe	shod	shod
shoot	shot	shot
sell	sold	sold

tell	told	told
get	got	got
make	made	made
stand	stood	stood

Some are made up of different radicals, which have been united for the sake of relieving the monotony of frequent use.

am	was	been
go	went	gone

Such as take three different forms from one root.

bear	bore	born
swear	swore	sworn
tear	tore	torn
wear	wore	worn
blow	blew	blown
grow	grew	grown
know	knew	known
throw	threw	thrown
fly	flew	flown
draw	drew	drawn
see	saw	seen
begin	began	begun
speak	spoke	spoken
break	broke	broken
weave	wove	woven
arise	arose	arisen
rise	rose	risen
fall	fell	fallen
steal	stole	stolen
drive	drove	driven
strive	strove	striven
smite	smote	smitten
rite	wrote	written
re	gave	given
eze	froze	frozen
forgive	forgave	forgiven

forget	forgot	forgotten
choose	chose	chosen
do	did	done
shake	shook	shaken
take	took	taken
lay	laid	laid
pay	paid	paid
say	said	said
bite	bit	bit
hide	hid	hid
slide	slid	slid
bid	bid bade	bid
abide	abode	abode
ride	rode	rode
stride	strode	strode
lie	lay	lain
slay	slew	slain
tread	trod	trodden
come	came	come
run	ran	run

Several of these verbs have additional forms of the past tense or participle, still partially retained, but gradually going out of use, or acquiring a specific application.

The following were formerly irregular, and are still occasionally so used; but there is a prevailing tendency to give them regular endings, and this may be considered the best practice.

awake	awoke	awaked
bereave	bereft	bereft
catch	caught	caught
chide	chid	chidden
cleave	clove	cloven or cle
clothe	clad	clad
crow	crew	crowed

dare	durst	dared
dig	dug	dug
drink	drank	drunk
dwell	dwelt	dwelt
grave	graved	graven
hang	hung	hung
hew	hewed	hewn
lade	laded	laden
mow	mowed	mown
show	showed	shown
sow	sowed	sown
strow	strowed	strown
saw	sawed	sawn
rive	rived	riven
shape	shaped	shapen
shave	shaved	shaven
shear	sheared	shorn
shine	shone	shone
spill	spilt	spilt
swell	swelled	swollen
thrive	throve	thriven
wax	waxed	waxen
work	wrought	wrought

Hear, heared, is a regular verb, though *heard* is often seen in books, and repeated in conversation as if spelled *herd.* Several of the London dictionaries give the noun *heard* defined as a herd of cattle, but the word thus corrupted as past tense of the verb *hear* is not English. Mr. Walker, in the first editions of his dictionary, gave it his sanction in a note ; but he very properly rejected it afterwards; and the best lexicographers in England have for years omitted this counterfeit word, leaving the verb *hear,* like *clear, fear, rear, sear, shear, smear,* and others of its class, to form the regular past tense.

ᵑeard, pronounced *beerd,* is the only word belonging to the En~ ʌ language ending in *eard.*

If the preceding exposition of verbs is substantially true, and well nderstood, it prepares the way for a scientific development of *mood* and *tense,* which will reconcile all their varying forms in words with immutable principles founded in the nature of *things*. The distinguishing of actions by the relations they bear to their causes, is philosophic, obvious, and common to all languages. To make a consistent division of *moods* or *tenses*, by the specific meaning of words, in their endless variety of combination, as has been so long attempted, is beyond human power.

The more particular exemplification of moods and tenses is referred to the practical exercises, which are to follow.

CHAPTER VII.

OF THE REMAINING TERMS IN LANGUAGE CALLED PARTICLES, CONTRACTIONS, BROKEN WORDS, OR ADVERBS.

The list of these words presents a strangely assorted group, and the only thing which appears to belong to them in common is that they are all presented under some disguise by which their meaning as words was not understood. Being supposed to have no absolute signification, the expounders were easily led to consider them as mere connectors, modifiers, or hangers on, to qualify the meaning of such words as had a meaning, and a direct application to actions and things.

The attempted distinction between declinable and indeclinable words, as a principle in classing the parts of speech, appears to be altogether fallacious. Like every other theory, not founded in truth, it is as bad in practice, as in philosophy. Any part of speech is indeclinable, when by the frequency of its use, and the nature of its relative bearings, it becomes familiar in its application; and is declined when its associations are less uniform, or less understo. The word *cut*, in its matter of fact use, is known to every boy w.. has whittled a stick, or *cut* his finger.

"*TO CUT*, *verb neuter*. To make its way by dividing obstructions."—Dr. Johnson.

I *cut* an apple last week; I *cut* one now: I have *cut* one; I have it *cut* and *dried*; it is a *cut* apple; a *cut* is made in it.

The following is Mr. Murray's list of the words which he calls *adverbs*, subdivided into eleven sorts, ended with &c., and with the farther information that there are many more. Some writers have given upwards of seventy kinds of adverbs.

"Once, twice, thrice, &c. First, secondly, thirdly, fourthly, fifthly, lastly, finally. Here, there, where, elsewhere, anywhere, somewhere, nowhere, herein, whither, hither, thither, upward, downward, forward, backward, whence, hence, thence, whithersoever. Now, to-day, already, before, lately, yesterday, heretofore, hitherto, long since, long ago, &c. To-morrow, not yet, hereafter, henceforth, henceforward, by and by, instantly, presently, immediately, straightways. Oft, often, oft-times, often-times, sometimes, soon, seldom, daily, weekly, monthly, yearly, always, when, then, ever, never, again, &c. Much, little, sufficiently, how much, how great, enough, abundantly, &c. Wisely, foolishly, justly, unjustly, quickly, slowly. Perhaps, peradventure, possibly, perchance, verily, truly, undoubtedly, doubtless, certainly, yea, yes, surely, indeed, really. Nay, no, not, by no means, not at all, in no wise, how, why, wherefore, whether, more, most, better, best, worse, worst, less, least, very, almost, little, alike, &c."

Mr. Murray says, of these "*adverbs*," that "they *seem originally* to have been contrived to express, *compendiously in one word*, what must otherwise have *required two or more*." No such thing could *originally* have *seemed;* nor could such a plan have been *originally contrived*. Compendious expressions of several words in one, are not contrived in any such way. The plain forefathers of mankind did not, with anticipating wisdom, design the refinements of modern language. They did not manufacture words, in large lots, like a tea-table set of crockery, to match each other in their after applications. The motly assemblage of *adverbs* are *nouns, verbs,* and *adjectives,* blended and contracted, in a way which no finite wisdom could have foreseen. The words thus formed have been considered in their
ing character as *subordinate to verbs;* hence the name *ad-verb:*
.e same time they are subordinate to adjectives; and while per-
ning this minor office in two so very different sorts of words, they
a one, and by no means the least important of the nine distinct
parts of speech. We are farther told, that though these words per-

form very numerous other offices, they may be reduced to certain classes, the *chief of which* are those of *Number, Order, Place, Time, Quantity, Manner, Quality, Doubt, Affirmation, Negation, Interrogation,* and *Comparison.* It would perplex a disciple of Linneus to understand such a classification: but the classing of things in nature, depends on natural principles; and language, we are told, is "entirely conventional and arbitrary," "depending altogether on custom."

This set of terms can never be comprehended as adverbs. What is said about them in grammars only bewilders, and does not give any real information. It becomes very important to take up the subject in a different light, to examine first the interesting principles which form the basis of exposition, and next attend to the proper application of the words.

First, the "*manner of action,*" which is the prime office of the adverb. On this subject, those who prefer *authority* to every thing else, may have that of an English judge, who, with his accustomed elegance and perspicuity; has given, in half a page, more truth and more real information, respecting the *manner of action,* than all the expounders of *adverbs* who ever wielded a pen.

"When the Supreme Being formed the universe, and created matter out of nothing, He impressed certain principles upon that matter, from which it can never depart, and without which it would cease to be. When He put that matter into motion, He established certain *laws of motion,* to which all movable bodies must conform. And to descend from the greatest operations to the smallest, when a workman forms a clock, or other piece of mechanism, he establishes, at his own pleasure, certain *arbitrary laws* for its direction; as that the hand shall describe a given space, in a given time; to which law, so long as the work conforms, so long it continues in perfection, and answers the end of its formation.

"If we farther advance from mere inactive matter, to vegetable and animal life, we shall find them still governed by laws; more numerous indeed, but equally fixed and invariable. The whole progress of plants, from the seed to the root, and from thence to the seed again; the method of animal nutrition, digestion, secretion, and all other branches of vital economy, are not left to chance, or the will of the creature itself, but are performed in a wondrous involuntary *manner,* and guided by unerring rules laid down by the great

Creator." Blackst. Com. Sec. II. Of the Nature of Laws in General.

In the attempted development of adverbs, and of all other words, it is intended that, as far as circumstances will admit, constant regard shall be had to the following considerations :

1. The principles of natural science on which the phrases depend.

2. Their connection with the necessary operations of thought.

3. The prime and essential meaning of the words.

4. Their elegant modern associations and use.

The *manner of action*, in every possible case, is to be sought in one of three principles.

1. The *mind, plan,* or *intention,* according to which the action is *designedly* performed.

2. The *means* or *instrumentality* employed.

3. The resulting *effect* on an *object,* as distinctively exhibited to the senses.

All kinds, and every circumstance of action, and all differences, which, in fact, or in contemplation, can exist between them, must be referred to one, or other, of these three classes. What is the *manner of action* by which the earth *performs* its annual *circuit* of 600,000,000 of miles, and *completes* the tropical *year* in 365 days, 5 hours, 48 minutes, and 49 seconds ? The *manner of action* is as well regulated, in the *earthquake* and *whirlwind;* but, by human observers, not quite so well understood. All actions, in the order of nature, are the same thing : whether in the boundless machine of intervolving worlds, or the microscopic fiber in a mulberry leaf, the *manner* of *action* is the *wisdom* of that Eternal MIND, which *pervades, directs,* and *governs* all. So far as man acts according to the organization of his nature, his *manner* of *action,* in common with that of other things, comes under the first great law : and, within the sphere of his judgment and free will, it is merely the substitution of the human, for the unerring MIND.

Let us suppose a man arraigned before a court, to be tried for killing an other. This is a case where, in practice, it becomes necessary to institute the most rigid inquiry concerning the *manner* of *action,* on physical, moral, and legal principles.

The prime question, as all the books, and the judges will tell us, is, *With what mind* was this *action done ?* Was it with a deliberately *wicked intention;* by a sudden start of *passion;* a mere want of the care; or without any *design* at all? In the second place what *instru-ment* did he employ? was it a *club*, an *ax*, *dagger*, or *deadly weapon* of any kind? Third, what was the nature of the *wound* or *hurt* pro-duced?

No human skill can, in any language, devise a word, to denote any thing concerning the *manner of action*, except in conformity with these principles. If the reference is to the *mind*, or the *instrument*, then the "*adverb*" is a *noun*; if the *effect* is referred to, this "*ad-verb*" is an *adjective*, describing the *object*, as *affected* by the action, and always in relation to some other standard perception, with which the *object* thus *conditioned* is compared.

In the second place, we may consider the "adverbs of quality." A recurrence to *adjectives* will show what this *quality* is made of. The standing example which Mr. Murray employs to show the nature of an *ad-verb*, as prefixed to an *adjective*, to *qualify* its *quality*, is, "A *truly* good man." Most of the *adjectives*, and a large portion of the nouns in the language, may be used as *adverbs* expressing the de-gree of quality, in the same way. The *easiest* understood explana-tion will be by parallel examples.

A *truly* good man.
The *true* Cornish dialect.
A *good* hearted man.
Highland Scotch sailors.
A *pure* gold ring.
The *finest* wooled sheep.
A *snowy* white robe.
A *shaggy* haired dog.
Double refracting crystals.
General election dinners.
Gold headed cane.
Longest lived animals.
Russia iron cables.
Real diamond ear rings.
Hardest working people.
Early morning air.
Deepest crimson gauze.
Oldest commissioned officers.
Winter evening stories.
Benevolent intentioned copyists.
Night blooming flowers.
Alum drest buffalo skin robes.
Finest merino wool blankets.
Real tortoise shell combs.
Brightest pink colored morocco shoes.

Dark age technical theory inculcation.
Complete nominal quality adverbs.
Thorough going qualifying quality instruction.

The mistake in the whole doctrine of *quality* was alluded to before : yet *adverbs,* without *naming things,* or expressing the *effect of actions,* " *qualify*" the " *qualities*" which *adjectives* denote. This may do very well for *neuter technicality;* but, in *practice,* the reader will probably agree, that it is rather difficult to take the second step, while it remains impossible to accomplish the first.

Our college theory of speech, whether in the *learned languages,* or the *vulgar tongue,* is a curious display of the science of mind. The *quality of a quality* and the *manner of action,* are so very different from each other, that if the words which denote them both were any thing but *adverbs,* they certainly could not belong to the same part of speech. We might, with as much propriety, represent *humbirds* and *elephants* as belonging to the same kind of animals : but, if we admit adverbs at all, it follows, of course, that, except denoting *things, relations,* or *actions,* they can, under some of their seventy characters, perform one office as well as an other. It would be improper, therefore, to object to any classification which this kind of *technicality* is supposed to require. As adverbs are the drudging dependants of all parts of speech, their contractions need create no surprise; for why should they not grow thin, when put to such hard service.

A large proportion of the words *called adverbs* are formed by adding *ly* to an other word. They have been represented as *modifying* both *adjectives* and verbs. The syllable *ly* is from the same root, and means the same as the adjective *like.* The word so compounded is an *adjective,* describing the *object* of a verb, in reference to some *resemblance* which it acquires or holds, from the *effect* of the *action.* It may also be made a *secondary adjective* by use, according to the general principles before explained. The word *like,* is a compound *noun.* This is not the place for the long train of its etymology, and the interesting principles, in *matter, mind,* and *social intercourse,* with which it stands connected. The noun *like,* in its primary application, is *body.* In its first extension, it is *image, resemblance, picture, representation.* " Every *like* is not the *same.*" " We never shall look on his *like* again." The verb to *like,* or to *liken,* is to re-sem-ble one thing to an other ; to bring it into con-form-ity, or *similitude;* to *adapt* a thing, or ac-com-modate one's self,

13*

to some thing else ; to cause to *a-gree*. The participial adjective *like*, is *likened;* and *ly* is a mere contraction of the same word. *Man-ly*, or *man-like*, is man *resembled*. *Wedge-like*, is *wedge-shaped*, or *cunei-form*.

The *resemblance* denoted by *ly*, or *like*, may be close, or very remote. There is no rule for using, or omitting, this *word*, or *syllable*. It is entirely a question of *fact*, determined by *fashion* and good *taste*. The difference exists not only between verbs of *like* meaning, used in a *similar* way ; but in cases where the *same verb* stands in the *same construction*. It is worthy of remark, *likewise*, that the verbs called *neuter*, all take the words which are said to express the *manner of action*, in *like manner* as the acknowledged *active* verbs, so that if the *neuter verb theory* was true, there would be *manner of action* where there was *no action*.

Live-ly, or *quick-ly*, is *life-like*. The steam boat made its *passage* very *rapid-ly*. *Like* a *rapid*, a *quick*, or *quickly*, running place, in a stream. This post-fix *ly*, according to the artificial systems of grammar, without definition of its own, has a magical effect on other words. At the same time it *qualifies* the *quality* of *adjectives*, it expresses the *manner* of *transitive*, and of *intransitive, action ;* the *manner* of *passion;* and the *manner* of a "*condition of being.*"

> The man sleeps *soundly*.
> She sits *genteelly* or *perfectly well*.
> She sits *idle* and *contented*.
> She remains *quiet* and *undisturbed*.
> She lives *contented* and *happy*.
> She lives *virtuously* and *happily*.

> The new house is finished *elegantly*.
> It is made *elegant*.
> It is rendered *elegant*.
> It appears *elegant* or *splendid*.
> It looks *well* or *elegantly*.
> It looks *neat* and *substantial*.
> It shows *well* or *superbly*.

> Exercise *cures* the patient *completely*.
> It *makes* him *completely well*.
> It *makes* his cure *complete*.
> It *effects* his cure *completely*.
> It renders his cure *effectual*.

The best practical exemplification of the adjective *like*, and its contraction *ly*, is in its compounding with itself. *Like*, and its reduplication, *likely*, are, in all the principal English dictionaries, defined, both as *adjectives*, and *adverbs*, and both with the same meaning in each case: so that the weight of authority, when properly examined, shows that the addition of *ly* to an other adjective, does not make a different part of speech. The keen logic of nature, which goes far beyond conventional neutrality, makes a distinction true to the essential meaning, and the real principle. Where the *likeness* of one *substance* to an other is obvious to the sense, the single adjective is used to express the direct resemblance, as exhibited: but if we contemplate a *transaction*, as very *like-ly* to happen, it is not the image of one *corporeal substance*, *likened* to an other. The adjective is therefore let down to the second degree of *similitude*, the *mental* or *supposed resemblance*, founded on the principles of *analogy* to *material bodies*. *Like*, therefore, has its application to *similitude* directly *obvious*, and *likely* to that which *resembles a likeness*, or which is applied by analogical inference.

In the third place, words called " *adverbs of time.*"

Every intelligible communication respecting *time when*, or *how long*, must include a *noun*, and one or more *adjectives*, expressed or understood.

Time is not made of any thing absolute or essential. It floats on the successively changing relations of things, and affords no object of perception to which a name can be absolutely applied. The manifestation, taken as the point or duration of time, must be some standard appearance, with which others in the measurable order of events may be compared.

The essential meaning of the word *time*, is periodical or alternate *change;* tremulous or vibratory *motion*. The Greek verb *to fear*, the English word *timid*, and many others, are founded on the same idea. It is *wavering, trembling*, or *vacillation*, as the indication of *fear*. In most of the northern languages, of Europe, the word *tide* is *time* ; that is, the regular *alternations* in the ebbing and flowing of the sea.

The *time when* any transaction took place, was when some known *object of perception*, in the *definable periods* of its *changing states*, exhibited a standard appearance, capable of being taken as a *point* or *measure*, in comparison with other successive events. To *point out*

any *time*, either in reference to its *epoch* or *duration*, must necessarily be to *name* the standard appearance, to *identify* it by an adjective, and to denote its *relation* to the *event* with which it is *compared :* for as the *appearance* denoting the *time* is never *absolute*, it
must have its *correlative* circumstances, either *described,* or *understood,* by previous familiar *association*.

It does not consist with the plan of this work to go into systematic
detail on the words denoting *time*. The *time when* Ruth *returned* to
her friends, *was " in the barley harvest:"* not in the " season of
snows ;" not in the *spring* season, when the plants *spring* from the
earth, nor that in which the leaves *fall* from the trees : it was not in
the *rain month*, nor the *" month of flowers;"* not in the *hay moon;* but
in the *harvest month*, and next preceding the fruit *mooning—moneth,*
or *month*.

The noun *day* is, in its primary idea, the *darting*, or throwing out
the beams of light; and the *nig-ardly, neg-ht,* or *nig-ht,* is the *neg-a-
tion, noug-ht, nihil-ity,* or *an-nihil-ation* of the light.

All which can properly be called science is true to nature ; and
language, when rightly understood, is always in accordance with
both.

" Every different *degree of light* makes the object have a different appearance, and *total darkness takes away all appearance.*"

Dr. Reid.

The "substantive," *night,* is the German *"* adverb," *not ;* and
under various modifications, the same *word* may be traced, thro the
different languages, ancient and modern, from the river Ganges to
Iceland.

Noon is *non,* or *none ;* the place of *beginning*, at which *nothing* is
reckoned; because the sun has made no departure from it. The
noon time, or *noon tide*, is *when* the sun is at the *first meridian,* indi-
cated, in the practical science of astronomy, by a *cipher,* or *nought*.
" To day" is *this day*, contracted in pronunciation, and afterwards
followed in spelling, when *carelessly* and *familiarly* used. In expressions of particular *dignity,* and *sublimity,* the correct scholarship
should be preserved. " *This day* shalt thou be with me in Para-
dise." *Morning* is contracted from *morrow-ning,* and *morrow* is an
opening, dawning or *next coming day*. The phrase, *on the morrow*,
is, in the shortened expression, *to-morrow,* and by ordinary speakers
uttered as if written *t' morrow*. *Yester-day* is the past or gone, the
earlier, or, as the Hollanders appropriately call it, the *foreleading*

day, taking the *present condition* of the intelligent beings concerned, as the *standard*, in the com-*parative* reference to *preceding* or *after* events.

Having offered these suggestions, respecting the principles, in *nature* and in *thought*, with which the leading "kinds of adverbs" stand connected, it remains to attempt an explanation of the words, which, having never been defined, are found to present the greatest difficulty in their application.

As it is considered the prominent characteristic of "adverbs" to "modify verbs," it seems proper to begin with the terms which are supposed to be particularly confined to this office in language.

The words *how* and *mode*, or *mood*, are *nouns* of participial formation, and *names* of the *mind*. *Wise* is also a participial noun, and means the *wisdom*, *wit*, or *knowledge*, existing in the *mind;* the *plan*, *design*, *calculation*, or *device*, formed by that mental *intelligence*. The word *how* is very familiar in its contracted form, that is, without the associated words.

" *How* was the action done ?"

In what *mode*, *mood*, *mind*, or *wise*, was it done ? With what *mind*, or *intention*, was it done ? According to what *mind*, *plan*, *design*, or *purpose* was it ? By what *wisdom*, *skill*, or *knowledge*, was the performance *regulated*, or *directed* ?

The noun *home*, in its ordinary modern use, will exemplify this kind of familiar *adverbial contraction*.

He is *at* (his) *home*. He went (to his) *home*. He left (his) *home*. "He is gone *to his long home.*" In this latter expression, the omission practised in common social intercourse would not suit the nature of the assertion, and it becomes necessary to use the associated words.

Manner is a compound word, and in its exact analysis, signifies *hand work*, that is, the *abil-ity*, *dexter-ity*, or *habit-ual* skill of the hands in the performance of an action. Like other words it readily extends to other equivalent *instrumentality*. The word *man-age-ment* is nearly synonymous with *manner*, and translated into undisguised English, is *hand-act-ing*. By a very easy transition, also, according to the general philosophic principles of action, explained under the verb, the instrument becomes the operator, or immediate cause of the performance. *How* many *hands* does the shoe-

maker employ in his *manu*-factory? That is, *how* many *workmen* does he employ? The word *how* is very often a *secondary* adjective, as it is used in the two preceding questions.

Why, formerly written *qui*, qua, quæ, and various other forms, is *what*, with the associated words, for *what* reason? from *what* cause? with *what* design?

It some times happens that a number of the words called adverbs come together; as,

Have you learned your lesson?

Ans. Not yet quite well enough, perhaps.

It probably will not be necessary to dwell on the philosophy of the remaining kinds of adverbs. It is said that "An adverb is a part of speech joined to a verb, an adjective, or to an other adverb, to express some quality or circumstance respecting it." We are not told of any "adverb" in the *case absolute* or *independent*, and therefore are to understand, that adverbs take the application which the grammatical theory contemplates. Adopting these definitions, then, and applying them on logical and algebraic principles, the "adverb of quantity," if made secondary to the *verb*, expresses the *quantity* of an *action*, of a *suffering*, or of a *state of existence*: if "joined to an *adjective*," it is to express the *quantity* of a *quality*; and joined to an other adverb, it denotes the *quantity* of a *circumstance*. In like manner an "adverb of doubt," according to its three kinds of application, is, first, the *doubtful modification* of *acting*, or *suffering*, or of *existence*; second, the *qualifying doubt* of a *quality*; and, third, the subordinate *circumstantial doubt* of a *circumstance*.

The noun *worth* is an instance of the kind of contraction which takes place by dropping associated words, It has been a source of much perplexity in the schools. "The horse is *worth* a hundred dollars." *Of the worth of* a hundred dollars. The word *of* coming before and after the noun *worth*, makes the expression too clumsy for repetition in familiar use, and where no important distinction requires it.

Al-ways, contraction for *in all ways*; in all modes, and by slight incidental variation, at all times: for whatever passes thro all successive manners or ways of action or "being," must endure thro all *times*. In the national idioms, therefore, which vary this "*ad-*

verb" to *all-days, all-time,* and others, the difference is only in the appearance.

As. This may be considered the most difficult word in the language, to explain in the various elliptical forms in which it is used. In its logical application it points out the identity of a general fact, thing, or circumstance, in comparison with a connected fact or proposition. To give its extensive etymology would be a show of learning easily made; but to no useful purpose. In grammatical character, this word in its modern use is an adjective referring to the noun *fact, thing, way, kind, degree, reason,* or other equivalent word; but, having a second reference to a proposition, for which the single word is the summary name. *As* signifies, as a defining adjective, *this, that, these, the same, the said,* with the *noun understood* after it. Such men *as* Cesar was: the same (kind) Cesar was. He believes *as* Lilly taught: *the same* (thing) Lilly taught. I will go *as* far *as* you will: the same degree far, the *same* (degree) you will. The water is *as* cold *as* ice: *the same* degree cold; *to,* or *in, the same* (degree.) It rains; and, *as* that is the case, I must stay at home: and, for *the same* (fact, reason, or thing,) I must stay at home. He went home, *as* he found it difficult to remain longer: for *that* (reason), he found it difficult.

So, formerly written *sa, sua,* and *swa,* is an adjective, nearly synonymous with *as,* and the words may be substituted for each other, in frequent instances. They would have it *so :* have it *that* (way). All-so, *all the same* (thing); *all in the same* (way).

And is a participial adjective, from a verb signifying to join. It is a modification of the same word *as* the number *one. John, James,* united, go to school. *John, James, to-gether-ed,* or *gathered to* each other, go to school. John, James, Peter, *connected, joined, united, oned, and,* go to school. John *united* Peter, go; John *and* Peter go. The peculiarity in the modern use of the adjective *and,* is that fashion has conveniently placed it between the things which it describes as being united, instead of setting it before or after them all. The eminent Horne Tooke developed the etymon of this word; but with his transcendant vigor of intellect, the defectiveness of his plan led him to mistake its grammatical and philosophic application.

First is *farest,* or *fore-est ;* and *last* is contracted of *latest :* the *time* or *thing* which *lags* most *behind.*

Ever. In the earliest languages of which alphabetic writing remains, the essential meaning of this word is *life.* By an easy transition, it became the *period,* or *measure* of *life,* that is, an *age ;* and, *ever* (*during the ages*) since the time of the Romans, this meaning has been preserved. It does not appear to have, *ever*, (in any *age*) been changed. "For *ever*:" (for *ages*.) "For *ever* and *ever*:" (for *ages* and *ages*.) *Ages of ages*, is the idiom, in most known tongues. Like other words in the same familiar use, it is mechanically and habitually transmitted thro the social intercourse of life, without the proper consciousness of its import. The whole mass of society acquire the habit of taking phrases all together, without attempting to analyze, or assign to each word, its due share ; and the same familiarity which causes the unemphatic associated words, when pronounced, to be uttered with a lightness and rapidity, intelligible only to an accustomed ear, by a slight extension, enables the hearer to supply them for himself, when wholly omitted. This is the principle which explains a large portion of the *adverbial contractions ;* or rather the whole of those made by dropping associated words.

Ever is a noun, *singular,* or *plural,* used to denote *time when,* or *how long ;* and is to be parsed by supplying such *adjectives* as the sense of the phrase requires.

Never is ne *ever ;* in no age ;.at no *period* or *time.*

Here, there, where. These are compound words, each made of an *adjective* and *noun.* The latter part of each is the word which we now write, *area.* It is an enclosed *yard,* or any *surface, open,* but *circumscribed* in its dimensions. It becomes extended, on the ordinary principles of analogy, to any *place, condition,* or *state,* real or imaginary, which can be designated or *pro-posed,* in the comparison with other things.

There is the, or *that, area.* He *left there,* yester day. He *left that area,* or *place.* He went *there : to that position.* He stayed *there : at,* or *in,* that place. The idea or explanation is precisely *there :* in that *condition,* or *state.*

Where, is *which,* or *what, area.* He went *where* he pleased: *to what place. Any where :* in any (the) place. The defining adjective contained in the word *where,* is in this instance superfluous ; but the redundancy does not appear as aukwardness ; because, without a rigid investigation, it is not perceived, and both words in the compound being reduced to one syllable, no farther contraction can be made.

Here. The prefix to this word is a former *ad*-jective, meaning *the, this,* or *that :* but which, for more than seven hundred years, has been disused in England. He departed from *here*, last week : from *this place*. He lives *here* : *in the described village, township*, or *city*. We rest these observations *here* : *at this position* of them.

For. This is one of the many important and difficult words in language, all attempts to explain which, have hitherto failed. The master etymologist, before referred to, says that it has the same meaning as *cause:* but this only brings us to the material question, what does either word mean ; for all which is said about them in dictionaries, will not make any person, in reality, wiser than he was before. This "*substantive,*" *cause*, by the least *action* upon it, turns into effect ; and there is no stopping place, or line of demarcation between them.

It has before been said that there is but one independent CAUSE ; that all created things are a series of *causes* and *effects*, existing as mere *relations;* and that, in every definite or possible *conception*, respecting a *cause*, the *idea* is *inferential*, the *noun* is only a *relative name*, and it is, from the unavoidable necessity of the case, a *derivative word*. This term *cause*, can have no exemption from a principle which is essential to its class. To explain the word *for*, in its important bearings, it is proper to begin ; not,

4thly. In modern *fashion*, with compilers of grammars ; nor

3dly. In mere *verbal etymology*, with Tooke and others ; nor

2dly. In *metaphysics*, with Aristotle, Locke, and a host of splendid men, who spent their lives in prying at the treasures of intellect, without a fulcrum for their levers ; but

First ; in the science of nature, as instituted by that WISDOM which never errs, never falls short, never changes its "*customs,*" nor controverts one fact by another. Language, as existing in these principles, will not be the subject of dispute, when once explained, and will have no exceptions to its rules.

That *unseen*, and *untangible, thing*, which is termed a *cause*, is inferred to be such, for the reason that an *effect* takes place, whic have learned from experience to understand, must have a and that no other thing in connection with the result produced, i probably *efficient*. The writers on the *science of sciences* may have, from nature, the demonstrative lesson, to begin with, that every *name* of a *cause, actor*, or *contriver*, as such ; of the *mind* and its "*qualities;*" of the *Deity* and his *attributes ;* is a *derivative* or *compound* word ; no matter with what *utterance*, in what *form*, or under what mistaken *exposition*, modern *fashion* may employ the *term*.

Each sublunary *cause* turns into *effect*. The *production* of this instant, or year, becomes the *producer* of the next. Every *causa-tive influence* is but the *effect* of a previous *agency*. The thing which *acts*, or *operates*, does so, because it has, *collected* or *reposited* within it, the *enlightening* or *reason*, the *force* or *vigor*, the *strength* or *adjustment* of *cords*, the *power* or *solidity*, to *produce* such re-*sult*. It is because it is *pre-pared, fitted, adapted, enlivened, qualified*, or made *wise, skilful, suitable, adequate*, and *proper*, to *produce* the *effect*. If we ascend the graduated scale of *being* or *acting*, to the FIRST CAUSE, then, so far as language, or the laws of thought, on *natural* principles, are concerned, the mind turns back on itself, and from comparison, and former habit, infers a *Deity*, by withdraw-ing all *restriction, error*, or *defect*, as contemplated in *created things :* for, according to the light of nature, this CAUSE must be adequate to the production of effects, innumerable, endlessly varied, and in-conceivably stupendous.

Cause and *effect* are convertible terms ; every secondary *cause* is itself *caused, effected*, or *produced ;* and to *effect* a *cause*, is to *cause* an *effect*.

For and *force* are modifications of one *word*, found in the lan-guages of northern and of southern Europe, as far back as letter wri-ting can be traced. Numerous collateral branches of the same etymon, are distributed thro the various modern tongues. The *rea-son, for, force, power* or *impelling cause*, where-*for* an *effect* takes place, is the accumulation of *knowledge, skill, vigor, life*, or *activity*, in which the *action* has its spring.

It will be found, then, that this *transmissible force* has no appro-priate *habitation*, or *resting place*. It pervades all bodies, without being detected in any, except by the results which follow its opera-tions. That versatile *thing*, which was *cause* in the agent, is trans-formed into *acting*, in the *verb*, and *effect* in the *recipient* of the ac-*tion*; as the *wheat* put into the hopper, comes out *flour*, in the trough below. The *name* of a *cause*, therefore, in its distinctive character, as such, can never be the *object* of a *verb*. Those who strongly feel for the advancement of science, may look back with regret to the extent of error into which the most gifted of the human family have been led, by employing these words as arbitrary signs, while overlook-ing the extremely important natural principles to which they apply.

It may seem at first view, an extravagant paradox in language, that the word *cause* does not mean *cause*. Nothing is more clear, however, as every expert linguist must see at once, than that the word *cause*, as *direct*, or *incidental*, *object* of a *verb*, stands in the re-

lation of effect, instead of *cause*. It does, in point of fact, cease to represent the *idea of a cause*, as hitherto explained by the writers on *natural* and *mental science*, thro the learned world. When it is found that a *word* of such importance, and generally supposed to be well understood, fails, in half its uses, to *mean its own meaning*, it is time to scrutinize, very closely, that principle of *matter* and of *mind*, which can *produce* such an *effect on a recipient*, or *passive, cause*.

It has before been said that the *cause* of all *material operations*, is ONE; the sole CAUSE, who is not *caused;* the Divine Author, acting thro the whole. The all pervading *principle* of *activity*, in its *essential nature*, human science *has not yet* invented instruments to weigh, to measure, or inspect. What *philosophy* can know of any *cause*, is learned from its observable *effects* on *material bodies*. This *causing principle, force*, or *activity*, is really *cause*, in its *general relation*, as producing a perpetual succession of *effects:* but our views of it are *partial* and *inferential*, as it is *received*, or *communicated*, by different *material bodies*, thro which it is transmitted. When we conceive the *idea* of this *active principle, cause*, or *force*, as a something *striking*, and *influencing*, a natural *body*, this *idea* comes under the explanation of the word *cause:* but when the same *force*, or inter-communicated *acting principle*, is, according to the general understanding of mankind, *forced* or *imparted*, from one *mass* of *matter* to an other, this same *general cause*, or a conceived *portion* of it, takes the character of an *effect*, in the *specific relative* connection in which it is presented: but so beautifully and sublimely is language conformed to the all governing *laws*, that *each word* applicable to this case is *modified* and *adapted*, in its *relative bearings*, to the *special fact*, while its broader *meaning*, and *rules* of *construction*, are exactly accordant with the sublimest *principles* which an omnipotent CAUSE, acting thro the universe, offers to philosophic contemplation.

The language being understood, the seeming contradiction is reconciled: it is found, here, as elsewhere, that Divinely regulated opposition produces harmony, and "All nature's discord makes al nature's peace."

The application of these principles, in their grammatical construction, may be seen in the use of the words.

1st. The word *for*, as a " *conjunction*."

1. "I submitted; (*for*) it was vain to resist."
2. We ran; (*for*) a superior foe was near.

3. I can not call words conjunctives; (*for*) explanation is better than such a substitute.

In the preceding sentences, the noun *for* is used without the associated words, as their ideas are understood by familiar habit.

1. *I submitted*; (the *for*, the *reason*, which induced me to submit, was,) *it was vain to resist.*
2. *We ran;* (the *for*, the *impelling cause* which *forced* us to run, was,) *a superior foe was near.*
3. *I can not call words conjunctives;* (the *for*, the *force* of conviction, the restraining *for*, or *cause*, which prevents such practice, is) *that arbitrary name would be a miserable substitute for explanation.*

2d. Arguments would be superfluous to prove again that the specific *relation* of any thing to a *cause*, or to an *effect*, must be a *produced relation;* and with the proper understanding of this principle, as belonging equally to the *science* of *matter* and of *thought*, there is no need of *etymology*, in the first place, to tell us that the *preposition for*, is, by *formation*, a *past participle*, and, as a part of speech, an *adjective*, describing the *object* of a verb, in the "*condition of being*," in which an *action* has placed it.

The crown was made expressly *for* the king.
The tailor made the coat *for* the man.
He made the coat, *adapted, prepared, adjusted, fitted, suited,* (*to*) the man.

Whether the word *to* is to be *used*, or *omitted*, after *adjectives* of this kind, depends partly on the special nature of the related things, but chiefly on familiar habit in the use of the expression. Still more is to be allowed for the degree of accuracy in the knowledge of the relations signified. Thus we say *opposite* (to), *up* (to), *in* (to), *near* (to), *on* (to), *like* (to), and a multitude of combinations with other words of this kind, which it is needless to repeat. The meaning of *for*, when understood, shows why this word has been so obstinately preserved by the mass of English people, before the *infinitive verb*, long after that use had been declared inelegant by polite scholars.

He was ready (for) *to go.* He made the watch (for) *to keep* time : *suited, adapted, prepared, forced, to go,* or *to keep* time. For the same reason the correspondent word is retained by several European nations, in elegant modern use, as a concomitant of the infinitive mood.

Be-cause. This "*adverb,*" or "*conjunctive,*" is merely two unaltered words put together. *Be,* is a verb, in the indicative mood, present tense, used in place of *is;* which latter word chiefly prevails in modern practice. This use of the verb *be,* in the indicative mood, is now somewhat *unfashionable;* but not *obsolete.* "These *be* the heads of their father's houses." What *be* these two olive trees? "Few there *be.*" "Many there *be;*" "The powers that *be;*" "If our definition of the verb *be* correct."—*Murray.* "I *be* here." Where *be* you? "If thou *be-est* he."—*Milton.* The parts of grammar *be* four, Orthography, &c.—*Martin,* "On Grammar and Language," London, 1776. "They that *be* whole need not a physician, but they that *are* sick." Whether they *be* good, or whether they *be* bad. "If there *be* any among you." "For we *be* brethren."

"If I *am* right, thy grace impart."
"If I *am* wrong, O teach my heart."—POPE.

Many writers, not particularly inelegant, in other respects, still, following the ancient practice, prefer *be,* to *am,* in expressions like the above.

Be-cause; there *be cause;* there *is cause:* the cause *be;* the cause *is: be cause* of unbelief: there *be,* or there *is,* the cause of unbelief. This statement may be depended on, *be-cause,* it is true : the cause *be,* or *is,* the statement is true.

The compilers of grammar have supposed that the word *be,* after *if,* had something peculiar in its character, under the name of the subjunctive mood; but that those who copy such opinions from each other, are not to be depended on in their expositions, is seen by reference to Matthew, xv. 14, and a multitude of other authorities, which it is needless to adduce.

Even. This word is by formation a past participle, and an adjective, as a part of speech. It describes something as being *even,* or *evened,* with some thing else; and commonly, in what is considered the adverbial use of the word, the *even* thing is evened with some *degree, position,* or *state,* supposed, or with some definite *time.* There is frequently an omission of several words, the ideas for which are supplied by the familiar train of thought. This *practice* was so formerly, and *it* is so *even* now : the *practice, evened* with, or *brought* up to, the *present time,* remains so.

Platina is *even* heavier than gold. It is *evened* with, or *equalled* to, a specific gravity, heavier than gold.

In-deed ; in very deed. Call the words any thing, but adverbs, and they need no explanation.

Now, is an adjective, and a trifling modification of the word *new.* It refers to the word *time,* understood. The *new time,* or *now time.* The *perfection* of *newness,* in any thing, is that its *finishing period* shall *precisely* reach the *present time.* The adjective of specific relation must be supplied, where the sense requires it.

Nay, no, not : these terms have come from different languages. *Nay,* is contracted of the old French, or Norman, *ne ay,* or *ne ayes,* have not, as explained under the verb *yes.*

No, is an *adjective ;* and when the *noun* to which it refers, is not *expressed,* it is *understood* in construction. In answer to a question, it is the single word, used *in the stead* of a whole proposition ; because it is the term, on which, as connected with the question, the entire answer, if expressed, would turn. Will you agree to go with me ? *No :* that is, I make *no* such *agreement.* I agree to *no* such *thing.* I have *no intention* to go. This response *no,* like its antagonist, *yes,* is proper only when the interrogation is so formed as to reduce the answer required to a single point. Will you go *to-day;* or *to-morrow ? No.* This word *no,* as used here, is not appropriate : it should be the adjective *neither.* That is, I shall *neither* go to-day, nor to-morrow. I shall go on *neither* of the days. Shape the phraseology of this answer as we please, the word *neither,* or *not either,* must come into it. "*This distributive adjective pronoun,*" then, is just the same kind of "*negative adverb,*" as the adjective *no.* If the person to whom the question is addressed, says, "*both,*" this word is an "*adverb of affirmation,*" on precisely the same principle as before. With these few guiding hints, every person of good talents can increase the illustrations to any requisite extent for himself.

Not, is a common noun, and a modification of *nought.* It is of great importance, and from its frequent repetitions, became in part of its uses, contracted in pronunciation, and afterwards in spelling, conformed to the utterance. To call it a "*negative adverb,*" is a total mistake of the meaning of the word, and of the principles with which it stands connected. Many writers of eminence, and whose works have had extensive influence thro the learned world, have treated what they call *positives* and *negatives,* as fundamental principles, in reasoning. There are, probably, very few erroneous assumptions which have had greater sway than this, in misleading the mind of man, respecting its own exercises and powers.

Not, is the name of a *thing ;* and so far as any essential *meaning* or *principle* is concerned, is no more *negative*, than *house, tree, valley, cave,* or any *thing* else : nor is any *word,* or *assertion,* in any language, more *positive,* or *negative,* than an other.   Before any person objects to this word, that it is not applied as the name of a "*substance*," let him take a little pains to observe what proportion of nouns, if a division should be made on this principle, must leave the "*substantive*" side, in his long list.

If that *unsubstantial something,* called a *nothing,* did not *ex-ist* with its *distinctive character,* and *means of perception,* its *idea* could not exist in the mind, nor stand *defined* in our dictionaries as "*a mental image,*" a *picture,* or *representation* of *nought,* or *nothing.*   If the word *not,* or *nought,* has either *meaning* or *use,* there must be some definite means of perception, by which it acquired that meaning, and by which, as a common *standard* of intelligence, it is *transmitted,* in social life.   There must be some way to *make* the *nothing,* or it could not exist, nor have its *likeness* depicted.   The only way to obtain the definite knowledge of any *sign,* is to learn its application to the *thing* which it *signifies.*   This principle applies with equal force to the *nothing,* and to all other things.   The noun *invisibility,* or *vacancy,* is as good a *noun,* and name of a *thing,* as any other.   What is a *hole* thro a board, or a *gap* in a fence ?   Could there be such *gap,* if there was not a *fence* at *each side* of the *gap.*   What is the *presentation* to the senses, and what the *perception* drawn from it ?   The fence *belongs together,* and some *agency* has *gaped,* or *gapped,* it ; made a *gap,* or *gapped place* in it.   This *gap* has its *dimensions,* and its *distinctive perception,* in comparison with its bounding substance, as a *material body* has when encompassed by seeming *vacuity.*   The way to make a *nothing,* is to set up *something;* to grow familiar with it, as occupying any assignable *locality;* and then *knock* it away.   The *perception* is the *contrast;* the *vacuity,* the *noug ht,* the *knock-ed away thing.*

It is proper here to examine, for a moment, a philosophic principle, which, in its misapplication, appears to have been connected with a vast extent of false reasoning, from the time of the Grecian schools, to colleges and judgment seats at the present day.

The reader will recollect that the general design, of which this work forms a part, is to show, that the system of exposition in language, as taught thro the civilized world, is extravagantly wrong; not merely in its incomprehensible, and ever disputed *specialties ;* but in its *entire structure,* and the *foundation* on which it is built.

Language is not "*founded*" on "*custom,*" or "*general practice,*" as we have been so often and so erroneously told. Human wisdom could never discover order, nor draw its boundary lines, thro the moving chaos of words, on the plan so long, so ably, and so fruitlessly attempted.

No theory of speech can be otherwise than bad, if it does not accord with demonstrative science, which "*changing fashion*" can not change. The question of *positive* and *negative*, is not one which *grammar* is *primarily* to explain. What is a *negative term*, or *negative quantity* in algebra. Can it exist, or is it *negative*, except merely in its *relation*, as set off against a *positive* of *equal*, or *greater amount*? Any expert mathematician will readily solve this *problem*, and put his *Q. E. D.* to the answer. The *principle* is *universal* in its application, not only thro the *world of matter*, but the higher *world of mind;* for the plain reason that the INFINITE WISDOM which presides over both, never forms contradictory laws.

What is a *negative?* "A *denying;* a proposition by which some thing is *denied.*" Can there be a *denial,* till there is some thing to *deny;* or except from the mere *relative* fact that it does *deny some thing else?* Certainly not. Then, most clearly, the *negative* does not consist in the *absolute meaning* of the *word,* or *phrase;* and no *single term,* or *proposition,* taken by itself, is more *positive,* or *negative,* than an other. The whole legal theory of *positive* and *negative testimony,* is a mistake of the *incident,* for the *essential principle,* and leads to much false logic in the courts.

Was the man *present,* or *absent?* He was *ab-sent.* Is the house *finished,* or *un-finished?* It is *un-finished.* Do you assert that, as a *positive* fact? I do *affirm, positively, absolutely,* and as a *fact* within my own *certain knowledge,* that the house is *not finished.* Then, Sir, I must take the liberty, flatly to *contradict* you, and *deny* your very *positive assertion,* by telling you that the house *is finished since you saw it.*

It would be needless to multiply examples, to show that the ideas of *positive* and *negative* do not depend on the *absolute meaning of words,* nor their *grammatical collocation;* but on the nature of assertions, *in relation to each other.*

Naught, is a modern alteration of *nought.* The *naughty* boy is so, because he is contemplated as *worthless,* or good for *nothing.*

Not, is very often a *secondary adjective;* as, *Not many, not good, not much. Not able, un-able, partially able, fully able.*

Oft, often : at *oft,* or *often,* times : adjectives. " He is *often* there." At *often,* or *frequent* times.

Or, contraction for *other,* an *adjective,* meaning the same thing as *other,* and with a following noun understood. The adjective *other,* refers to a *noun,* expressed, or sufficiently alluded to, in concomitant words; and *or* to the noun *wise, manner, way,* or *other* equivalent *word,* understood by habitual familiar association. " John (*or*) George will go." John, (in *other* case) George will go. This is either right (*or*) wrong: in *other* wise.

Nor, is *ne or ;* not otherwise; *not* in *other way,* or *manner.*

Other wise ; in other wise. The word *wise* has been before explained. It is used as a noun, both in contraction and without: as we say, in any *wise;* slant *wise ;* length *wise ;* in this *wise.*

Not-withstanding. This word, as used in its compound form, is often placed at the end instead of the beginning of the phrase to which it belongs. In legal procedings it is correctly used. "Any former law, *in any wise,* to the contrary not-withstanding" (this law): that is, not effectually *withstanding,* or *opposing* it.

Perhaps, per chance, per adventure. These terms are a mixture of the Latin *per,* by, with an English word in each instance. They have become established in use, and are easily explained when analyzed.

Once, one time : *twice,* two times.

Since, the past participle *seen,* and the adjective *as : seen as, seen that,* or *the same,* (*time,* period, state, or condition of things.) Ever *since* the first of January : ever from a *period* of time, *so* called, *so seen ;* so contemplated : ever from a period *seen,* viewed, named, or contemplated, *as* the first of January.

Still. This is the participial adjective *stilled.* The reason why it is said that a person *still* remains, or remains *still* in a place, is because he is quietly placed there : he is *fixed, stationed,* and free from *annoyance* or *agitation,* which causes him to remain.

Hence, thence ; from this place, from that place ; each " *adverb*" containing three constituent words. *Thither, whither : that other, what other,* with the word *place* understood, after, and *to,* before, each. The word *hither* is partially modified by imitation of the two preceding words. *Hitherto,* is *to hither,* or *to this place ;* for the word *other* does not in propriety belong to it.

Straight-way : by a straight way, in a direct course, without loss of distance, and by easy inference, without loss of time.

Then, when ; " We seen nowe bi a miror in darcnesse : *thanne* forsothe, face to face. Nowe I know of partye: *thanne* forsothe schal know as I am knowen."—1 *Corin.* xiii. *Translation* 1350.

Per annum, a year, *th' anne ;* the year ; any definite or set *period of time. Then,* that time, at *that time :* when, what, or at *what period,* or *time.*

Than, the ane, the one ; *than,* the one *thing : then,* the one *time.* This apple is better *than* an orange. The one orange ; this apple is better.

While. Wheel ; time or period in which some thing *wheels* its round. All the *while :* thro all the *while,* or *time.* Stay here *whil* he goes and returns : during the *while, time,* or *period.* They *while* away the *day* in idleness : *wheel,* or *pass it* away.

Till, is *to while.* In the contractions of words, by quick utterance, *w* and *h* very naturally fall out, unless their sounds are particularly necessary for some purpose of *distinction.* The letter *i* does not appear to have anciently had the two very different sounds which it represents in modern English.

Whether. Which either, or *which alternative,* of two or more transactions, or things. *Whether* of the twain : *which either* of the twain, or two. This expression is not accordant with elegant modern practice. *Whether* they will hear or forbear : *which either* of the two alternatives. They may do *either* of them : the question is, *which either* they will do. *Whether* is a defining adjective, referring, *alternatively,* to the several propositions, but more directly to the interposed word *thing, event,* or *alternative,* understood.

The more compounded words of this description, are to be resolved into their elements, as before explained.

Whatever, is to be analyzed ; *what* (thing, fact, or event,) (in any) *age :* or, for greater ease and simplicity, it may be considered as one plain adjective, *whatever thing : whatever fact,* or *circumstance.*

When-ever ; (at) *what time,* (in any) *age.*

Where-ever ; (at, in, or to,) *what place,* (at any) *time.*

If the hints suggested in the foregoing pages, respecting the words called *adverbs,* are well founded, they show that a vast extent of error has long prevailed, in some of the most sublimely interesting principles of language, of nature, and of thought. They show the want of some thing very different from what any nation has yet had in this department of learning. They make us feel the evils of that technical perplexity which could so pervert the operations of reason, and degrade the highest subjects of human contemplation.

It is the beauty and glory of speech, so connected with the wel-

fare of man on earth, that its essential rules are not the artificial invention of finite contrivers; but that their foundations are laid in
those unalterable laws, which operate alike, from atom to atom, and
from world to world; few, simple, clear, harmonious, and limitless,
like the Divine Wisdom which formed them. The real power of
man, is the skill to direct the physical energies subject to his controll: his enjoyment, so far as earthly considerations are concerned,
is to know himself; to appreciate correctly the true end of his being; to improve his social condition; and adapt the means within
his reach to his own best good. The science of speech, is the science
of mind; and the instrument of nearly all which men can know or
do. There can be no reasonable doubt that, when the principles of
language shall be ably developed, in their own true nature, that
event will do more to benefit the human family, than any other,
except the invention of letters, and the art of printing, which has
ever been accomplished by human means.

IRREGULAR AND IMITATIVE SOUNDS, CALLED *INTERJECTIONS.*

Many words in language are formed of imitative sounds, more or
less true to nature. One bird is called a *cuckoo,* and an other a *whip-
perwill.* The *dove* is said to *coo:* formerly represented by the letters *w-oo,* or *u-oo,* to *woo;* and which, as pronounced, was the *short, indistinct,* followed by the *full,* sound of double *o.* This is a nearer *imitation* than the modernized English *verb.* The *emblems* alluding to
this bird, need not here be described to Pagans or Christians, who
read. One animal is said to *chatter,* an other to *chirp:* owls *hoot;*
the goose *hisses;* hens *cluck;* and chickens *peep.*

The *reasoning being* takes these *sounds,* and their first *meaning,*
from his inferiors, adopts them in regular language, and branches
them into extensive forms.

Man, in common with other animals, has also *indistinct utterances,*
which fall below the boundaries of *regulated speech.* Such is that
audible breathing, which we call a *groan,* and which writers attempt
to imitate by the letters *O, oh, ah,* and others. We see the letters
ha, ha; or *he, he, he,* employed to represent laughter. We have
bow, wow,' wow; quack, quack; caw, caw; and *bah;* to represent the noise of a *dog, duck, raven,* or *sheep.*

The only rule applicable to these sounds is, the matter of fact, and common good sense. If they acquire a definite sound and meaning as words, so as to be intelligibly employed in construction, then they become *nouns, adjectives,* or *verbs,* according to the manner of their application. If they do not rise to this description, they are neither words, nor parts of speech. Noises the farthest removed from regular speech, may convey very important ideas, and a rushing train of thoughts may be excited by a single sound; as, for instance, the firing of a cannon on an enemies' frontier. It would be difficult for the lonely African traveller to express, in a word, or a sentence, the ideas called up in his mind by the roaring of a lion. What single part of speech is to *typify* the precise *thought* awakened in a mother's breast, when, during the sacking of a city, she hears her frightened children *scream,* as their murderers approach? How fallacious, then, to say that sounds of this kind are parts of speech, because they convey ideas to the mind! When people *laugh,* and *cry,* and *shriek,* and *groan,* by *rule,* grammar may explain what the utterances called "*interjections*" mean.

.CHAPTER VIII.

SYNTAX.

All human knowledge may be divided into two kinds.

1. Distinctive *entities, relations,* and *facts,* as *presented* to the *senses,* in the *natural world :*

2. Signs acquired to represent the objects of perception, direct or inferential.

Tho' all which we know, or can conceive, depends on the *first* class, in this division, the *second* is far the most extensive in *practice,* as it must exist in the mind of nearly every individual. The *signs* employed in *social intercourse* are the best experience of *all ages,* made the common stock of the *present:* and the share which a single person obtains, soon transcends the measure of knowledge which the longest life would enable him to acquire by *direct observation.* The following couplet, tho not strictly correct, has much of reason in it :

"Tis to the press and pen we mortals owe
All we believe, and almost all we know."

The *signs* employed in the social interchange of *thought*, being extremely important, it becomes a matter of vast interest that they should be

1st. *True* to the *objects of perception* in nature, from which they are derived.

2d. *Definite* and *well understood*, in their transmission.

3d. That the *laws* of their *combination* should be *few, simple,* and *clear*.

First. In deriving ideas from objects of perception, the mental image must be true to the original, in the main features, so far as the object is itself definitely presented, provided there is no illusion of the senses, in making the observation.

Second. In reference to the second of these considerations, all which could be said, amounts in substance to this: So far as any sign fails to represent the thing which it is designed to signify, it is futile; and so far as by wrong understanding, or wrong application, it represents any thing different from what is intended, it is false.

Third. This latter consideration is the more immediate subject of inquiry in what may be offered concerning the principles of language, which come under the head of syntax.

Persons accustomed to close scientific research, are led to observe more and more, that our acquisitions in every department of learning, are facilitated in proportion as the elementary principles of that department are few and well understood. The reason may be readily perceived. We judge of every thing by comparison. To learn what is new, it must be referred to what was known before; and to preserve a consistent judgment, so as to give each subject its due estimation, it is requisite to maintain some common standard of reference, with a comprehensive and rational plan. If the standard is variable, the judgment will be false; and if the foundation is unsolid, the superstructure, with all possible repairing, can not be firm. The multiplicity of single facts, when arranged in due order, according to enlightened views, presents no corresponding proportion in the difficulty of their acquisition, compared with the increase of inapplicable divisions and rules.

The individual components, which make the aggregate of language, are almost limitless. The first suggestions of reason, therefore, might lead us to suppose that, in this amazing variety of detail, it would be impossible for any community to converse, intelli-

gibly, with each other, unless they have, in some way, guiding principles of extraordinary excellence in their adaptation; and that
these must be infixed with the native logic of the mind, whether
learning has ever detected and explained them or not. In this in-
cipient belief we become strengthened, by analogy in those sciences
which have been considered peculiarly demonstrative, or susceptible of obvious proof. Passing other examples, unnecessary to cite,
all which music can perform, depends on the variations of seven
notes. In mechanics, how few, and strikingly simple, are the principles which govern such stupendous operations in nature and art !
and geometry readily shows that all possible forms are but modifications of length, breadth, and thickness.

In language, we have three classes, or parts of speech. Their
uses are distinctive, and their divisions clear. The subdivisions also,
are remarkably few, and their nature such, as always to harmonize
with the primary classification.

Entering the field of language, then, no matter how extensive
or various, the progress is limited only by the boundaries of human
power; for when the traveller, understanding the plan of his route,
is able to project his own guiding lines before him, there is hardly
an excuse for getting bewildered, or greatly wandering from the
right course.

Before we procede to the rules of Syntax, it appears requisite to
examine a question which has hitherto received very little attention,
if thought of at all.   What is a rule ?

"RULE. *Substantive.* Government, sway, supreme command;
an instrument by which lines are drawn: canon, precept by which
the thoughts or actions are directed; regularity, propriety of beha-
viour."—DR. JOHNSON.

This *definition,* like numerous others, means too many things to
mean any thing *definite.* When all of them are abridged to one,
and that the *reg-ht,* or *right,* one, we shall have a real definition;
and not before.

The *reg, reg-le, reg-ula,* or *rule,* is *the "instrument by which lines
are drawn;"* and the *reg-se, rec-se, rek-s, rex, rule-man,* or *rul-er,* is
he who uses the *instrument* to *draw* the *lines,* for his people. All
supposed difference of meaning is but the extended application of
this one. The *principle* always supposes the *ruling instrument* to be
straig-ht, streg-ht, reg-ht, or *rig-ht;* with competent power and wis-

dom to employ it. Whatever allowance is to be made, in human affairs, for unavoidable error, the rules which pervade the natural world, are all drawn in absolute perfection.

A rule, then, is not merely a prevailing *fact ;* but, in the greatest extension of the idea, must suppose *di-rec-ting* wisdom, producing an orderly disposition or arrangement of things, in conformity with some *reg-ular* plan.

If, for example, a man should state, as a general rule, that, on a thousand acres of wild land, there are more oak trees, than of any other kind of timber, this may be *fact ;* but it is his mistake to call it a *rule.* So, with seeming plausibility, it might be declared a *general rule,* in our national geography, that the *Rivers of the United States run to the south ;* as, the *Connecticut, Hudson, Delaware, Susquehannah,* and others: but to this *rule,* there must be *thirty one* exceptions ; because we distinguish *thirty two* points of the compass, and there are rivers running towards each of these points.

Whatever body of *Syntax* may be laid down as the supposed *rules,* to explain the structure of speech, will be easy, appropriate, and efficacious, as a guide in practice, in proportion as they are conformed to those laws of perception, on which both thoughts and words, in all their applications, depend. On the contrary, they will be perplexing and mischievous, in the same degree as they are artificial and technical, or as they deviate from the consistent simplicity of nature and truth.

The unerring plan of nature having established three classes of perceptions, and consequently three parts of speech, we know, demonstratively, that all different combinations which can be made with them, as distinct parts of speech, must be limited to *six.* It is also undoubtedly true, that [the prime rules of construction, which apply to the three general classes, can not be invalidated by subordinate ones, to explain the minor divisions. On this principle, therefore, as well as the one before alluded to, that which has an exception is no *rule.*

STRUCTURE OF SENTENCES.

Syntax teaches the proper arrangement of words in a sentence.

Agreement is the connection of two or more words in the same constructive relation.

RULES OF SYNTAX.

Rule I.

The noun is agent, or object of a verb, or follows a preposition.

Rule II.

Two or more nouns, connected by *and*, are taken as a collective plural, in their relation to other words.

Rule III.

Pronouns take the same relations in a sentence, as the other nouns they relieve, would do in the same place.

Rule IV.

Adjectives refer to nouns, expressed or understood.

Rule V.

The indicative verb agrees with the person and number of its agent.

Rule VI.

Each verb has one or more objects, expressed or implied.

Rule VII.

Participles in *ing* are either *nouns* or *adjectives*, according to the manner of their use.

Rule VIII.

A preposition shows the relation of two or more things to each other, and in construction, must have a preceding, and a following objective word.

These eight propositions are placed thus together that they may all be seen at one view. It is not pretended that they are all of them *rules*, according to the principles before explained; but so strong and general is the impression that a grammar must contain a large body of syntax, that it seemed necessary, so far as could be done, without sacrifice of truth, to make the greatest possible number of something to call rules.

RECAPITULATION OF THE FOREGOING RULES.

Rule I. The noun is *agent* or *object* of a verb, or *follows a preposition*, as

The *teacher* instructs his *pupils* in *logic*.

EXAMPLES.

"*Henry* defeated *Richard* in the *battle* of *Bosworth*."

Henry,	proper noun, singular number, masculine gender agent of the verb defeated.
defeated,	a regular verb, indicative mood, past tense, agreeing with its agent, Henry, which is third person, singular.
Richard,	proper noun, singular number, masculine gender, object of the verb defeated.
in,	preposition, showing the relation between Richard and battle.
the,	defining adjective, referring to battle.
battle,	common noun, singular number, neuter, object after the preposition in.
of,	preposition, showing the relation between battle and Bosworth.
Bosworth,	proper noun, singular number, neuter gender, object after the preposition of.

"*Hope* animates *us*."

"A peaceful *mind* is virtue's *reward*."

True politeness has its seat in the heart.

Charles learns Latin at his school in the city.

The judge dispenses justice with dignity.

Note. This rule applies to nouns in their proper connection in a sentence. They are sometimes employed without this connection; in which case, they are said to be *absolute* or *independent*. Nouns absolute are used in three ways.

1st. In titles, labels, or notes, where the name, without assertion, gives the idea required.

2d. Style of personal address. In this use of a noun, it merely designates the person spoken to; but is otherwise unconnected with the sentence.

3d. In a detached phrase, to explain an attendant state of things; as, "The *premises* being admitted, the conclusion is certain."

Noun independent or absolute.

EXAMPLES.

First, *Titles.* "*Latin Dictionary.*"

These words placed on the back of a volume, convey a distinct
15*

idea, as well as if it was asserted, that the thing so marked, is a book distinguished by that title.

So, if a small piece of paper, with the words "Madeira wine" written upon it, was fastened to the neck of a bottle, it would be readily understood, that the thing so labeled, was a bottle of Madeira wine, without a more formal assertion of the fact.

Second. Style of personal address.

" Forbear, my *son*, the hermit cries."

This personal designation has no connection of agreement or government with the sentence. It merely shows to whom the speaker is directing his discourse. It is only necessary in parsing, to say that such word is the noun, or pronoun, independent.

Third. Detached phrase.

" The *sun* being risen, it will be warm."

Here the first phrase, does not amount to affirmation, but supposes a condition of things, in the fewest words, as standing in some kind of connection with the whole assertion contained in the other part of the sentence. The noun included in this phrase, is not connected with any verb as a word.

The *inhabitants* amounting to 60,000, Congress admitted them, under the Constitution, as a new state.

An adjournment took place, the *members* being too few to form a quorum.

Oranges being plenty, we laid in a good supply.

Oranges,	noun absolute, because contained in a detached phrase, and not connected with a verb.
being,	participle from the verb *be*, describing the condition of oranges.
plenty,	adjective, describing the state or circumstances of oranges, at a time indicated by other words.
we,	pronoun, first person plural, agent of the verb *laid*.
laid,	verb, indicative mood, past tense, agreeing with its agent we, first person plural.
in,	preposition, having an objective word implied, as in the *ship, store, basket*, or whatever they were put *in*, or *into*.

a,	adjective one, referring to the noun *supply*.
good,	adjective, describing *supply*.
supply,	common noun, singular, object of the verb *laid ;* we *laid* a good *supply into our vessel.*

Rule II.

Two or more nouns singular, united by *and*, are taken as a collective plural, in relation to other words; as, *Guy* and his *brother are chants.*

The word *and*, is a past participle, signifying, *joined, united, added. Eke, aec,* and *ac,* were formerly employed in the same way; but these are no longer retained for this purpose, and the word *and* is left to stand alone in its present use.

Examples.

" *Simon* and *Andrew were* casting *their* net into the sea ; for *they were fishers.*"

" *Ainli* and *Ardan,* valiant *sons* of Ulna, *were* at the banquet. *They* pledged *their* word, upon *their* arms, *they* never more would give me cause of pain."

Shem, Ham, and *Japhet, were* the *three sons* of Noah.

Hengist and *Horsa were* the Saxon *leaders who established themselves* in England.

Note 1. When two or more names, for the purpose of clearness, or emphasis, are applied to the same thing, they are said to be in apposition, and do not form a plural; as,

" My earnest *desire,* and *prayer* to God, *is,* that Israel may be *saved.*

" *Catiline, the leader* and *contriver* of the plot, was there.

Nouns in apposition, agree with each other, and stand in a common relation to other words. They are agents or objects, according to the sense in which they are understood with reference to the verbal action.

Examples under Rule II.

Socrates and *Plato were* wise *men.*

Socrates and *Plato,* wise *men,* once *existed.*

Socrates,   proper noun, singular, masculine, coupled with *Plato,*
                by the word *and.*

and,   participial adjective connecting *Socrates,* and *Plato.*

Plato,   proper noun, singular, masculine, and together with
                Socrates, agent of the verb *were.*

were   irregular verb, part of the verb *to be,* in the indicative
                mood, past tense, agreeing with its two connected
                agents, *Plato* and *Socrates.*

wise,   adjective, referring to *men.*

men,.   common noun, plural, in apposition with *Socrates* and
                Plato, as agent of the verb *were,* because that the mere
                act of *exercising* the vital functions, did not make them
                wise men.

"She walks a queen."

Queen, is agent of the verb, in apposition with *she ;* because the
act of walking does not make her a *queen.*

"He *proved himself* a Roman citizen."

"Nero *rendered himself* a detestable *tyrant.*"

Tyrant,   is *object* of the verb, in apposition with *himself,* because
                it is the name of what he *rendered himself,* and not of
                what he was independent of that act.

"The duke *made himself king.*"

"This said, he *formed thee, Adam, thee, O man, dust* of the ground."
"The *people* of Nantucket *are* chiefly enterprising *whalemen,* or
connected with the whaling business."

Are. The action denoted by this verb, that is, *breathing,* or in-
haling *air,* does not make these people *whalemen ;* if it did, all people who *are,* or *air themselves,* would probably be whalemen, for the
same reason.

Inference concerning nouns in apposition.

Any noun, after, as well as before a verb, may be agent, and not
object, when that noun does not denote the thing which the verbal
action produces or affects.

Rule III.

Pronouns take the same relations in a sentence, as the other nouns they relieve would do in the same place.*

Who did this thing? " *It* was *I*."

Who,	pronoun, standing for the person, or persons, suspected; male, or female, and first, second, or third person, as the fact may happen to be shown.
did,	verb, past tense, and it may take its form, number, and person, according to the prevailing idea of the speaker.
this,	defining adjective, referring to thing.
thing,	common noun, singular, object of the verb did.

Note. Pronouns sometimes stand for characters, personated only by description; as, " *He* is wise *who* speaks little."

It,	meaning *the said person or thing*; pronoun in apposition with I.
was,	indicative verb, past tense, agreeing with *it*, third person, singular.
I,	pronoun, first person, singular, in apposition with *it*.

Rule IV.

Adjectives† refer to nouns expressed or implied; as, " *Many* are *called*, but *few* are *chosen*;" that is, few and many *persons*.

Examples for Practice.

" A time there was, ere *England's* griefs began,
When *every* rood of ground maintained *its* man."

---

* The rules of syntax given for nouns, apply equally to the kind called pronouns; and this is to be understood, throughout the explanations here offered, without the repetition. ·

The right pronoun should, of course, be used to represent the noun for which it stands. This is, in substance, all which can be said respecting its agreement with " *antecedents or substantives.*"

Pronouns meaning the same thing, may be of different grammatical persons, according as they are used under different ideas of existing relation. .

† English adjectives never vary their forms for number, gender, or position.

a *good* man,	*good* men.
a *good* woman,	*good* women.
a *good* book,	*good* books.

A,	defining adjective, referring to *time.*
time,	common noun, singular, agent of the verb *was.*
there,	adverbial contraction, including a noun, in apposition with *time.*
was,	irregular verb, taken as a part of the verb *to be;* indicative mood, past tense, agreeing with its agent *time,* third person, singular number.
ere,	contraction, meaning the *dawning era, period,* or *time;* and, by present use, *the time before.*
England's,	defining adjective, from the name *England,* to " point out" what griefs, to whom related, or by whom suffered.
griefs,	common noun, plural number, agent of the verb *began.*
began,	irregular verb, from *begin; begin, began, begun;* indicative mood, past tense; agreeing with its agent *griefs.*
when,	contraction, *the period which,* referring to the whole line following.
every,	*each one of the whole, taken separately;* a defining adjective, referring to *rood.*
rood,	common noun, singular number, agent of the verb *maintained.*
maintained,	regular verb, indicative mood, past tense, agreeing with its agent *rood.*
its,	defining adjective, referring to *man,* to point out the one who, with reference to every particular rood of ground, was the occupant of that one, or was, in some way, maintained by its productions; *not the man who belonged to the rood of ground, as the possession which is owned, as legal property.*

" Turn thee unto me, and have mercy upon me ; for *I* am *desolate* and *afflicted.*"—*Ps.* xxv.

desolate,	adjective, referring to the pronoun *I, describing* by *condition, circumstance,* or *situation.*
afflicted,	past participle or adjective, describing the state or condition of the person represented by the pronoun *I.*

" *Great Pompey's* shade complains *that* we are *slow,* and *Scipio's* ghost walks *unrevenged* among us."—*Addison's Cato.*

Pompey's,   adjective, formed from the noun Pompey, used to point out what shade; which was the shade, or disembodied spirit, that had once animated *Pompey.*

that,   adjective, referring to *complaint,* or an equivalent word understood: *complains that complaint,* or *makes the complaint,* we are slow.

slow,   describing adjective, referring to the pronoun *we.*

Scipio's,   defining adjective, to particularize *what ghost* is meant.

unrevenged,   adjective, referring to *ghost.*

"And *all mine* are *thine,* and *thine* are *mine ;* and I am *glorified* in thee."—*John,* xvii.

"In *any* point *which* (point) discretion bids you pursue, and *which* (point) has a *manifest* utility to recommend it, let not difficulties deter you : *rather* let them animate *your* industry. If (*that* supposition) *one* method fails, try *a second* (;) and *a third* (;) *Be active,* persevere, and you will certainly conquer."—*Sir R. Steele.*

rather,   adjective in the comparative degree, from *rath,* early, seasonable, and refers to the whole following part of the sentence : let this state of things be, *rather, earlier, sooner,* than permit the alternative evil.

your,   defining adjective, to point out industry; *that special industry, which ought to actuate you.*

Men must be *taught* as if you taught them not,
And things *unknown, proposed as* things *forgot.*

" *The* farm is well *wooded* and *watered.*"

IMPLIED ADJECTIVE.

The adjective is sometimes omitted in expression, and is indispensably necessary to be supplied, in order to complete the sense.

"Caroline would be very happy if she could *have her wish.*"

Any lady, in her right mind, can *have* her *wish,* whenever she pleases. A *wish* is as easily *had,* as it is *made ;* and by just the same process ; that is, simply, by *wishing it.* The only difficult or doubtful part of the question is, whether the *wish* is to be *gratified.*

RULE V.

The indicative verb agrees with the person and number of its agent; as, "*Homer warms* us; *Milton fixes* us in astonishment. *They are* both sublime, and *excel* other poets." " *You* and *he go* to school." " *Thou art* the man."

Note 1. A noun of multitude may be deemed *plural*, in refer-ence to its const·tuent parts, or *singular*, as a collective whole: but the leading idea, in either case, should be preserved; as, " The *as-sembly was* adjourned by *its* own vote;" " The *assembly were* divi-ded among *themselves; they* closed *their* session last week."

Note 2. A verb, having two or more agents in apposition, may agree with either; as, "I am the man who command you, or who commands you."

Rule VI.

Every verb has one or more objects, expressed or implied; as, " They *try* to *learn;*" that is, " They *try* their *skill* to *learn* their *lessons.*"

" *Read*, (   ) not to *contradict* (   ) or confute; (   ) nor to *believe* (   ) and *take* (   ) for *granted;* but to *weigh* (   ) and *consider* (   )."—*Lord Bacon.*

Read (the *opinions* here offered, or any *other;*) not to contradict, or confute (*them;*) nor to believe (*them,*) and take (*them*) for grant-ed; but to weigh and consider (*them.*)

" *Ask*, (   ) and *it* shall (   ) be (   ) given you; *seek*, (   ) and ye shall (   ) find (,); *knock*, (   ) and *it* shall (   ) be (   ) opened unto you."—*Matth.* vii.

Ask (*what is needful*) and it shall be given to you; seek (*salva-tion*) and ye shall (*the necessary consequence*) to find (*it;*) knock (*the door of mercy*) and it shall (   ) be (*itself*) opened unto you.

" They sow not, (   ) neither do (   ) they reap, (   ) nor gather (   ) into barns."

" Man *wants* (   ) *but* little here below,
 Nor *wants* that little *long.*"   *Goldsmith.*

but,   imperative verb, *be-out,* leave out, except: the word *not,* or *nothing,* is understood before it. Man wants *nothing, except* a little; he wants "next to nothing;" with a *trifling exception,* he wants *nothing.*

long,   contraction for " *a long time.* "

Note. Imperative and infinitive verbs, in English, are invariable in form, and future in meaning ; as, " *persevere* in goodness ;" " *stay* here ;" " *depart* in peace ;" " *prepare* yourself to *meet* your friends.'

> " *Rise, rise,* my soul, and *leave* the ground ;
> *Stretch* all my thoughts abroad ;
> And *rouse* up every tuneful sound,
> *To praise* the eternal God."

Rise,   imperative verb, addressed by the psalmist to his own soul ; according to the plain sense, it implies that his soul is not yet risen, or not so to a sufficient degree ; and, therefore, like all other imperative verbs the action required, cannot be complied with, till after the wish is expressed ; that is, in the future tense.

my,   defining adjective, referring to *soul.*

soul,   noun absolute, as being the style of direct personal address.

and,   contraction, for *added,* referring to the following phrase, *leave the ground.*

leave,   *stretch,* and *rouse,* the same as *rise.*

to   is a contracted word, signifying *act, performance ;* and on account of this meaning is placed before a verb in the infinitive mood, for clearness of understanding, to distinguish the word as a verb, from the same word, when it is a noun.

to praise,   a verb, in the infinitive mood, which is always consequent on some existing, or supposed condition of things, and always future, either in relation to the present time, or to the state of things supposed.

Rule VII.

Participles in *ing,* are either *nouns,* or *adjectives,* according to the manner of their use.

> He is engaged in *erecting* a house.
> He is engaged in the *erecting* of a house.
> He is engaged in the *erection* of a house.

The true principle in this use of the participle *erecting,* appears to be, that as a noun, it is the name of an act, fact, circumstance, or

16

thing. That the *thing* so named is the "*substantive*" called *action*, or *acting*, does not vary the *principle ;* but is the *incident belonging to*, or the *belonging incident in*, the special case. It is shorter, and more fashionably elegant, to say, he is engaged *in building a house*, than *in the building of a house ;* and from habitual familiarity it is equally well understood.

It will be remembered that all *adjectives* are *nouns* or *participles*, employed to denote the relations of things to each other: and nearly every participle, whether present or past, may be made an adjective by use.

> " Less *dear* the *laurel growing*,
> *Alive, untouched*, and *blowing*,
> Than *that* whose braid
> Is plucked to shade
> The brows with vict'ry *glowing*."

Penelope *is loved* by me.

Pompey *was conquered* by Cesar.

Penelope *is sensible, loving, lovely*, and deservedly *loved* by all her friends. She *is seated* by her little sister.

My oxen and my fatlings are *killed*, and all things are now *ready*.

Rule VIII.

A "*preposition*" shows the relation of two or more objects to each other, and in construction has a *preceding*, and a *following*, *objective word ;* as, He threw a *stone into the water*.

The direct effect of the action is to place the *stone*, which is its *object*, in a new *condition of being*. The *adjective into*, describes that *condition ;* but the condition so *described* is one of specific local relation, and the *correlative thing* must be mentioned, before the description is complete.

It has been supposed that the *adjectives* called "prepositions" *governs* a following *objective word*, when it is expressed. To declare a total disbelief of this position is to start a question of vast importance in language, and which deserves to be well examined.

It is proper in the first place, to see what is the philosophic principle on which this doctrine is supposed to be founded.

Taking the word *into*, in the example above given, it is evident that the phrase, "*into the water*," does describe the *condition* in which the action places the *stone*. Description is the appropriate office of the adjective. The word *water* is not here an adjective. The *stone* is not *water*, nor is it a *water stone*. The adjective *the*, refers to *water*, and does not describe a *the* stone, nor a *the* " condition of being." Therefore the description, manifestly implied by the phrase, essentially belongs to the adjective *into*.

We can have no rational conception of *government*, without the *exercise* of some *governing power* or *influence*. To place any *word*, or *thing*, or " *cause it to be*," in any " *case*," in which it was not before, or would not otherwise be, is, most clearly, to *perform* an *action*, and to make use of necessary *means*, to *produce* this *effect*. The adjective *into*, as employed above, or any other word of its class, does not express the *active exertion* of *power*, or *influence*, to produce *change*, and therefore does not *produce change*, in a *following word*, or any other object.

In the third place, we may consider this adjective *into*, in its connection with the above sentence, in reference to its *matter of fact*, and as *practically contemplated* by the common understandings of men. The *first effect* of the *action* of *throwing*, falls on the *stone*, as its *direct object*. The unavoidable nature of this *effect* is, to place the *stone* in a new *position*. This *position*, in order to be understood, must be *described*. The adjective *into*, with its *correlative bearings*, expressed or understood, does describe it. The *stone* can not, and does not take a *new position*, without producing an *effect* on *something else*. It does, as a consequential result of the *throwing*, produce an *effect* on the *water*, by displacing so much as its own bulk occupies, and agitating a greater or less portion of the rest, as plainly manifested to the sense. The fluid called *water*, is, therefore, the *second object* of the *action*, and the noun, *water*, is the *incidental object* of the verb *threw*.

In the last instance, we may test the *principle of language* by the substitution of other *adjectives* for the " preposition," *into*. He *threw* the stone, up, down, high, low, far, distant, off, out, nearer, abaft, nigh, opposite, athwart, adjacent; *abaft* the *chains, near* the *window, adjoining* the *boat, opposite* the *ship, into* the *water*, and *down* the *fathomless abyss*.

It will be perceived that what is here offered under the head of *Syntax*, and all which could be said on the subject, is but the repetition of principles before explained. The proper understanding of these principles is vastly important, not barely as an interesting subject of science, and taste, but as practically necessary to the expert and correct transmission of thought. If the speaker has a just knowledge of each single word, in its essential and collateral meaning, then the less formal syntax he is perplexed with the better: for properly understanding the sign in its adaptation to the thing signified, brings all syntax to the rule of fact and common good sense, that any one, in speaking or writing, is to choose such signs, and so to combine them, as to convey the ideas he intends to express.

That the action has a necessary dependence on the acting power by which it is performed, applies to the nature of the verb, as explained under that class of words.

It is equally true, therefore, whether taken as a principle belonging to that part of speech, or as a rule of syntax, that an indicative verb agrees with its agent. This proposition, which really is a *rule of syntax*, has a practical and useful application. In every language which has made any considerable advancement, the verb, for the sake of proper distinctions, takes different forms as referred to different persons and numbers. If it has not a distinct form for each, this is no contradiction of the rule. The only material point is that it shall not have a form inconsistent with the relation in which it is placed. So, when we say that every adjective refers to a noun, it is true as a rule, tho, in English, it can not have much practical bearing, as the adjective never varies, on account of the noun.

PART II.

CHAPTER IX.

CRITICISM, AND PRACTICAL EXERCISES.

There are few propositions received thro the learned world with such unquestioning submission, as that " *custom, in language,*" is the monarch,

> " Whose *arbitrary sway*
> *Words*, and the *forms of language must obey.*"

From the time of *Horace,* this assertion is echoed, till a person accustomed to philological pursuits becomes tired of its repetitions. Open a hundred books of grammar, and rhetoric, this *technical axiom* stands forth, nearly in the same words, and it is in the mouth of almost every person who attempts to display his skill in the nine parts of speech. The man whose misfortune it is to differ in opinion, from such a weight of authority, or not to have a clear view of what others so generally believe, ought to be very distrustful of his own powers.

Dr. Campbell, a very sensible writer, where false principles did not mislead him, says, "Every tongue whatever, is *founded* in *use* or *custom.*" He then re-echoes, as it seemed almost necessary to do, the hackneyed quotation from Horace,

> " Quem penes arbitrium est,
> Et jus et norma loquendi."

We learn abundantly from our grammars, that a prime rule of syntax may have from ten to fifteen exceptions, and still be a good rule. It may be allowed, therefore, without objection to this kind of logic, to offer some reflections which appear to stand connected with it.

1. *Custom,* or *fashion,* in language can not exist, till language itself is brought into *general,* and in some degree, into *fashionable use.* This foundation, then, is laid, after the superstructure is erec-

16*

ted; which appears to be against the *customary* rules of architecture, according to "*reputable, national, present, use.*"

2. As it is allowed, on all hands, that this *fashion*, or *custom*, is very "*fluctuating*," and that "its *caprice* is apt to get the better of analogy," it appears to afford too loose a foundation, for an edifice of such vast importance.

3. It is submitted to the consideration of learned men, whether it is, strictly speaking, a good figure of rhetoric, to call a thing a foundation, while it shows such a prevailing disposition to run away.

In the hands of a good technical expositor, these doubts may perhaps be reduced to form as exceptions to an excellent general rule.

There will probably be a time, when those who teach *rhetoric*, and *logic*, will agree that the following *syllogism* is substantially just:

There is no real *elegance* in language, if it is not *correct*:

It is not *correct* if it has no "*foundation*" in *nature*, or *truth*: therefore,

Language *founded* merely in "*capricious fashion*," is not *elegant*.

In speaking of the theory of language, as now taught among all civilized nations, it is intended to treat the subject with fairness; but, at the same time, with freedom, as truth, science, the public good, require. Believing it to be absurd and mischievous, it is certainly allowable, if possible, to show it to be so. In the remarks which may be offered, it will be needless to occupy the reader's attention with trifling details, or to dwell on the countless discrepancies of ever varying expositors. The objections are not to the *commentaries*, but to the *text*.

The system has been taught, and apparently believed, for centuries. No individual, or single community, is answerable for its defects. The world at large is interested in getting rid of it, if, as a system, it is wrong. Mr. Murray is taken as the head, and representative, of what the learned world is now employed in studying, under the name of grammar. No compiler, in any country, or language, appears to have been more honest, diligent, or successful, thro a long course of years, in collecting and arranging the received opinions on this subject. His work has been the text book for two nations, during thirty years, and received extravagant praises from a large portion of the reviewers in the three kingdoms, as the one, "*beyond all comparison, superior* to any other in the English language." Mr. Murray's grammar is therefore the standard model, as this branch of learning is taught in colleges, and schools; and what is said of this, will substantially apply to the teaching in all the languages, ancient and modern, as now explained, wherever grammar is taught.

It is not intended here, to call in question what individuals may have done; but the grammars which have received the sanction of national, or of the highest scholastic authority, will all be considered as belonging together.

What is this grammar? "The *art* of *speaking*, or *writing* a *language* with *propriety*."

A doctor is not to suffer for a long time, by the disease which his own medicine is recommended to cure. This judicious and industrious compiler, with the unparalleled encouragement of two most enlightened nations, carried his work thro near forty editions, with all possible chance to explain it, as he wished it to be. We are to presume that this grammar, in such a length of time, taught Mr. Murray, as it was intended to teach others, to speak with propriety; and, by necessary consequence, to say what he meant.

Into how many parts of speech does this grammar divide words? Nine. What is the foundation of this division? Custom, or fashion. Does the fashion of language often change? Yes. And why not the division with it?

What is the first of the *nine* parts of speech? *Articles.* What are *articles* ? "Words prefixed to substantives to point them out and show how far their signification extends." A very important office in language. Is the class numerous? It consists of two words only. What, can two words point out, limit, determine, settle, and define the extent of nouns in all their various applications? Is there much difference in the meaning of the two words? There is no difference in their meaning; because neither of them means any thing; but their manner of meaning is directly opposite to each other. How then do they both belong to the same part of speech, in grammatical distinction from other words? They both *point out, determine*, limit, define, and fix the extent in which the noun is to be understood. Let me understand you; are they both *defining* words? Yes; but one *defines definitely*, and the other *indefinitely :* one *points out*, or *ascertains*, in a *certain*, and the other in a totally *uncertain* manner; one *limits* without *limitation*, and the other with.

What farther rules are there respecting *a* and *the* ?

"A *substantive* without any article to limit it is generally taken in its widest sense; as, "A candid temper is proper for man ;" that is, for all mankind."

What did you buy this morning? *Paper* and *ink*. All *paper kind*, do you mean? No. Then the purchase was not grammatical. What would you like for dinner? *Beef* and *pudding*. *A beef*, or *the beef?* No, neither: but *beef*. Then you wish them in the "*widest extent*." "*Cash* paid for *hides* and *lumber*." "*Man* is mortal." *Quadruped* is mortal. *Bird* is volatile. *Ox* is stout. *Goose* is noisy. *Book* is wrong. "*Kid* wont go."

How is the *indefinite* article used to *point out* or *define* a noun, and show, in an *unlimited* manner, *how far* its *limits extend* ?

If *a* yard of satin costs *three* dollars, what will *nine* yards cost, at the same rate? If *nine* yards cost *twenty-seven* dollars, how many yards can be had for *an* eagle, at the same price?

The adjective *a*, or *an*, means *one*, and that only. The *one* thing to which it refers, may be *identically specific*, or it may be *any one* among ten thousand. Whether it refers to *a* particular thing, or not, has nothing to do with the *meaning*, or *character*, of this adjective; but depends on some thing else used with it.

Mr. Locke wrote *an* Essay on the Human Understanding, which is *a* very able work. This assertion does not lead us to suppose that Essay which Locke wrote to be *any one* among fifty Essays on the Human Understanding; but the very *one* which he did write. *The* is an article. This can not mean that *the* is *any* article, uncertain what *one*; but the *identical article*, which this *adjective* is.

NOUNS, OR NAMES OF THINGS.

Why are these words called "*substantives*," in the grammars? Because they are supposed to be the *names of substances*. What kind of *substances* are denoted by the nouns, *vacancy*, *nonentity*, *emptiness*, *blank*, and *space* ?

GENDER.

Why are things, not *male* nor *female*, made *masculine* or *feminine*, by the rules of English grammar? To give richness and dignity to the language. How are they applied? By a figure of speech. What is *ship*, according to this figure? *Feminine*. Why so? Because *she* is particularly "beautiful," "delicate," and "amiable."

Is there not a little impropriety in this figure, when it is said of the beautiful, delicate, and amiable, ship *Thunderer*, *Jupiter*, or *Royal George*, that, " *She* sunk the Admiral's ship; but *she* had *her* rigging much shattered :" or of the steam boat, *Chancellor Livingston*, that " *she* broke *her* shaft," or " burst *her* boiler ?"

NUMBER.

Does the plural form always denote mere increase of number ? So our grammars lead us to suppose. When a merchant advertises "*sugars*, and fresh *teas*," does he mean that he has *five teas*, and *four sugars ?* I never thought of that before. It is a pretty broad principle to think of: he means *different kinds* of tea and *sugar ;* for no *one* sort, whatever the *quantity* might be, could form a *plural number*. It is mere *variety*, without any idea of *counting*. *Drugs* and *medicines, paints* and *dyewoods, hopes* and *fears*, and multitudes of other plurals, are of the same kind.

CASE.

What is a *noun ?* A *name*. And *nominative* means *naming ?* Yes. Then the *nominative* case of a *noun*, is the *naming* case of a *name*. Are there any *names* which are not in a *naming* case ?

ADJECTIVES.

" These apples are not *good ;* but they are *the best* that I have." How does it happen that this *superlative* degree, "*the best*," instead of increasing the *positive* "*good*," does not come up to it in "*quality ?*"

ADJECTIVE PRONOUNS.

On what principle can *one* word be used in *two parts* of speech at the *same time*, and, of course, in *one place ?* How can an other word stand for a *noun*, where the *noun* is *standing* for itself, in its own place ? " This is *his* book." What *quality* of book does the word *his*, by the *adjective* part of its character, express ? As a *pronoun;* in what *case* is it ?

VERBS ;

Active, transitive, denoting a real operation, passing over and producing an effect on an object.

" Their chairs *support* them." Two pillars stand side and side. They *sustain* the superincumbent *weight*, and each one *equals* the *other*. How do the columns perform these *actions ?* The captain *received* a very severe *wound*. The lady has the tooth ake. The child *has* blu*e eyes*, and brown *hair*. The man *has lost one* of his *horses*. How ? He *had him* stolen, last night. *Neuter grammars*, and the *walls* of neuter school rooms, *contain* strange *doctrines*.

PASSIVE VERBS.

"It seems, by his vociferation, that he *is determined* to *be heared*. What is a "*passive verb ?*" That which shows that the *agent suffers*, or *receives*, the *effect* of an *action*, performed by an other. It is made by placing the verb *to be*, before the past participle of an *active verb ;*" as,

> "Penelope *is loved* by me."
> Thunder *is heared* by me.
> The blow *is received* by me.
> The blow *is given* by me.
> Penelope *is seated* by me.
> The pain *is suffered* by me.
> His violence *is felt* by me.

Does this mean that Penelope *receives* the *effect* of the *love* that *I exercise*, and the thunder *suffers* the *effect* of the *noise* which I make? If not, what is the meaning? Does the *effect* of the *loving* pass over from *me* to *Penelope*, and the *effect* of the *hearing* pass from me to the *thunder ?* The man *is determined*, at all events, *to be heared*. How does this *recipient agent suffer* the *effect* of *being heared ?* By his own *boisterous passiveness* in *making* a *loud noise*.

What is the *matter of fact* in this business of *hearing ?* How is it *acted* or *suffered ?* Some operation, as the *firing of a gun*, or the *filing of a saw*, puts the *air* in *motion*. This *agitation* of the air extends, from particle to particle, till it comes to the *hearer ;* and entering his *ears*, *strikes* upon the thin membranes, called *tympans*, or *drums*. This *action* of *ear-ing*, or *hearing*, then, is really *being acted upon*, by an *external cause ;* or *suffering* the *effect* of an *action*. It is so; but it is *acting*, too : for if the *organs of hearing* were not kept in tone, to *receive* this *effect*, and did not *act* in *co operation* with it, the person certainly would not *hear*. This *hearing*, then, is *active*, and *passive*, both at once. So is every operation of *seeing*, *feeling* or *suffering*, *taste*, and *smell*. To *suffer* is an *active verb*, according to the *neuter* and *passive grammar*. To *feel*, to *receive*, and to *bear*, are also *active*. How, then, can an other *verb*, which *means* the *same thing*, in the *same way*, be a *passive* one; or where is the dividing line between *action* and *passion*, when they so mingle that the same *action* is *half one*, and *half the other ?*

" Those mighty spirits *lie raked up*, with their ashes, in their
urns ; and not a spark of their eternal fires glows in a present bo-
som."   *Johnson. Sejanus.*

What is the grammatical difference between *lie raked up*, and are
raked up ?

Grammars are written to " teach the *art* of speaking and writing
correctly." Do these same grammars mean what they say ? What
is the verb *to lie*, called ? Neuter ; because it is said to *express no
action*, but simply a *state of being*. Does it express any *different
state* of being, or any *less action* for a sick person to *lie* on a *bed*,
than to *keep* his *bed?* What are the verbs to *sit*, and to *stand ?*
They are said to be neuter. If a soldier, *standing* in his ranks, has
a ball shot thro his heart, he instantly *falls ;* because he *loses* his
strength. Then, most clearly, he *used* his *strength*, before, in order
to stand. Can an ordinary man *stand* on a rope dancer's cord ? If
not, why ? Was there not a time when the rope dancer, himself,
could neither *do* this, nor even *stand* on the floor ? If so, then he
had *to learn the art* of *performing* both of these *non-actions*. If an
infant, of a month old, should be placed *sitting* in a chair, and destitute of a *supporter*, it would instantly *fall*, for want of *strength* to
support itself. If a lady, *sitting* in a chair, should faint, or, in other
words, should lose the strength which she exerted before, she would
fall. That every exertion of strength, whether much or little, is
action, is known to children, if they are not falsely taught. Both
strength and skill are required, to sit, or seat one's self, or to preserve the sitting posture ; and an elephant, with all his strength,
would not be able to perform that *action*, for want of *knowing
how*.

When it is said that the verb *to be*, " expresses a *state of being*,"
we can not dispute the assertion : but it is equally clear that the
verb *to love*, denotes a *condition of loving*, and to tell the scholar so
is precisely as instructive in one case as in the other. The same
kind of *neuter* teaching, among such as can be satisfied with it, may
be carried to any extent. It can easily be said that, if a man *plays*,
or *plays* a *tune*, on a *violin*, that verb clearly implies *fiddling*, or a
state of fiddling. It is difficult for any person to teach what he never
knew, and there is large allowance to be made in such cases. There
is, however, much comfort in the *neuter* plan of instruction, on this
account. If, for instance, a neuter teacher, should meet with the

statement that "a sailor *harpoons* a whale ;" tho he might never have seen this *verb* before, and knowing nothing of its *meaning*, but supposing it to have no *meaning* at all, would naturally infer that it did not mean "*action*, nor *passion* ;" yet he would feel tolerably sure, in his own mind, that, at least, it expressed a *state of harpooning*, or some thing about a condition of that nature, in some way or other. This would be precisely the same kind of grammar as that which is now given under the name of neuter verbs. When doctors, in high places, solemnly declare that " the verb *to be* expresses a *condition of being*," mere learners are in duty bound to admit it, and make the best possible use of such a sage lesson.

To put the matter beyond all dispute, there is a verb in *Latin*, and an other in *Greek*, meaning, *in substance*, nearly the same thing, or the same nothing, and almost in the same way.

INTRANSITIVE VERBS.

What is an *intransitive action !* That in which there is a real *movement*, or *change*, and nothing *moved* or *changed.* In the name of common sense, did any one ever hear of such an *action ?* No where except in *neuter*, or *inoperative*, grammar : but that is a matter which very wise men have settled, in a way that common sense has nothing to do with. It is proved by an overwhelming throng of great scholars, that there are four thousand verbs, in English, expressing this kind of " *intransitively active*" operations. It is the fundamental principle of all the grammars and dictionaries. A man would deserve a place in a mad house, if he was crazy enough to talk about common sense, in opposition to so much authority and learning.

We may *think* upon this subject, then, if we do not *think any thing ;* and *talk*, too, if we avoid *uttering words*, or *sounds.*

EXAMPLES OF INTRANSITIVE VERBS.

" *Strike*, while the iron is hot. "—*Old Proverb.*

The person to whom this is addressed, is to take care not to *strike* any *thing.*

A blacksmith hires a journeyman to *blow* and *strike.*

"I came, I *saw*, I conquered. "—*Cesar's letter.*

The man *has* many *workmen* employed ; some to *plow* and *sow*, others to *chop* and *split ;* some to *mow* and *reap ;* one to *score* and *hew ;* two to *frame* and *raise.* In his factory, he *has persons* to *card*, *spin, reel, spool, warp*, and *weave;* and a clerk to *deliver* and *charge*, to *receive* and *pay*. They *eat* and *drink*, three times a day; and. as they *work* hard, and *feel* tired at night, they *sleep* and *dream* comfortably, and *rise*, or *get* up, with the dawn, to *go* to their work again. In the morning, the children *wash*, and *dress*, and *prepare* to *go* to school, to *learn* to *read*, *write*, and *cipher*.

The celebrated horse, Corydon, will *perform* (   ) on Tuesday evening. He will *leap* (   ) over four bars, separately, in imitation of an English hunter. He will *lie* (   ) down, and instantly *rise* (   ) at the *word of command*. He will *move* (   ) backwards, and sideways; *rear* (   ) and *stand* (   ) on his hind feet; *sit* .(   ) down, like a Turk, on a cushion. To *conclude*, (   ) he will *leap* (   ) in a surprising manner, over two horses.

SELF ACTIONS.

The verbs, which have been called reflective, denote actions that recur upon the actor, or in which the person *does something* to *himself*. The great mistake is in supposing that any action.is *confined* wholly to the *agent*.

The thief *helped himself* to an other man's *cloak*.

It is very evident here that, if the thief *obtained* a new *garment*, an other person *lost it*.

"Let loose the murmuring *army* on their masters, to *pay themselves* with *plunder*."—*Venice Preserved*.

Would not an army let loose, to *pay themselves with plunder*, most probably *extend* the *effects*.of the action *to* some other *object?*

He *supports himself* by his *labor*.
He *cut* his *finger* with a *knife*.
He *broke* his *arm* by *accident*.
He *ruins* his *health* by *intemperance*.
He *poisoned himself* with *arsenic*.
He *destroyed* his own *life* by *poison*.
He *hit* his *head* against a *beam*.
He *exerts himself* with great *diligence*.
He *uses* his *feet* to *walk*, and his *hands* in *splitting* logs.
He *froze* his *ears* in *travelling*.

17

He *takes exercise* to refresh *himself*.
He *refreshes himself* with *exercise*.

They have gone to *breathe* the mountain *air*, for the *benefit* of their *health*.
They have gone to *recreate themselves* in the mountain *breeze*.

> ——" The July sun's collected rays,
> *Delight* the *citizen*, who, gasping there,
> *Breathes clouds of dust, and calls it* country *air*."
>
> *Cowper.*

At the battles of *Wagram, Austerlitz*, and *Waterloo*, the *agents* were the marshaled hosts on each side. Their *actions* operated on *themselves*, or· on *each other*. According to the *neuter* philosophy, they were *ineffective actions*. The armies *arranged themselves ;* the officers *commanded*, subalterns *obeyed ;* they *loaded* and *fired ;* the balls *flew ;* they *charged* with bayonets *;* they *cut*, and *stabbed*, and *slashed ;* men and horses *fell ;* they *weltered* in blood. Heads and limbs of men and beasts, with fragments of shattered carriages, *lay* in heaps. The earth *sustained* the *bodies*, and *soaked up* the blood of thousands who *yielded* their *lives* on these ensanguined fields.

OBJECTS OF VERBS,

AND

AGENTS AFTER VERBS.

" Thou shalt *call* his *name John :*" or shalt *call him* John.

Name,   This word is here the direct *object* of the verb *call*.
John.   This word, tho apparently standing as object, is really agent, being connected with a verb, which, in relation to it, is merely declarative.

In the phrase, " Thou shalt *name him ;*" the sentence is complete as a grammatical assertion: but it is necessary to know what the name is, which is therefore added as an explanatory word.

Again, it is not supposed that the name itself is created by the act of naming, nor that it is in any way contemplated as the object of the action ; but the name is previously made, and is barely to be specified in connection with the act of naming the person.

In the third place, it follows from the preceding remarks, that the name should be in an unaltered form, or what is called the nominative case, or it would not be the genuine designation. This is the general principle of nouns in apposition, and of the agent after the verb.

"*We, we,* the *consuls,* are wanting in our duty."

We are the *consuls who* are wanting in our duty. "*Ye* are *they.*" "*I* am *he.*" "*I* am the *man* whom *ye* seek." "*I, Dion,* am the man ; what more ?" "*I, John Doe, yeoman,* do hereby declare." *I* am *John Doe, yeoman,* and do hereby declare.

In the above instances, the second and third name of the agent is added, to ascertain the personal identity. Whether such explanatory title is placed before, or after the verb, does not alter the grammatical principle; but is a question of *brevity, perspicuity,* or *harmony,* in utterance.

"*He* reigns *king.*" His being a *king,* is not the *effect* of his *reigning.* *King* is therefore not the *name* of the *man,* in character as the *object* of the *action ;* but that which belonged to him prior to the action, and independent of its *resulting influence.*

Whether the person, or thing, named, stands in the relation of agent or object of an action, is a question of fact, to be determined in each case, in order to apply any grammatical rule : and not a matter of arbitrary form, or depending on any select number of words.

The arbitrary "rule" given in grammars, that the verb *to be,* has the same case after, as before it, is not true : nor has this, or any other verb, any peculiar character in this respect.

Be an honest man, and not barely *profess* that *character.*

"If a man would seem to *be* any thing, let him really *be* what ( ) he would seem to *be.*"

"Almost thou persuadest me to *be a Christian.*"

Almost thou persuadest me to *change myself* into a *Christian :* to make a *Christian* of *myself.*

Whatever may be thought of Agrippa's theology, there seems very little reason to mistake the import of his language ; and certainly as little in the original as in the translation.

The examples which follow, will serve as exercises in parsing verbs, in reference to the question whether they denote action, and whether they have objects.

"One *star equals* an *other* in glory.

The roof *shelters* the *family;* the floor *supports*, and the walls *enclose them.*

Windows *exclude* the *cold*, and *admit light.*

"And God said, ' Light *be ;*' and light *was.*"

If it was any *action* to create the sun and stars, with their attendant orbs, that *action* is signified by the short sentence above ; and if the sentence denotes *action*, it is *"expressed"* entirely by the verbs *be* and *was.*

be, imperative verb, *exist; spring* into *being; assume position, order*, and *acting influence*, in the system of wheeling worlds.

was, indicative verb, past tense, denoting that the fiat of Almighty power and wisdom, " Light *be*," was instantly obeyed.

And GOD said unto Moses, "I AM THAT I AM; and thus shalt thou say unto the children of Israel: I AM hath sent me unto you."

Exod.

> I AM the first, and I the last,
> Through endless years the same ;
> I AM is my memorial still,
> And my eternal NAME.

Dr. Watts; Hymn 45.

The compounded word which, through its varying forms, we call the verb *to be*, though in all its parts both noun and verb, and exceedingly significant as such, has been so long unexplained, and, by the force of tradition and habit, unconsciously used, that to develop its forcible, sublime, and true meaning, is necessarily to exhibit it in an *unfashionable* point of view.

> "I am the *I am*, or that *I am.*"

am, verb, expressing self action, the action of sustaining one's self in life. Never having any variation in its *object*, it is unnecessary to express it, for the sake of perspicuity, or distinction. No word, therefore, is retained in use for this purpose. In parsing, it is only necessary to have the principle well understood, without dwelling upon it in practice.

the I AM, *Vitality itself; uncreated, boundless, unending Being ; Life-giving Power; Self sustaining Existence; the eternal, uncontrolled, unassisted, self acting Principle of Life.*

I am, as here used, is taken together, as a noun ; and such a noun as never had a parallel in expression. It could not be translated, from the original, into any language, without greatly lessening its force.

I am, as a noun, could never be used, but by the *Ever-living God ;* and, without verbal reasoning upon it, the unavoidable necessity of the case shows that it can be taken only as a *nominative word*, or as the *actor :* because that, as the Supreme Being has no " variableness or shadow of turning," and is above all influence of inferior *actors*, he can not in strictness be contemplated as the *object* of any *action :* for the nature of action is unavoidably to produce change in that on which it operates.

In the use of language, the *name* of the *Deity* frequently becomes the object of a verb ; but this mode of expression is to be understood as growing out of the necessity of the case, and the mere *relative* and limited conceptions, which finite beings must have of the Sovereign Lord.

For similar reasons, no *past participle* can ever apply to the Supreme Being, for what he *absolutely is*. We can say, *relatively*, of the Most High, " He has *been* our Protector, ever since we had existence :" but, in all which pertains to his own Divine Attributes, it can not be said that he ever has *been* any thing which he is not now; because the *past participle*, in every possible form of its use, denotes the resulting *effect* of action or change.

" *City of New-York, ss.* The People of the State of New-York, to Timothy Trusty, Greeting ;

We COMMAND YOU that, all and singular business and excuses being laid aside, you *BE* and *APPEAR*, in your proper person, at the next court of common pleas, to be held at the City Hall of the city of New-York, on the third Monday of January next, at ten o'clock in the forenoon of the same day, to testify all and singular, what you may know, in a certain cause now depending in the said court, then and there to be tried, between John Doe, plaintiff, and Richard Roe, defendant, of a plea of trespass on the case ; and *this* you are *not to omit*, under the penalty of two hundred and fifty dollars."

Two hundred and fifty dollars *penalty* for not *performing* the *action* of *being* in court at the time commanded.

198 CRITICISM AND

You *be* and *appear*, that is, you *have*, and *present*, *yourself*.

On what principle is the military law founded, that if a sentry, in time of war, "shall be found *sleeping* at his post, and be thereof duly *convicted*, before a court martial, he shall *suffer death*."

"You may (   ) also know a well bred man, by his *manner of sitting* (.) Ashamed and confused, the *aukward man sits* (   ) in his chair, bolt upright; whereas the man of fashion is easy in every position. Instead of lolling (   ) or lounging (   ) as he *sits* (,) he leans (   ) with elegance, and by varying his attitudes, shows that he has been used to good company. *Let it be* one part of your *study*, then, to learn (   ) to *sit* (   ) *genteelly* in different companies, to loll (   ) gracefully where you are (   ) authorized to take that liberty, and *to sit* (   ) up respectfully, where that freedom is not allowable."—*Lord Chesterfield's Letters.*

"Go (   ) and *sit* (   ) down." "*Sit* farther that way." "*Sit* (   ) up straight." "Come (   ) here, and *sit* (   ) down by me."

"*Sitting*, the *act of resting* on a seat."
"*Session*, the *act of sitting*."

                        Johnson's Dictionary.

"How is your little brother to-day?" "Very weak yet; not able *to sit up* long enough to have his bed made."

He *sat* (   ) *up* too long, and the *exertion fatigued* him very much.

I *had* a bad *pain* in my head; but I *slept it* away.

They *slept away the fumes* of their wine.

"They slept, and eat, and drink'd; what then?
Why eat, and drink'd, and slept, again."

                        Prior's Contented Couple.

"When I *lay me* down *to sleep* (   ) I recommend myself to his care; when I *awake* (   ) I give myself up to his direction. Amidst all the evils which threaten me, I will (   ) look (   ) to him for help, and question not that (   ) he will (   ) either avert them, or turn them to my advantage. Though I know neither the time nor the manner of the *death* I am to *die*, I am not at all solicitous

about it; because I am sure that he knows them both, and that
(   ) he will not fail (   ) to comfort and support me under them."

Addison, Spectator.

"Then, having shown his wounds, he'd *sit him* down,
And, all the livelong day, discourse of war."

Tragedy of Douglas.

"He *sat him* down by a pillar's base,
And drew his hand athwart his face."

Lord Byron.

"I *sat me* down and wept."

Old Song.

"Why Gloster, Gloster!
I'd speak (   ) with the duke of Cornwall and his wife:
The king would speak (   ) with Cornwall:
                    But *wherefore sits he* (   ) *there?*
Death on my state ! *This act* convinces me
That this retiredness of the duke and her
Is plain contempt. Give me my servant forth:
Go (   ) tell the duke and 's wife I'd speak (   ) with 'em
Now, instantly. Bid 'em come (   ) forth and hear me ;
Or, at their chamber door, I'll beat the drum,
Till it cry (   ) *sleep* (   ) to death."

King Lear.

"*sleep* (   ) *to death."* This must necessarily mean *sleep* (some
thing or some *person*) to *death :* because it needs not the
highest kind of philosophy to tell us that there can be no
death where there is no *object* to suffer death. To form a conjecture, therefore, according to the probable meaning of the
writer ; what were the *sleepers,* in this case, more likely to
sleep to death, than *themselves.*

"*Love not sleep ;* lest thou come to poverty."

Prov. xx.

"The hare *sleeps* (   ) with its *eyes open ;* because it is (   )
very fearful ; and, when it hears the *least noise,* it *starts* (   ) and
pricks up its long ears. If it hears a dog coming (   ) it runs

(   ) away very swiftly, stretching its legs, and soon leaves him far behind."

The sick man *slept a good deal*, last night, and it *had* an excellent *effect upon him*.

He *slept* a good deal of *sleep*, and the *sleep* which he *slept* had a good *effect* on him.

" Then cometh he to his disciples and saith unto them, *sleep on* now and take your rest."

" The *workers* of iniquity *lie in wait* for my soul." *Ps*. lix.

" We ordered the oarsmen to *lie down* as close as possible to their benches, to avoid being seen by the enemy." *Telemachus*.

Lie still, children, and *go to sleep*.

" To live (   ) soberly, righteously, and piously, comprehends the whole of our duty." *Murray's Grammar, Parsing Lessons*.

to live, this verb must certainly include the active exercise of the qualities and functions which pertain to us as living and accountable beings, or it could not " *comprehend the whole of our duty*."

If I could *live* my *life* over again, I should *try to employ it* to better advantage.

We have but one *life* to *live* on earth: how important that we should *improve it* to the best purpose !

"The *life* which I now *live* in the flesh, I *live* by the faith of the Son of God." *Gal*. ii. 20.

He *lives* a very comfortable *life*, by his industry and good conduct.

" *By these things* men *live*." *Isa*. xxxviii. 16.

" He *died* for all, that they which *live* (   ) should not henceforth *live* (   ) unto themselves; but unto him which *died* (   ) for them, and *rose* (   ) again." 2 *Cor*. v. 15.

"It is pleasant and glorious *to die* for our country."

"I choose *to die* innocent rather than *to live* guilty."

"Reader, go, tell at Sparta, that *we died* here in obedience to her laws." *Inscription at Thermopylæ.*

died : Did Leonidas and his companions *perform any action* on the memorable occasion to which this monument alluded, and which Dr. Goldsmith intended in the translation to *express* by the verb *died ?*

"Seest thou a man diligent in his business? he shall *stand* (   ) before kings: he shall not *stand* (   ) before mean men."

Prov.

"Who will rise (   ) up for me, against the evil doers; or who will *stand* (   ) up for me, against the workers of iniquity."

Ps. xciv.

At my right hand he *stands* (   ) *prepared*
To keep my soul from all surprise,
And *be* my everlasting guard.

Doct. Watts.

"*Watch* ye; *stand* (   ) fast in the faith; *quit* yourselves like men; *be* strong."

"Your *walk* to school is a long one." "Yes; but I *walk it* in a short time."

"For I know the *thoughts* that I *think* toward you, saith the Lord; *thoughts* of peace, and not of evil, to give you an expected end."

Jer. xix. 11.

It is stated, as a fact, that Mr. Reaumur, the celebrated naturalist, contrived by means of experiments in galvanism, to make a grasshopper, not only leap a considerable distance, but actually sing, after it was dead.

"*A verb passive expresses* a *passion* or a *suffering*, or the *receiving* of an action, and necessarily *implies* an *object acted upon*, and an *agent* by which it *is acted upon ;* **as,** to *be loved ;* Penelope *is loved by* me."   *Murray's Grammar.*

Penelope is *sensible, loving, lovely,* and deservedly *loved,* in a high degree.   She *is seated by* her little sister.

" My oxen and my fatlings *are killed,* and all things *are ready.*"

The members *are* chiefly *assembled,* and *making* arrangements to commence their session.

The mother *was delighted,* yesterday, with the prospect of her son's return ; but she *is anxious* today, because her hopes *are* not *realized.*

" Confide the secret to no person *living ;* but *be prepared,* at one o'clock, without fail, to go with me."

be prepared ; have yourself *prepared ; put yourself* in preparation ; *perform* the *actions* necessary to change your present unprepared condition, into one of complete readiness to go ; and *do this* without the knowledge of any other person.

" He will, by his turbulence, *cause himself* to *be heared.*"

That is, according to the passive verb doctrine, he will suffer the action of being heared, while he is wholly passive.

The candidate *is* totally *unqualified* for the station ; because he *is ignorant* of its duties.

" Penelope *is loved by* me :" " I *love* Penelope."

Pompey *was conquered by* Cæsar.

The army *was encamped by* the river Tweed.

" The retreat *was favored* by the fog."

The traveller *was robbed* by broad day light.

The letter is *written, sealed,* and *lying* on the desk, *ready* for the boy.

Dialogue.

A. Poor Scoggin *was drowned by* the side of India wharf.

B. Did the *side* of India wharf *drown him ?*

A. O, no; how could that be?

B. How was it then?

A. Not having strength of mind to bear his misfortunes, *he jumped* into the dock, and *was drowned.*

B. What was the verdict of the coroner's jury?

A. Suicide, or *self-murder.*

B. O, I thought by your speaking, that he only *suffered* the *action.*

A. To be sure, it is the *passive verb ;* but we *ought* to *exert ourselves* to *be* better *acquainted* with what it means.

" Guy Fawkes *was prepared* with a dark lantern, to blow up the king and parliament."

The thief *was concealed* in a potato bin, where he *was found, lying stretched* by the wall, and *waiting* for a chance to pilfer something from the house.

She lives, *respected, contented,* and *happy.*

The fire grows *hot, glowing,* and *cheerful.*

He stands *convicted, penitent,* and *confessing.*

The fear of the Lord tendeth to life : he that hath it, shall *abide satisfied.*

If the influence of wrong teaching and habit was not extensive, very little illustration would be required to show that, in what is called the *passive* verb, the past participle is a mere adjective.

One of the difficulties which every teacher must encounter, is the want of explanation in dictionaries and elsewhere, of the meaning of words. Definitions are wanting, particularly in those words which are most disguised, because of their great importance and consequent frequency of use. Among others, the verb to go is represented as neuter, from the circumstance that its meaning as a word is wrongly given.

To go signifies, not merely progressive motion ; but any kind of violent exertion, to produce movement. It is nearly synonymous with the verb to *act*. It is still used with its governed object expressed, tho it is now most fashionable to omit the object.

"With weeping shall they *go it* up." Who *goeth* a *warfare* at his own charge?" "You can not *go that.*" It was anciently used with conscious understanding that it meant *work, labor, toil, operation. Ago* (Latin), is a cognate word.

The verb *go* is irregular. This irregularity is made in part by its being united with the verb to *wind* or *wend.*

"The lowing herd *wind* (   ) slowly o'er the lea."

"O'er hills and dales they *wend* their way."

"Shall we *wind* along the streams, or walk the smiling mead ?"

"They *went* their *ways*, one to his farm, an other to his merchandize."

"*Go* your *ways;* behold I send you forth as lambs among wolves."

wind themselves, in a long serpentine string ; or *wind* their *circuitous way* o'er the lea.

wend their *way:* this is the same word as the other, with the slight change of *i* to *e.*
Such splitting and multiplication of words is very common in the progress of language.

went their *way. Went* is the past tense of wend, as *send* makes *sent; bend, bent,* and others. These are the ideas connected with travelling, not only as cattle *wind*, or *string themselves*, over the lea ; but as the early framers of speech must *wend* their way, round hills and fens, before cities are built, or roads made. It is the same idea which gives rise to the expressions to take a *turn;* perform a *circuit;* and make a *tour,* which is but the French word for the same thing.

go your *ways. Go* signifies to *act;* to *exert* one's *self;* to *exercise vigor;* to *move* forward. For a man " to *go* his *way*," means the same as to *work*, or *make* his *way* through a crowd, or through any difficulties which oppose his progress; or to *force himself,* or *force his passage* through the evils which beset him. The joining of the two verbs *go* and *went*, obviates the monotony which would otherwise take place, by their frequent use.

The words *go* and *wend* both had their origin and grew into extensive use, before people rode in coaches on turnpike roads.

> " And *panting*, *labor* to the farthest shore,
> The *toiling* caravan."

"And choked with sedges, *works* its weedy way."

" The man has a hard task, but he *works himself* along."

> " The dark way-faring stranger breathless *toils*,
> And often falling, *climbs* against the blast."

If the tight shoe *pinches*, let the wearer say whether this verb has an object or not ; and if the theory of intransitive actions is totally destitute of truth, let those who believe in it say how it can be made useful in practice.

It is not always necessary in parsing, to find a precise object for the verb; but it is necessary to know that every verb has one or more. A mistake respecting the noun *self*, has led to much error. This *self* is a personage of far more consequence than the compilers seem to imagine. The modern fashion of joining adjectives of personal relation to it, in myself, herself, and others, makes no change in the meaning. It would be better to write the words separate, as is necessarily done when a descriptive word is used.

" Each was to each a dearer self." " His other self." " Whose very self art love." " Spain, the shadow of her former self." " From our own selves our joys must flow."

The improper compounds of this noun *self*, with different adjectives, has deceived those who take words, by first appearance, as presented to the eye.

"I use *his self*, and *their selves*, instead of the corrupted words *himself* and *themselves*, in *which usage* I am justified by the authority of *Sidney*, and of other writers in the reign of Elizabeth. *Self* seems to have been originally a *noun*, and was, perhaps, a synonymous word for soul."—*Sir William Jones' Persian Grammar.*

If such a man as Sir William Jones had examined this particular word a little more minutely in the Persian and Arabian languages, as he was abundantly capable of doing, he would have left out his *perhaps* in the passage just quoted.

"*Self* is that *conscious* thinking *thing*, which is *sensible* or *conscious* of *pleasure* or *pain*, capable of *happiness* or *misery*."—*Locke's Essay*.

Self, soul, and *person,* are interchangeably used, at present. "London contains 1,200,000 *souls*," that is, *persons*.

Lovers of their own *selves,* more than lovers of God. "He worships his own dear self."

The verbs considered most distinctively *intransitive,* are occasionally used with their *objects expressed.* This is almost necessarily done, when they take new and striking applications, to things out of the range of common place utterance. In a skilful employment of such words, much of the beauty of poetry consists. Thompson is particularly happy in this use of verbs.

> "Still in harmonious intercourse they *lived*
> The rural *day,* and *talked* the flowing *heart,*
> And *sighed,* and *looked* unutterable *things.*"

Every writer of genius finds out, in his practice, that "*intransitive*" verbs *have objects,* whatever stupid lesson to the contrary he may study in his grammar.

"A sensible wife would soon *reason,* and *smile him* into good humor."—ADDISON.

"Even Sunday *shines* no *sabbath day* to me."

IMPERSONAL VERBS.

These verbs denote such actions as are familiarly understood, in connection with some agent and object habitually associated. If varied from the common use, the connected words must be expressed.

It *rains.* What do you speak of? The *rain.* What of it? what does the *rain* do? It *pours* down. How does it *pour* down? It *rains* down. *What* does it *pour* down? *Rain.* Then the *rain rains rain.* To say *it rains* is sufficiently understood. This latter expression is shorter, less monotonous, and more fashionable; and for all these reasons, more elegant. The person who would understand language, otherwise than as a mere smatterer, should know *why* it is so.

"With store of ladies whose bright *eyes*
Rain influence, and judge the prize."—MILTON.

"Then the Lord said unto Moses, behold, *I* will *rain bread* for you, from heaven."—*Exod.* x.

"Then the *Lord rained* down, upon Sodom and upon Gomorrah, *brimstone,* and *fire,* from the Lord, out of heaven."

MOOD.

IT is not difficult to understand that every action must depend on some agency to perform it: and yet this proposition, simple as it is, seems to have been very remarkably overlooked by those who teach others "to speak and write correctly." If any thing but "custom" is to be the foundation in dividing moods, the choice appears to be natural and plain.

If we look into language, as founded on principle, we see actions represented as being performed by some agent or actor: or, secondly, one intelligent being commands or solicits an other to do or avoid some thing: or, thirdly, an action takes place, as consequent on some previous state of things taken together, and operating as a collective whole, to produce the event which the infinitive mood expresses.

Mr. Harris, the most learned writer in England, who has attempted the science of technicality, gives fourteen moods.

These moods are the *declarative* or *indicative,* the *potential, subjunctive, interrogative, requisitive, imperative, precative, optative, enunciative,* &c. It is unnecessary to trouble the reader with a longer list. The *philosophy* on which moods are taught, may be seen in a short quotation from the very learned author before mentioned, whose work abounds with erudite quotations, and appears to possess almost every excellence, except *truth,* and common *sense.* It may probably surprise some of the compilers of grammar, that the exceptions should be so very few.

"If we do not strictly assert, as of something *absolute* and *certain,* but as of something *possible* only, and in the number of *contingents,* this makes that *mode,* which grammarians call the POTENTIAL; and which becomes, on such occasions, the leading mode of the sentence."—HERMES, p. 141.

"Yet sometimes the *potential* is not the leading mode, but only subjoined to the indicative; as, Thieves *rise* by night, *that* they *may out* men's throats.

"Here, that they *rise*, is positively asserted, in the *declarative* or *indicative* mode; but as to their *cutting men's throats*, this is only delivered *potentially*, because how truly soever it may be the *end* of their rising, it is still but a contingent, that may never perhaps happen. This *mode*, as often as it is *in this manner subjoined*, is called by grammarians, not the POTENTIAL, but the SUBJUNCTIVE."—p. 143.

Again, page 144, "And thus have we established a variety of modes, the INDICATIVE or DECLARATIVE, to assert *what we think certain;* the POTENTIAL, for the purposes of *whatever we think contingent;* the INTERROGATIVE, *when we are doubtful*, to procure us *information;* and the REQUISITIVE, to assist us in the gratification of our *volitions."*

The difficulty with this kind of *explanation* is that it requires an extraordinary degree of talent to comprehend and apply it. Instead of using the *rule* to discover the fact, it is hung on the fact, after that is fully ascertained: but surely no judge, who is master of the whole case, can have patience with such special pleading.

It will be seen that the *names*, and the attempted *divisions*, of these *moods*, are made to depend on the supposed meaning of a *preceding verb:* potential, because formed, in part, by the word *can*, which conveys an idea of "*being able*," in some way or other. The dictionaries, too, tell us that *can* is a *sign* of the *potential mood*, which is an additional reason why the *potential mood* should follow the verb *can*. The case seems as plain as what we read in children's books; "*Harry* was *brother* to *Lucy*, and *Lucy* was *sister* to *Harry*." The number of moods, however, is very deficient. The *fourteen* should at least be multiplied by *ten*. The word *need* comes before an other *verb*, without the *preposition to*. It is therefore an "*auxiliary*," and unquestionably a *sign* of the *indigent mood;* as the verb *dare* is of the *courageous*, and *feel* of the *sensitive*, or *passive* mood: but to all attempts to explain moods or comprehend them, by this kind of technicality, we may apply a quotation from an other eminent scholar,

"Strange such a difference there should be,
'Twixt tweedle-dum and tweedle-dee."

The frivolous and absurd verbiage, respecting moods which nature forbids, are troublesome to those who are compelled to task their memories with such ridiculous attempts at explanation; but fortunately they are soon forgotten. None of them has much effect in perverting the language in its practice, if we except the singularly aukward and inconsistent expressions taught under the name of the *subjunctive mood.*

"If a book *does* not appear worthy of a complete perusal; if there *be* a probability that the writer will afford but one prize to divers blanks, &c."—DOCTOR WATTS.

The verb *be* is here in the indicative mood, or the sentence is bad English.

No man has yet attempted to use a *subjunctive mood* in the English language, without contradicting both himself and the expounders in applying its absurd "rules."

"A tame serpent was taken by the French when they invested Madras, in the late war, and was carried to Pondicherry, in a close carriage. But from thence *he* found *his* way *back again* to *his* old quarters, which it seemed *he* liked better, though Madras *be* distant from Pondicherry, above 100 miles."—LORD MONBODDO.

"Taste is certainly not an arbitrary principle, which is subject to the fancy of every individual, and which admits no *criterion* for determining whether it *be* true or not."—*Blair's Rhetoric.*

Whatever a *criterion can determine,* is not *contingency.* The verb *be,* as here used, is either bad English, or it is in the indicative mood, agreeing with its agent *it.* If it is intended to be *future,* then the criterion of time will, at the proper period, determine whether it *is* true or not.

The following is probably the best statement of the *subjunctive* mood which can any where be found.

"It may be considered as a rule that the changes of termination (for the subjunctive mood) are necessary when these two circumstances concur:—1st. When the subject is of dubious and contingent nature; and, 2d. When the verb has a reference to future time. In the following sentences, both these circumstances will be found to unite: 'If thou *injure* another, thou *wilt hurt* thy self. If he *conti-*

nue impenitent, he *must suffer.*"—*Murray's Grammar,* 8vo. vol, i.
p. 207.

It does not require a very penetrating logic to see that the *positive
assertion,* in the *indicative* mood, "thou *wilt hurt* thyself," wholly
depends, for all the *certainty* it can have, on the *contingency* of the
other member of the sentence, "*if* thou *hurt* an other." In the second sentence, what kind of justice is it to make the *certain* punish-
ment depend on *doubtful guilt,* or *contingent repentance.*

All which is said to explain the *subjunctive mood,* harmonizes in
one *incidental property.* It is *uniformly inconsistent.*

The indicative mood may express the action in an *affirmative,
negative, interrogative,* or *suppositive* manner: but whether one, or
the other, makes no difference in the grammatical character of the
verb, being wholly a *matter of fact,* and depending on associated
words susceptible of almost endless modification.

Whether the *imperative* mood is to be understood as *command* or
entreaty, is a *question of fact,* which grammar can not explain.

"*Give* me some bread."

This is the *imperative mood :* but it necessarily belongs to *intelligent beings,* one of whom can *utter it,* to an other, who can *understand it,* else the expression would be *nugatory.* In practice, the *relations* of these persons *to each other* are supposed to be known ; and
on the *fact* of that relation, depends all the difference in the imperative mood. The expression, addressed in a becoming tone to a
parent, is *entreaty;* to a *servant,* it is *command ;* and in ordinary social intercourse, *polite request,* especially by adding, "if you please,"
or some equivalent phrase. In most instances, it would be impossible to determine, by the *verbal form* of the imperative mood, whether it is *supplication* or *command. Grammar* can not teach these
collateral facts. It does not belong to rules of language to tell whether the *speaker* is *master* or *servant ;* and it answers no better purpose to occupy scholars with such verbiage, than to perplex them
with pretended *rules of speech* to explain the difference between a
tadpole and a frog.

The *imperative mood* depends on the volition of a speaker, or first
person, addressed to a second, to do some thing, or omit some thing,
in a different way from what would otherwise be done.

It seems an entire mistake to suppose that the imperative mood is part of an elliptical phrase in the indicative; for, of all the uses of the verb, the imperative is the most natural and simple. Its utterance in cases of urgency is the most prompt, and the reasons are numerous and strong for believing, not conjecturing, that it is prior to other forms of the verb.

The *infinitive mood* appears to have been the subject of remarkable mistake. According to the long taught theory, it is *governed* by whatever word happens to come before it: but why should this *infinitive verb*, which, according to the *Stoics* and *peripatetics*, both, is the most dignified part of human utterance, be thus domineered over by all parts of speech, and all other forms of the verb?

When language is taught according to science and truth, we shall not learn, as an *arbitrary rule*, that one word governs an other, in any case. Each *word* represents an *idea*, drawn from an *object of perception*. It accords with that perception, under whatever relation, appearance, or state it may be presented; and the words in language will, as signs, harmonize with each other, like the objects which they signify.

To make the principle more clear, suppose a thousand maps were drawn by a common scale, to represent different parts of the earth. If each map was truly drawn to represent the outline of the country, no matter how irregular, then these maps might be put together, and would be found exactly to fit each other; but it could not be said that one of these maps required an other to come to it, with crooked edges, to fit its own outline, or caused it to be farther north or south than it would otherwise be: for, as each map has its own locality and topography, to which it must be adapted, it would still be the same if no other map had ever been drawn. *Ideas* are "*mental images*," each like the originals; and *words* are their *types*, following the same *natural laws*.

An *action* must have a *cause*. In the indicative and imperative moods, the agent, *expressed* or *implied*, is the cause. The infinitive verb has no agent. The action which it denotes must then have some other cause.

They had a fire made in the stove to *warm* the room.

The cause of the action which the infinitive mood denotes, is the whole *transaction*, preparatory *circumstance*, or *state of things*, from which a *second action* takes place, as consequential. The expression is often elliptical, and some times to a great degree : but the principle is the same, in all languages. The infinitive mood is frequently expressed without mentioning the preparatory condition on which it depends; because that, for all necessary purposes, it is sufficiently understood.

" *To see* the sun is *pleasant."*

It would be idle to tell a person of common intelligence, what is necessary to be performed in order to see the sun. That point is supposed to be gained, without the necessity to go back and repeat the process ; or to recount the steps taken to arrive at it. The intention is, in the shortest form, to connect the two ideas of *pleasantness,* and of *seeing the sun.*

It is a *pleasant* circumstance *to see* the sun. We can open our eyes, and look up, *to see* the sun ; and this is a pleasant sight ; the *thought* is a pleasant reflection ; gratitude to Him who bestows this blessing, is a *pleasant* exercise.

———

TIME OR TENSE.

An allusion has already been made to what we understand by the word *time,* in its philosophic principle. Some notice has also been taken of it in its practical application, as interwoven with the laws of thought. It remains to speak of its modifying influence in the structure of speech.

Time is not confined, in language, to verbs, as has been so mistakenly supposed. It belongs to all sorts of words, as it does to all sublunary things. The *infant* must, before long, cease to be an *infant,* or be a *child* for the second time : *sons* and *daughters* will lose the relations which constitute them such ; *young* persons *may* be *old,* and *rosy* cheeks *pale ;* the hearts, at present *agitated,* will become *quiet;* and *you* and *I,* who now speak and hear, will soon be *they* and *them,* of whom a few *successors* in the scene may, perhaps, sometimes converse.

Time, in its general application to changing things, is to be learned and considered, not as a principle of speech, but as a law of nature, to which words are to be appropriately applied from previous knowledge of facts: but tense is here to be examined as one of the modifications of the verb.

In the systems of grammar, as taught among different nations, the number of tenses is varied, commonly from six to fifteen. Harris ingeniously exhibits twelve tenses. Mr. Murray has twelve, consisting of six primary ones, each subdivided into *definite* and *indefinite*. The French writers, who have paid great attention to this subject, generally make more. Mr. Bauzee, in his very learned work, has *twenty. tenses.* Doct. Beattie makes *thirty-six*, in his English grammar, and thinks that a less number would produce a defective view of the language, and create *confusion* in the *grammatical art.*" The royal academy of Spain give an elaborate and methodical explanation of *seven future tenses*, in that language.

As the learning of tenses, according to such a scheme, must be a greater undertaking than the building of a house, it becomes a matter of serious importance to begin by counting the cost, as far as practicable, and then to make some kind of estimate what the acquisition will probably be worth when it is gained. The whole school theory of *tenses* procedes on the attempt to find out whether an *action* took place, at, after, or before, the period of one or more other *events*. The *principle*, on this plan, is easily settled; and the compilers will need to be diligent in *counting their tenses*. They are equal to the number of *distinguishable successions* from the beginning to the end of *time*, and these multiplied into each other, according to the various forms in which they are to be combined.

The appropriate business of grammarians appears to be to explain the *tenses of verbs*, not " accurately to mark" all " the *distinctions of time*," " in which *actions* or *events* occur."

From the bewildering technicality of *twelve, thirty-six*, or *ten million*, tenses, let us take a hint from a practical man on whom the hand of nature stamped the genuine, original character of greatness.

" The condition of human nature would be lamentable indeed, if nothing less than the greatest learning and talents, which fall to the share of so small a number of men, was sufficient to direct our judg-.nt and our conduct: but Providence has taken better care of our happiness, and given us, in the simplicity of common sense, a rule for our direction by which we shall never be misled."

Lord Chatham.

After employing the every day commodity here recommended, to find out what the *tenses* really are, we can better examine the *collections of opinions* laid before us, under the name of *grammar*.

First, let any person, at all accustomed to *reflect*, ask himself whether, in the common affairs of life, he ever thinks of *time*, otherwise than as *past*, *present*, or *future*.

Second. Has any nation, in practice, formed a large number of *words*, to denote *ideas* which do not *exist in* the *mind*?

Third. Do we *perceive* that an *action takes place*, while it *does take place*, after it is *finished*, or *before it begins*? If it is agreed that the action is *perceived*, only when it is *perceivable*, that is, when it *takes place*, then the *first step* is accomplished, and we may consider as settled, the fact that every *radical verb* is in the *present tense*.

If the action has *taken place*, been *perceived*, and *has ceased*, how is the *idea*, without the direct *perception*, called up, in the *mind*? By *memory*. How is this *past tense* expressed? By a *modified utterance* of the *present tense verb*, or by some *appendage* to *compound it*.

The early practice was, to *double the verb* of the *present tense*, either to *denote* the *repetition* of *action*, or to *recall* the event which was *passed*. A few hints will afford a sufficient view of this subject, for our immediate purpose. The reduplication of *verbs*, to express *repeated action*, is partly on the *imitative principle*, alluded to in speaking of the *sounds* called *interjections*. The same practice is continued, in some modern languages, to a great extent, tho its present use, in English, is very limited. The heart is said to go, *pit-a-pat*, to represent its *successive pulsations*. So we have *tittle-tattle*, *fiddle-faddle*, *clitter-clatter*, and other similar expressions. The reduplication is somewhat common in that form of *Latin verbs* called the *perfect tense*.

The regular *past tense*, in English, is made by post-fixing the verb *do*. This *verb* was anciently the letter *d*, followed by a *vowel sound*. What that sound was, can not be known; for there is no certain dependence on the *letter*, as presented to the eye. It appears in the forms *da*, *de*, *do*, and others. This was *doubled* to make the *past tense*; and *da da*, or *de de*, pronounced doubtless broader than at present, was *twice do*; repeat the *doing*; and, by easy transition, *did*, or *done*.

This verb, thus thrown into the *past tense*, was *appended to others*: and the *vine* which they *plant-ed*, and *water-ed*, was then *plant-dede*, and *water-dede*; or, in the modern form, *plant-done*, and *water-done*; such as the *done act* of *planting* and *watering* had made it.

If this mode of expression had not already been adopted, and grown into familiar habit, it would immediately take place, without any thing new, except an other word of equivalent meaning affixed. To say that a man *salt-dede*, *salt-ed*, or *salt-affected*, his meat, is the same, in principle, as to assert that he *iron-shod*, or *wood-shod*, his sled, *steel-plated* a sithe, or *water-rotted* his flax. These *past tense verbs*, in each case, turn into *adjectives*, by a slight change in their use; as an *iron shod* sleigh, a *steel plated* ax, *water rotted* hemp, *grass fed* cattle.

The *append-dede* verb, by familiar *coustoume*, *droppe-dede* its *fyrste d*, and afterwards the *final e*, whiche broughte it to its *preasante forme*.

Within the last hundred years, the *ed* has ceased to be pronounced as a separate syllable, unless it follows a sound with which the letter *d* will not coalesce.

The principles here hinted at are common to all languages. They belong to the laws of perception and of thought.

In speaking of *tenses*, it is to be remembered that it is the *tenses of verbs* which is the subject, and not the *temporal divisions* of all *possible facts*. Each *verb* is *one*. No *simple indicative* proposition can contain more than *one*. Every *indicative verb* is either *present*, or *past*; and an *imperative*, or *infinitive* verb, is inevitably *future*. This is not the place for exemplification in foreign tongues, or it might easily be shown how tenses *supposed* to differ from this statement, are made, and what they are made of. The English scholar will not depend on any other language, to apply these principles in his own.

FUTURE TENSE.

There is no *future tense* of an *indicative mood*, in any language. A few elementary truths, properly understood, would have saved a prodigious labor of learning on this point.

The *indicative mood* is so called, because it "*indicates*," "*points out*," or "*declares*," an *action*, or *event*. That which *indicates*, must have some *index*, as the means of "*pointing out*," or "*declaring*, a thing;" and a *future index*, instead of aiding *instant knowledge*, would ...ed a *present index*, to show that this *future* one was going *to exist*. It is equally a contradiction, in terms, and in fact, to talk of a future indication. What is *future* is not *indicative*.

That the action which has not yet taken place, can enter into any possible conception of the mind, appears to depend very simply and

uniformly on principles which may be understood by a single example.

The blooming trees *will* yield fruit in its season.
The trees *promise* to yield fruit.
The trees *have* the *nature* to yield fruit.
The trees *encourage us* to expect fruit.

The *indication*, in these instances, is the *appearance* of the *trees*.
It is no matter whether that *indication* is called *will*, *nature*, or
encouraging promise : for in either form of words, the same thing is
meant. The *future* event, *imperceptible* in itself, and beyond the
reach of *indication*, is *inferred* from comparing some existing *manifestation* with past *experience*. Whatever the *index* may be in the
special modification, or however the *verbal utterance* may be shaped
to *assert it*, the *principle* remains unchanged. It is the *present indication asserted*, and the *resulting* future *action inferred*.

The trees are in *blossom*. We have seen them so before ; have
seen the *succession* of *events*, following that *appearance ;* and learned to *understand* that, by a *natural law*, the *fruit* is likely to *suc-
cede*, in due time. The regulated *principle*, by which the fruit grows,
in orderly course, from the *bud*, is considered as some thing *inherent*
in the *tree ;* and this *principle*, in forms as various as the separate
components of the universe, pervades all objects. It passes under
the names of *will, volition, choice, judgment, caprice, nature, quality,
aptitude, inclination, leaning, disposition, longing*, and many other
similar terms. Probably no *idea* or *principle*, belonging to language
to settle, is more extensively misunderstood, nor, at the same
time, more important to be known, than what is called *volition*, or
will. However various the *degrees*, or *modes*, of operation, *will*, or
volition, belongs to all created things ; and *absolute free will* to none.
The man *will* go to the wedding, to marry the woman he loves ; he
wills to go out of the house which is burning : he *will* be sick ; *wills*
to suffer pain ; and *will* die, in opposition to his *will ;* for the *complex* being, man, "wonderfully made," has different *wills*, which
may concur, or stand opposed. The child, *born "without ideas*,"
and with a *mind* " like a sheet of *blank paper*," " arbitrarily *chooses*,'
in what is most necessary for its sustenance, and acts, with a skill
beyond what reason can teach. The hop vine *searches* for a support, and *wills* to fasten itself by a double turn, where a single one
is not sufficient. The *lively, inanimate* needle, *senselessly cunning*,

wills to aid commerce and science, by *indicating* the darkened poles, to the wise lords of the earth.

Sparks *tend,* or are "*prone* to fly upward," and water *wills* to run downward : and if this was the place to dwell on the subject, it might be seen, how unnecessary is any distinction, in language, on this point, and how futile the attempt to make it.

It is an advantage that, in the English language, two verbs are not artificially compounded, as they are in many other tongues. The *indicative* mood is always distinct. It is the expression of *will, intention, power, skill, aptitude, preparation,* or *tendency,* presently *manifested,* and from which, according to settled rules of judging, a consequent action is inferred.

This view of the words called *auxiliaries,* in its main features, is not new. It has been ably treated of, by several writers, particularly by Doct. J. P. Wilson, in his Essay on Grammar, a work which displays not only great erudition, but an originality and vigor of thought, rarely met with under the degraded name of grammar.

A slight view of the *tenses,* as they are explained in the *standard grammar,* will close this subject.

"Tense being the distinction of time, might seem to admit only of the *present, past,* and *future* ; but to mark it *more accurately,* it is made to consist of six variations, viz. The present, the imperfect, the perfect, the pluperfect, and the first and second future tenses."

Murray, 8vo. vol. i. p. 68.

To mark time with still greater accuracy, however, the author, (page 73,) adds six more tenses, to *point* it out "*indefinitely.*" In the elucidation of this subject, the compiler has displayed a "*sagacity*" which has drawn forth the loudest praises from the strong phalanx of British reviewers, and of all whose literary consciences are left with these critics, for the sake of convenience, dignity, or safe keeping.

PRESENT TENSE.

"*Indefinite* present tense denotes action without limiting it to a given point ; as, virtue *promotes* happiness."

Definite. "This form expresses the present time with precision; as, "He *is meditating,*" "I am *writing,* while you *are waiting.*"

It will be seen that these supposed definite tenses are made by taking an adjective with the verb, as being part of it.

In the first place, admitting that it takes half a dozen separate words to make one verb, the expression still is not necessarily *definite*, in reference to time, any more than the verb would make it. "The pyramids *are standing* near Memphis." "When did they *begin* to *stand*, and when will they *cease?*" As long as they *are pyramids*, they must *remain standing*, in the proper form to make them so. What is the difference in the tense, to say, I *am sitting*, or I *am seated*; he *is sleeping*, or he *is asleep*; he *is sick*, or *well*, *making* a voyage of discovery, or any thing else?

In the next place, if we should attempt to put some thing else with verbs, it would be impossible to tell what to select. Hardly any two sentences are alike, in all the collateral facts and circumstances, and there is no end to the perplexity resulting from attempted distinctions of this kind, where no distinction can be made, except that which belongs to the specific fact, in each case, thro the endless variety of expressions. To blend all the attendant circumstances, in a phrase, or sentence, with a verb, is to mistake the whole carriage and harness for a part of the horse; and to *elucidate* in a way too *mysterious* for human comprehension.

"The *imperfect tense* represents the action either as *past* and *finished*, or as *remaining unfinished*, at a certain time past: as, "I *loved* her;" "They *were travelling* post when he met them."

To ordinary observers, it appears rather unaccountable that the "sagacity" which could split time by rule into twelve parts, should have left the "*finished*" and the "*unfinished*" action together, instead of splitting again.

"He *perfected* his work, *delivered* it, and took his pay for it."

In this sentence, what *imperfection* is there, either in the *time*, the *fact*, or the *form* of utterance? If neither of them is *imperfect*, then why is it called the *imperfect tense?* Translated into Greek, Latin, or other language, it must be in the *perfect tense*: then why *imperfect* in English?

If Mr. Murray's grammar has any defects, they probably are not the errors of haste or inadvertence. The division of tenses is not said to be technical; but it is professedly accordant with fact. Does it not vary from fact, in a remarkable degree? Is grammar the art of writing correctly; or is it any part of correctness for a writer to mean what is true, and say what he means? The absurdities of this system are not Mr. Murray's fault. The crazy edifice, from its tottering foundation in " *custom*," is so wretchedly constructed, that ten thousand mendings could not make it appear otherwise than bad.

" The perfect tense *refers* to what is *past*," and " *conveys an allusion* to the *present time ;* as, I have finished my letter."

The definition of this tense *has* very carefully *stated* the *terms* in which it is conveyed; or, it *has* the *terms* very carefully stated ; but with all care, it *has*, and *exhibits*, but very little *evidence* of *perfection*. It *refers* to the *past*, and conveys an allusion to the present. Why does a verb, in the perfect, or second degree of past tense only refer to past time ; and why can it not be cut off from the present ? For a very strong reason; that is, because the only verb which it contains is in the present tense. This principle has been mentioned before, and need not be repeated.

" The pluperfect (or more than perfect) tense represents a thing not only as past, but also as prior to some other point of time specified in the sentence: as,

"I had finished my letter before he arrived."
He *arrived* before I *had finished* my letter.

" He had received the news before the messenger arrived."
The messenger arrived before he had received the news.

An experiment *was tried* on Mr. Murray's two pluperfect sentences, and it *was* easily *perceived* that after they *had been* changed, with the imperfect tense first in order, they remained just as good English as they *were* in their previous state. This imperfect is always perfect ; and no part of grammar which is *true* can be *more than perfect :* so that a *pluperfect tense* is as useless in practice, as it is inconsistent in principle. In the forms called *imperfect* and *pluperfect* tenses, either may stand *first*, in the order of arrangement, and of time, as the fact, in the special case, happens to be : nor is this to be understood of the English alone ; but of other languages in general. Enough has been said of the *future*, whether *first*, *second*, or *tenth*. Each tense is *perfect* in its kind : it is *present*, *past*, or *future*.

Leaving this technicality of a *dozen tenses*, we may turn to facts and practice, as they are exhibited before us.

Tho the *present tense*, in strictness, is without measure of continuance, and only the *dividing line*, between the *past* and *future*, yet the *action*, and the *tense* which expresses it, *continue* to be *present*, from the time of its *commencement* to its *termination*, whether that period is long or short.

"The earth *is* round."'

At whatever time this sentence may be uttered, from the creation to the end of the world, the verb *is* remains equally *present*, and the assertion equally true. Most of the confusion, and false reasoning respecting the *present tense*, have come from blending ideas which did not belong together, and from the misunderstanding of words.

Truth *is* everlasting.

Mr. Johnson *teaches* school.

It *lightens*.

The man *says* " Yes."

He *sails* to-morrow, for Europe.

is,   In the first sentence, from the nature of the assertion, denotes an *eternal present*. At each successive period, it is coeval with the ever advancing now.

teaches,   denotes an action begun, and not finished. This action, like many others, is not continuous, but intermitted. He follows that business as his usual occupation : but the assertion would be made, as well on the day when he does not, as when he does, teach school, till he relinquishes that employment.

lightens.   The single action denoted by this verb is very short in its continuance ; and the assertion, in the present tense, would hardly be made, if the idea did not extend to its repetitions.

says.   The man *says* " Yes," instantaneously, and without repetitions. In the assertion of the fact by an other, the two actions are so nearly cotemporaneous, that no purpose of utility would be answered in noticing the distinction.

In a grammar founded on nature and truth, *past tense*, means an *action* which is *finished*, or so far finished as it is necessarily contemplated in the expression. The following examples, with what has already been said, will give a sufficient idea of its principle.

" Socrates *died* like a philosopher."

Socrates *was* instructing the young Athenians.

Socrates *was* killed at Athens.

Socrates *is* in an eternal world.

died :   *past* tense, denoting a single *terminated action.*

was :   this verb denotes the condition of being, the functions of which Socrates performed as a living man.

was :   this verb, in the third sentence above, affirms the state in which the mortal part of Socrates, for some time, *preserved itself,* after the act of destroying his life; but which corporeal personality has since passed away, so that nothing earthly now remains to which the identity of Socrates can be affixed. The affirmation must therefore be in the past tense.

is :   the assertion expressed by this verb, is the unending present tense, in reference to that Socrates whom the poisoning cup of his misguided countrymen could not destroy.

He *has* gone to Washington.

He *is* gone to Washington.

He *is* going to Washington.

He *is* living in Washington.

He *is* coming from Washington.

These five verbs affirm, alike in the present tense, the condition or situation of the person denoted by the pronoun *he.* He *has, retains, exists,* or *sustains himself,* in the condition in which the finished *act* of *going,* or the unfinished *act* of *going, living,* or *coming,* has placed him.

In what has been called the " *perfect tense,*" after understanding that *have* is the only *verb,* and the *participle* used with it an *adjec-*

tive ; that this *verb* is *principal,* and not *auxiliary;* with an *object implied,* if not *expressed ;* no farther explanation will be required, to make the application in all its forms.

"I *have sat* half an hour in this chair."

Half an hour ago, I passed through the *action* or *change,* the *termination* of which *placed me sitting* in this chair. I yet *have myself seated* or *sat* in the same situation.

" He *has* resided four years in this place."

has. The man still *resides* here, and *expects* to *spend his days* among us, so that he only *remains* in the situation in which he *placed himself* four years ago.

They *have* lived six years in France, and since that they *have* lived ten years in Boston, where they now *live.*

have ; these two verbs are with propriety, both in the present tense. They now *have* or *continue themselves* under the circumstances, the benefits, and disadvantages, whatever they may be, which a residence in France, and a ten years' residence in Boston, since, *has produced upon them.* No *subsequent change* is taken into the contemplation. We can not say of a man *who is dead,* he *has lived* four years in France ; because the proposition affirmed of him as a *living man,* will not apply in the *present tense,* after he *has passed into a different state of being.*

We may say, Cesar *was killed* 1800 years ago; but not with propriety, Cesar *has been killed* 1800 years ; for, excepting an Egyptian mummy, nothing which could *be killed* 1800 years ago, can now be spoken of by the verb *has,* in the *present tense.* These ideas will readily explain the long standing grammatical paradox, that an English verb, in this mistaken "*perfect tense,*" unavoidably "conveys an *allusion to the present time.*"

The imaginary *pluperfect* depends on the same principle.

The binder *had bound* my book, and the blacksmith *had shod* my horse, when or before I sent for them.

These expressions are alike the simple *past tense.* The blacksmith *then had* my horse *shod ;* he *was* as the act of shoing had made him ; and all additional circumstances respecting time, are only to arrive more nearly to the period *when,* as it relates to concomitant events.

A few examples will enable teachers to explain the *future* with consciousness of truth, and with profit to their scholars.

He *is* to finish, *can* finish, *wishes* to finish, *shall* finish, *may* finish, *has* to finish, *will* finish, *must* finish, and *ought* to finish his Greek grammar next month.

In each of these examples, the first verb, in *italic,* is in the *indicative* mood, *present* tense; and the second, in Roman letters, is *infinitive,* and consequently *future ;* because, it is a law of language as well as of nature, that one action can *not* happen both after an other, and at precisely the same time with it. When, therefore, we say, He *wishes now* to *embark next year* for South America, it seems hardly correct to teach pupils that these verbs express two actions, *both* in the *present tense,* at the *same time.*

The *second future* tense will not require much explanation.

" The two houses *will have finished* their *business* when the *king comes* to prorogue them."—*Murray's Gram. 2d Fut. Tense.*

The above sentence means, " The two houses *will have* their *business finished* before the king will *come to prorogue them.* Before the *time* at which the king *wills* to come."

Did the idea occur to the distinguished gentleman quoted above, that his "*future beyond a future*" happens to denote an action *prior* to that expressed by the verb *comes,* in the *present tense ?*

The phraseology called "the second future tense," is a modern grammatical invention ; artificial, inelegant, and very little used. "*I shall* or *will have loved,*" and a large portion of the other examples of this kind given, it is believed are no where seen or heared, except in the perplexing and inapplicable tables of verbal conjugations. Let a person of discriminating mind, and well versed in literature, scrutinize these tables, which have caused so many tears in schools, and so much puzzling among compilers, in counting tenses and moods. He will be surprised to find how little concern they have, with any purpose of utility in practice.

He *will have written* the letter.

He *will have* the letter *written.*

It *will make void* the contract.

It *will make* the contract *void.*

You *may get ready* the packet.

You *can get* the packet *ready,* or *prepared.*

You *are to get ready* the packet.

You *ought to have* the packet *prepared.*

Concerning the words called *adverbs,* and *prepositions,* enough has probably been said. An other *part of speech,* belonging to the customary system of grammar, appears to require some notice.

CONJUNCTIVES, or CONJUNCTIONS.

A person who has not given considerable attention to philological studies, would be amazed at the extent of learning which, during more than 2000 years, has been employed to explain this set of words. A slight glance at the subject may give some idea of what learning can do, when fostered by national aid, and exerted under the guidance of fashionable technicality. The "*Hermes*" of Mr. Harris, before referred to, has been considered by his fellow-laborers as one of the " most splendid efforts of human genius ;" and, as compared with most of the erudition in this department, it certainly does exhibit a very extraordinary degree of talent. This very learned and ingenious writer says, (page 238,) " Now the definition of a CONJUNCTION is as follows :—a part of speech, void of signification itself, but so formed as to help signification, by making TWO or more significant sentences to be one significant sentence :" and, in continuation,

" This therefore being the general idea of CONJUNCTIONS, we deduce their species in the following manner." He then, at considerable length, and supporting himself by a prodigious weight of authority, procedes to characterize these various "*species* of conjunctions."

This distinguished author then, in due form, gives the synonyms, character, and locality, of these various *species :* but as some of his names differ from those of other eminent grammarians, the following list is offered, as being the one in which many learned men of different nations, appear to have agreed. The words are here given in their English form.

Conjunctive, adjunctive, disjunctive, subdisjunctive, copulative, negative copulative, continuative, subcontinuative, positive, suppositive, causal, collective, effective, approbative, discretive, ablative, presumptive, abnegative, completive, augmentative, alternative, hypothetical, extensive, periodical, motival, conclusive, explicative, transitive, interrogative, comparative, diminutive, preventive, adequate preventive, adversative, conditional, suspensive, illative, conducive, declarative, &c. &c. &c.

It is difficult to conceive, without the aid of great learning, how a word which has no meaning, should be of such extensive use; or how it can exercise such vast and various influence on other terms. If no *meaning* at all, then why such *manner of meaning*; and such *difference* of *signification*, between one *conjunctive word* and an *other?* Has any person sufficient skill in Arithmetic to find such a *difference* between two *noughts?*

Probably one reason why an oracular *image* uttered *responses*, was because the heathen *priest* was in it; but no man who honestly believes his lessons in grammar, would be likely to suspect that a most important *noun* or *verb* could *lie hid*, in the *shell* of a *conjunction.* Horne Tooke, with a master hand, has settled this question, and left no room for argument upon it.

Our model grammar informs us that the " conjunctions are *principally* divided into two sorts; the *copulative*, and the *disjunctive*." The list is furnished, consisting of *twenty-two* words.

According to the account of these *conjunctives*, they perform offices nearly as multifarious, in proportion to their number, as adverbs.

1. They *join* other words, both in a *joining*, and in a *disjoining* way.
2. They *govern* a *conjunctive*, or *subjunctive*, mood.
3. They bring two sentences into one.
4. They unite singular nouns, and form a plural, by the aid of a long rule of syntax.

5. By the operation of an other *rule*, they " connect like moods and tenses of verbs."

Besides these main considerations which have been so often and so variously elucidated, some queries of a minor kind yet remain to be answered.

1. When two *junctive words*, *dis* and *con*, meet in the same broken place, how is the business of joining and disjoining to be regulated between them?

2. When three conjunctives come together, as some times happens, what is the middle one to do?

Of the two "*principal*" divisions, the *dis-junctive conjunctives* form the *majority*. They are twelve in number; *but, or, nor, as, than, lest, though, unless, either, neither, yet, not-withstanding.*
The *con-junctive con-junctives* are, *and, if, that, both, then, since, for, because, therefore, wherefore.*

" The *same word* is occasionally used *both as* a *conjunction, and as* an *adverb;* and some times as a *preposition.*"—*Murray,* &c.

According to this theory, it must be very difficult, in a word without meaning, to distinguish the double, or perhaps triple, character under which it may offer. One or other of these cases will very often occur: *but if either, or even though both* should happen, the teacher, to prevent embarrassment, or loss of time, may call them either *adverbs, conjunctions,* or *prepositions,* and pass on. There is no need of understanding these words, in order to explain them to others. In two respects the instructer is always free from the danger of appearing ignorant or aukward.

1. If an inquisitive learner should be inclined to ask puzzling questions, he never will know where to begin.
2. Let the teacher give what answer he pleases, no human being can say whether it is right or wrong.

The whole college theory of grammar is a huge, complex organ, of which any one may turn the crank, or blow the bellows, without knowing the machinery within. Whatever discordant notes may come forth, or however often it needs repairing, the highest authority has declared that the organ is right. It is this beneficial circumstance that, under the school system of teaching "the art of writing correctly," renders many persons the happy instruments,

> "Who sharpen others, as the hone
> Gives edge to razors, tho itself has none."*

A man who could free himself from the thraldom, and survey the scene as a mere spectator, might be amused at the extravagant absurdities, propagated under the sanction of the highest authority: but the exhibition assumes a very serious aspect, when it is considered that the best period of life is spent over such grammatical dream books, and that millions are left to the miserable choice between no explanation in language, and such explanations as these.

After seeing the *philosophy* of *conjunctions*, we may devote a few moments to their practical application.

1. Their *joining* of other words, in a *joining*, and in a *disjoining* way.

Mr. Murray's explanation on this point, is too long and too blind, to quote. The idea intended is that one set of conjunctives connect both the words and the sense, and the other, while they connect the terms, express opposition in the sense. Example of the opposition.

"They came with her, *but* they went without her."

They came with her, *and* they went without her, is just as good English, and these *conjunctive* and disjunctive conjunctives may be substituted for each other, if the fact should require, in a great portion of the cases in which they are used. As a principle of language there is not a particle of correctness in all which is said about these two kinds of words, in any point of view under which they can be contemplated.

"Me he restored to my office, *and* him he hanged."
>> *Chief Butler to Pharaoh.*

John is good, *and* Peter is very bad.
John is good, *but* Peter is equally so.

---

* "Fungar vice cotis,
Acutum reddere quæ valet ferrum,
Exsors ipsa secandi."
>> *Horace.*

That one set of these words must join, and the other disjoin, the sense, is no more a rule, than that the last Friday in each month, regulates the weather for the next month : or, that, if a man first sees the new moon over his right shoulder, he will have good luck till the next lunar change.

Some learned grammarians have apologized for the contradictory terms, *disjunctive conjunctive,* as growing out of the necessity of the case. They do not seem so literally *pre-post-erous,* as the rhetorical *"post-positive pre-positions."*

With reference to the influence of conjunctions in governing an additional mood, and in connecting like moods and tenses, a few words will suffice.

The attempts to explain and follow an imaginary subjunctive mood, lead, probably, to more bad English in modern practice, than any other single cause.

" CONJUNCTIONS connect the same moods and tenses of verbs; as, *If* thou sincerely *desire* virtue, she *will be found* by thee."—*Murray, Syntax,* R. 18.

" Some conjunctions require the indicative, some the subjunctive mood, after them. It is a general rule that when some thing contingent or doubtful is implied, the subjunctive ought to be used ; as ' If *I were* to write, he would not regard it ;' ' He will not be pardoned unless he repent.' "—R. 19.

To speak of " some thing *contingent,* or *doubtful, implied,*" is rather talking backwards ; but it is not the design to criticise Mr. Murray's language. He is not happy in his style ; and this consideration acquires greater force when we advert to the length of time employed to re-write and correct. Want of clearness is *real,* not *implied,* doubt.

Rules 18 and 19, of Mr. Murray's Syntax, stand opposed to each other, and neither of them, as a rule, has any foundation in fact, ncr application in practice. The coincidence of the facts supposed, is one of those things which may happen or may not ; but whether the next month is rainy or fair, the last Friday has nothing to do with it.

The conjunction *if,* according to the theory, connects two propositions, and of course two verbs. The conjunction governs one in the subjunctive mood. If both are not so governed, then they are not in the same mood. I *will* not *go, if* he *do.* I *shall* not *believe* such doctrine, *though* an other Murray *say* it, and the reviewers declare it excellent "beyond* all comparison." The two members of the sentence, in each case, have a reciprocal and necessary dependence, and by every just principle of reasoning, are equally positive. The *doubt* or *contingency* "implied," is the *sole* "*foundation*" of all the certainty which can exist in the case. With regard to the eighteenth rule, that conjunctions connect like moods and tenses, the exceptions to it are very numerous.

1. As a rule, it is wholly untrue.
2. As a guide to practice, it is mischievously deceptive.
3. It stands contradicted by the examples given to illustrate it.
4. It is opposed to the necessary law of thought.

"As it *was* in the beginning, *is* now, and ever *shall be.*"—*English church service.*

"Thieves *rise* by night *that* they *may cut* men's throats."

"What I *do, have done,* or *may* hereafter *do, has been,* and *will* always *be,* matter of inclination, the gratifying of which always *pays* itself; and I *have* no more merit in employing my time and money in the way I *am known to do,* than an other *has,* in other occupations."—*Howard, the philanthropist.*

In the observations which follow Mr. Murray's eighteenth rule, there is a half-way exception made, which is, perhaps, not absolutely worse than the rule itself; but the impropriety is more directly apparent. It states in substance that, if the rule does not agree with the fact, in a particular instance, "the nominative must be repeated." So far as this expression can convey any meaning, it implies, that there may be a verb without a "*nominative case,*" unless a *conjunction requires it* to have one.

Having thus freely examined the *model system* of *grammar,* as arranged by Mr. Murray, it is proper to state that there is not the slightest intention of disrespect to the *man.* They who, professing to believe the theory, attempt to write it over, virtually impute the

---

* "Mr. Lindley Murray, the ingenious author of the best English grammar, beyond all comparison, that has yet appeared."—*Imperial Review.*

deficiency to him, as an individual. The system is such, from beginning to end, that ten thousand recompilations can not make it
otherwise than absurd. Nature will not change its laws to agree with
such expounders of language, more than the heavenly bodies would
alter their course, in conformity with the Alexandrian school. Tho
Mr. Murray possessed no extraordinary powers of mind, and origi-
nated no doctrines, wrong or right, he possessed one merit of a high
kind, which is most thankfully accorded to him. There is probably
no author, or compiler, whose numerous publications are more free
from every thing offensive to delicacy, or more uniformly on the side
of those great principles of religion and morals, on which the welfare of
a community so vitally depends, and, without which, the most bril-
liant talents are a fleeting meteor, dazzling to destroy. Whatever
may have been his errors of opinion, they did not reach the heart.
Throughout a long life, he afforded undoubted evidence of a benevolent disposition; and generously exerted the talents, respectable, if
not splendid, which his Creator had given, to promote what he
deemed the best good of his fellow beings.

ERRORS IN PRACTICE.

Most of what is called false syntax is error in fact, or merely an
improper selection of a word, rather than a deviation from any settled rule of language. The chief cause of the error is a dependence
on arbitrary rules, instead of ascertaining the true meaning of words,
and the remedy, to be effectual, should remove the cause, by teaching the knowledge of terms, in their adaptation to the object from
which they are derived, and which it is their appropriate office to
represent. The types will be easily applied, if the antitypes are
well understood. Most of the examples of false syntax set down in
books, are not made up of bad English, but of bad grammar. Some
hints have already been thrown out on this subject, in what is said of
the imaginary subjunctive mood.

Among the errors which really prevail, the most frequent is the
deviation from the rule that the indicative verb agrees with the
person and number of its agent.

Among persons elevated above the lowest ignorance, this deviation takes place chiefly, either where two, or more, agents, are connected, to form a plural, with which the verb is to agree ; when the
sentence is *inverted;* or when the *verb* is placed at some distance
from the *agent,* with intervening terms, so that the *connection* is not

clearly perceived. The *examples* which might be given under this head *is* very numerous; but the principle is in itself so simple, that it does not appear necessary to trouble a competent teacher with a long list.

"The *conditions* of the sale *is* cash, or approved notes at 60 days." "What *signifies* good *opinions,* when our practice is bad." "There *is* two or three of us who have seen the work." "We may suppose there *was* more *imposters* than one." "If *thou would* be healthy, live temperately."—*wouldst.* "If *he were* to write, I would not regard it."—*was.* "I knew that you *was* there."—*were.* "You *was* in Boston, I suppose."

Considerable talent and learning have been shown to prove that the pronoun *you* is singular, and that *you was* is a proper expression. If this pronoun was singular, not only "*you was,*" but *you art,* also, would be good English; but both are incorrect; and for a like reason. The pronouns *you* and *we* are both plural, though applied by courtesy, or arrogating self importance, to a single person. They are to be explained according to the fact ; not as altering the principles of language. If these constructive forms of politeness were now abolished, others would be invented; for there is a natural tendency to them. Without reference to what is practised among foreign nations, has no man who ever dealt in *English grammar* been addressed in the language of humble deference, "Will *the gentleman* have any thing else ?" "*Does the gentleman* think *his* boots will do?" "Shall I bring up *the doctor's* carriage for him ?" instead of the direct question, "Do you wish any thing of me ?"

"Full *many a gem* of purest ray serene."

This form of expression anciently prevailed to a considerable extent; but it is hardly used by modern writers. The sentence will be grammatical by adding the word *times* after "*many.*" Full *many times a gem,*" &c.: as we say, many times *three* or *five* gems. How *many times one* in seven ? How *many times five* in thirty ?

A wrong adjective is sometimes employed to express the relations of things.

"I do not mean that I *think* any *one* to blame for taking due care of *their* health."—ADDISON.

The word *their* does not properly show the relation between
"*any one*" and *health*. The English language is defective, by lack-
ing two or three words to represent a *single person*, whether *male*
or *female*. Where the sex is uncertain, the *masculine singular*, according to the best practice, should be preferred.

The agent of a verb is some times omitted, and the order of sentences is sometimes changed; as, "To fear no eye, and to suspect
no tongue is the great prerogative of innocence." This sentence is
inverted. *It* is the great prerogative of innocence to fear no eye,
and to suspect no tongue.

From the omissions, there is, in many instances, a difference of
opinion in reference to the words to be supplied. Frequently the
sentence may be completed in different ways without material
change of the import. "The arguments advanced were *as follow*,"
or *as follows*. We may supply the omission by saying, either, were
such as follow, were *as they here follow*, or were *as the statement of
them here follows*.

In the use of such defining adjectives as refer to a single thing,
whether *absolutely*, or *conditionally*, care should be taken to preserve
consistency of expression, thro the connected words. One of the
company *is*; not *one* of the company *are*. John, or James, *was*
there; not *were* there; because, tho *both* are mentioned, it is only
in reference to the *alternity*; and the *verb affirms* only of *one*. Each
of the brothers *is* employed; not *are* employed; because the assertion is not made of the *brothers* collectively, but essentially of *one*;
tho that *one* is which ever *one* may be named, and, by implication,
each other *one*, considered in successive order.

There is, in some instances, an inelegant and improper repetition of
the agent, particularly where it is employed to help out the measure of a rhyme; as,

> "My *dog he* is trusty and true."

> "My *banks they* are furnished with bees."

Concerning nouns of multitude, no rule can be given. It is an
exercise of judgment to determine whether the reference is to the
group, as an aggregate whole, or to the distinctive individuals who

compose it. According as one or the other of these ideas prevails, the verb is to be singular, or plural.

Pronouns are often improperly used for *adjectives;* as " see *them boys,*" "set back *them chairs.*" This awkwardness is confined to the *plural form,* as we do not hear any one say, " move *him chair.*"

Foreign terms are some times used for English. They are inconsistent with purity and elegance, and on these accounts should be avoided.

For the French, ten dollars *per* quarter : *a* quarter.

Questions frequently arise respecting the apostrophic *s,* in adjectives of personal relation, more especially when several of these adjectives refer to the same noun.

Jane's and Eliza's books. Jane and Eliza's books.

The first expression refers separately to Jane's books, and to Eliza's books, as different parcels, or those to which Jane and Eliza do not stand related in joint interest. Jane and Eliza's books are those with which Jane and Eliza have some joint concern.

The word *had* is often improperly used before the adjectives rather or better ; I *had* rather not *stay* —you *had* better *remain* here. Leave out the adjectives *rather* and *better*, the impropriety is then seen at once.

" What method *had* he best *take* in a circumstance so critical ?"— HARRIS—HERMES.

The past tense verb is improperly used for the participial adjective.

He has *went*. I should have *went*, if I *had have* known it.

" Two negatives, in English, it is said, destroy each other, and amount to an affirmative." Such a rule is altogether a mistake. A wrong use of words, however, frequently takes place, which it is the honest intention of this rule to rectify. If a person makes the assertion, " I dont want none," the probability is he does not mean what he says. The mistake is in the fact, not in the grammar. The person who knows the import of his words, may, *not unfrequently*, make this the most pithy form of expression.

20*

No, no ; or *no, not yet,* does not mean *yes.*

Did you ask the man's permission? *No,* I did *not ;* but my brother did. What was his answer? He did *not* say *no.* O, then, according to the grammar, he said "*yes,*" or, at least, gave an *affirmative* answer. *No, not* that, *neither.* Then he said *nothing,* did he *not? Not* so, *neither.* Pray how then? He told a long story, not directly to the point, either way. The cup is *empty ;* it is full ; it is *not empty, nor* full.

PUNCTUATION.

It may probably be expected, as a matter of course, that a work on grammar is to contain a set of " rules," to mark the pauses used in writing. Any person who duly reflects on the vast variety which the forms of expression assume, will readily perceive that if rules could be supposed applicable to all phrases, it would be difficult to say what set of men could *reduce them to order,* or where they would end. In examining the directions given, by a hundred persons, very little of a practical nature can be gathered from them. Like much of the exposition in grammars, the amount is, Find out the right of the case without the rule, and then fit the rule to it. Hardly any two persons can be found who agree in their punctuation. None, without concert, could uniformly agree.

After a full experiment, it would be found that the business of punctuation depends far more on judgment, taste, and practical skill, than on any set of formal directions which can be given. For any instruction which this work can offer, the reader is referred to the examples it exhibits, with such allowance as intelligent persons will make, for haste and accident, in a first edition, on an extensive and various subject.

DIRECTIONS FOR THE PLACING OF CAPITAL LETTERS.

Capital letters were formerly much more used than at present. every noun beginning with one. According to the best practice in modern writing, it is proper to use them,

1st. At the beginning of every sentence.

2d. To commence every measured line of poetry.

3d. In every proper noun; as *England, North Carolina, Delaware*, the ship *Golden Age*.

4th. Adjectives immediately derived from proper nouns ; as the *Grecian* fleet, the *Italian* language.

5th. All names of the living God ; and, as a part of Christian literature, including the words allusive to the *Savior, Holy Spirit*, Divine Providence, the Messiah, the Supreme Being, or whatever word may be intended as the appellation of the true God, according to any modification of religious creeds.

6th. The first word of any formal quotation, or example, intended to be distinctively set forth. This last use, however, is chiefly an exercise of judgment and taste ; for it would be too formal to employ the capital, in introducing one or more words, with the regular flow of the sentence.

7th. Principal nouns, or other words, in titles of books, maps, and other things; as, Murray's Grammar of the English Language.

PROGRESS OF LANGUAGE.

The following extract from a proclamation, by King Henry VIII. will serve at once for a parsing lesson, and for a sample of the English language at that period.

Henry VIII, by the Grace of God, &c., to all prynters of bookes within this oure realme, and to all other oure officers, ministers, and subjectes, theis oure letters patents, hering, or seing, greting : We do you to understand that wherein tymes past it hath been accustomed that theis bookes of divine service, that is to sey, the masse booke, &c. both in Latyn, and Englyshe have prynted by strangeres in strange countreys, partelye to the great losse and hinderance of oure subjects, who both have the sufficient arte, feate, and treade, of printing and imprinting suche bookes myghte profitably and to thuse of the commonwelthe be set on worke; and considering also the greate expences of so necessary workes as theis arre, and to the intente that hereafter we woll have theym perfectly and faithfully done to the honour of Almighty God, and safegard and quyetnes of oure subjectes, which dayly doo, and further may incurre no small parill and daunger of proclamacions and lawes, we have graunted and geven privelege to oure wel beloved subjectes, &c., the libertie to prynte the bookes above said, and everie sorte and sortes of theym, whiche either att this present daye arre in use, or hereafter shall be auctorised within any parte of oure realmes or domynions, &c.

INDEX.

INDEX.